LABORING IN THE FIELDS OF THE LORD

Laboring in the Fields of the Lord

SPANISH MISSIONS AND SOUTHEASTERN INDIANS

JERALD T. MILANICH

SMITHSONIAN INSTITUTION PRESS
Washington and London

Editor: Robert A. Poarch
Designer: Janice Wheeler

Library of Congress Cataloging-in-Publication Data
Milanich, Jerald T.
    Laboring in the fields of the Lord : Spanish missions and Southeastern Indians /
Jerald T. Milanich.
        p.   cm.
    Includes bibliographical references and index.
    ISBN 1-56098-940-8 (alk. paper)
        1. Indians of North America—Missions—Southern States.   2. Indians of North America—
Southern States—History—Sources.   3. Indians, Treatment of—Southern States—History.
4. Catholic Church—Missions—Southern States—History.   5. Florida—History—Spanish colony,
1565–1763.   6. Spain—Colonies—America—Administration.   I. Title.
E78.S65M55   1999
975.9′01—dc21   98-42319

British Library Cataloguing-in-Publication Data available

Manufactured in the United States of America
06 05 04 03 02 01 00 99   5 4 3 2 1

∞ The paper used in this publication meets the minimum requirements of the American National Standard for Information Sciences—Permanence of Paper for Printed Library Materials ANSI Z39.48-1984.

TO MICHAEL V. GANNON,
WHO HAS TRAVELED THESE TRAILS BEFORE

One of the last Popes who succeeded Saint Peter . . . gave these islands and mainlands of the Ocean Sea [Atlantic Ocean] to the said King and Queen [of Spain] . . . with everything that there is in them, as is set forth in certain documents. . . . We beseech and demand . . . that you accept the Church . . . and that you acknowledge the King and Queen . . . as the lords and superior authorities of these islands and mainlands. . . . If you do not do this . . . we warn you that, with the aid of God, we will enter your land against you with force and will make war in every place and by every means we can and are able, and we will then subject you to the yoke and authority of the Church and Their Highnesses. We will take you and your wives and children and make them slaves . . . and we will take your property and will do to you all the harm and evil we can.

—From the *Requerimiento* read by Spanish conquistadors to the native people of
the Americas in the sixteenth century

To err is human; to forgive, divine.

—Alexander Pope, *An Essay on Criticism*

CONTENTS

PREFACE

On a steaming mid-July afternoon, sweltering in the heat and humidity, I stood beside the parapet on the upper level of the massive, Spanish-built stone fort in St. Augustine, Florida. Below me on the green sward in the center of the fort people authentically attired and armed as Spanish troops and British infantry and officers reenacted the July 1763 ceremony in which Spain passed control of St. Augustine and the colony of La Florida to Great Britain.

A film crew recorded the event for an episode of *Archaeology,* the television series appearing on the Learning Channel. The show for which the scene was being shot—"Spain's Lost Empire"—focused on the missions of La Florida, Spain's name for the southeastern United States during the colonial period. I served as the show's on-camera mission expert.

Yes, there were Spanish missions in the southeastern United States. Between the 1560s and 1760s more than 150 Jesuit and Franciscan missions were established within the large region between modern Miami and the Chesapeake Bay. Especially during the seventeenth century, Spanish missions had dotted the landscape of northern Florida and southern and coastal Georgia.

These missions and the Spanish colonial initiatives of which they were an integral part have been one of the secrets of American history. Most people are familiar with the swallows returning yearly to mission San Juan Capistrano in California. Mention mission San Francisco and there is hardly anyone who would not equate that late eighteenth-century Spanish-Indian village with the city in California. Few, however, would know that a century and a half earlier, in 1606, another mission San Francisco had been established in northern Florida by the Spanish and was in existence for nearly a century. Santa Cruz, Santa Catalina, San

Diego—all of these missions existed in seventeenth-century Spanish Florida, long before there were missions in eighteenth-century California.

International politics in the eighteenth century led to the destruction of the La Florida missions and ultimately to Spain's loss of its colony. For two decades, 1763–83, La Florida would be a British colony, only to return to Spanish control until 1821, when it became a possession of the United States. American colonists soon began to settle what would become the twenty-seventh state and erase evidence of two prior centuries of mission history.

Today nothing remains of the missions that dotted La Florida's landscape. Ruins in Florida and Georgia once rumored to be remnants of missions have all been proven to be late eighteenth- and nineteenth-century, postmission constructions. Our knowledge of the Spanish missions of La Florida comes from archaeological excavations that delve beneath the ground and from historical documents filed away in archives in Spain and elsewhere.

Nothing original remains for cinematographers to create a television show about La Florida's missions. Indeed, nearly all buildings of any kind relating to the early period (1565–1763) of Spanish colonization of the southeastern United States have long since been obliterated. Only St. Augustine's stone fort, the Castillo de San Marcos, and a handful of other structural features in and around St. Augustine provide architectural testimony of that past.

But the future is bright. Today archaeologists and historians are applying their skills to finding, uncovering, describing, and interpreting the missions, the native peoples they served, and their role in Spain's control of colonial La Florida. Bioarchaeologists, scientists who study the skeletal remains of the mission villagers themselves, are also involved in this research, which since 1980 has resulted in an almost complete rewriting of scholarly understanding of the missions.

The view that has emerged is a somewhat contradictory one. We cannot help but admire the intentions and initiatives of missionary friars who labored, sometimes under extraordinarily difficult conditions, to bring Christianity and aspects of Hispanic culture to the southeastern Indians. We also recognize that the very process of conversion brought great changes to the lives of those same Indians. Missions, an integral part of Spain's colonial system, were a means of controlling native people by making them Catholic subjects of the Spanish Crown dependent not only for religious well-being, but for access to goods that originated far from La Florida. The desire to own colorful glass beads and sturdy iron hoes was as powerful as the desire to adopt Spanish religious beliefs.

The mission system also provided a way to harness native villagers as laborers. Nearly all of the La Florida colony's manual labor, both in St. Augustine and in the surrounding countryside where the missions and small military outposts were established, was performed by mission Indians. The institution of *repartimiento,* which gave the Spaniards the right to native labor in exchange for religious education, functioned in conjunction with the mission system; labor quotas and the conscription of people to serve on labor gangs were organized through mission villages.

Missions *were* colonialism. The missionary process was essential to the goal of colonialism: creating profits by manipulating the land and its people. This was true elsewhere in the Americas as well. From Argentina to the Yucatán, from California to Georgia, church, state, and colonialism were entwined. Conquistadors, missionaries, and entrepreneurs went hand-in-hand to conquer the lands and people of the Americas. All were, in part, responsible for the decimation of the native populations served by the missions.

In Florida and much of Georgia that decimation was total. Native populations were annihilated. Except for small groups of refugees who fled La Florida in the early eighteenth century, none of the native people of the southeastern missions survived the colonial period. The missions that had brought the native people a new life also helped to ensure their demise.

My purpose in writing this book is to introduce readers to the Spanish missions of La Florida and the native people they served, especially the Apalachee, Guale, and Timucua Indians. I also wish to acquaint you with some of the research projects and methods archaeologists and historians used to develop the new perspectives on the Spanish missions.

In the chapters that follow we will visit some of these research projects—projects whose scopes range from major excavations at an archaeological site (that the public can visit) in Tallahassee, Florida, to the interpretation of documents found in the Archive of the Indies in Seville, Spain. In learning about the missions we also will learn about the roles of the natural environment and the social, political, and economic institutions of Indian societies in shaping the nature of the La Florida mission system.

Still another part of the story is the impact of the missions on specific native American groups. We will closely examine, for example, what happened to the Indians who lived at the missions and worked for the Spaniards of St. Augustine.

All this information about the missions must be examined against the background of contemporary events taking place in Europe and elsewhere in the Americas. The competition among the colonial powers vying for supremacy in the western hemisphere was responsible for the formation of the La Florida colony, situated between the northern rim of Spain's Caribbean, Central American, and Mexican colonies and the new English colonies emerging along the eastern seaboard of North America. Wars, international disagreements, and treaties involving Spain, France, and England helped mold La Florida and its missions. Those same conflicts would destroy the missions.

My central theme is simple: the missions of Spanish Florida should be viewed not as a benign offshoot of colonialism, but as colonialism itself. Religious education was a calculated way to save souls while converting a potentially hostile population into a labor force that toiled in support of the colony and its colonial overlords. Today the shadows of the past are being illuminated by archaeologists and historians intent on revealing what really happened in the Spanish mission provinces of Guale, Timucua, and Apalachee. But even the light of knowledge cannot brighten one dark truth: missions and colonialism must take most of the blame for the disappearance of a significant portion of the southeastern Indians.

IN SEARCH OF A ONCE FORGOTTEN LAND

In the maze of T-shirt vendors and sunglass racks that defines the historical district of St. Augustine, Florida, the Castillo de San Marcos is an oasis of authenticity. Its massive coquina-stone walls convey to modern visitors the power once wielded by colonial Spain in La Florida.

The fort has always been one of my favorite archaeological sites. I enjoy strolling through its damp, interior rooms, pungent with the smells of human antiquity and the humid Florida climate. More than three centuries after it was constructed, this symbol of the conflicts that arose in the colonial period between Spain and England is still an imposing artifact.

Spain's grasp on the eastern seaboard of the United States once included the land between Miami and the Chesapeake Bay, but that hold was loosened after the English founding of the Virginia colony in the early seventeenth century and slipped even more after the Carolinas were settled later that century. Construction of the St. Augustine fort began only a few years after Charles Towne, modern Charleston, South Carolina, was established in 1670. Charles Towne's settlement was a clear sign to the Spaniards that the English had whetted their appetite for La Florida, and the wooden fort that previously guarded St. Augustine needed to be replaced by a more substantial fortress.

The Castillo de San Marcos served its purpose well. On two occasions in the early 1700s English armies took St. Augustine and laid siege to the fort, only to be quelled by its massive walls. It would be the 1763 Treaty of Paris, not gunpowder, that lifted the portcullis to the English.

A close look at this fort reveals quite a lot. If we use a lamp to peer into the shadows of the ill-lit interior rooms, ghosts from the past emerge, and we can

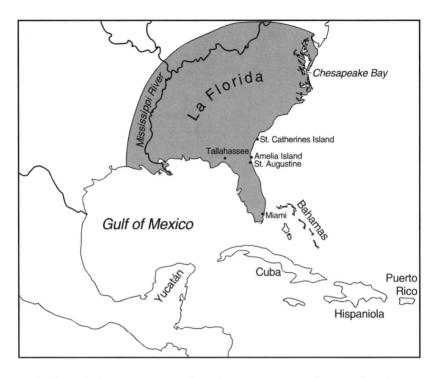

La Florida amid what was once part of Spain's American empire. (Some modern place-names are noted.) Early in the sixteenth century La Florida encompassed the lands north and east of Mexico, all of which were largely unknown. By the time of the first missions, La Florida had come to refer to what is now roughly the Southeast.

begin to understand what colonialism really meant. In one darkened corner we discover that the lumber used in the construction of the inner rooms was cut from forests well outside of town. Native laborers would have had to provide the muscle for hewing logs, transporting them to the construction site, and shaping them into timber and boards.

Shining a light into one of the narrow guardhouses, we see that huge coquina-shell blocks were used in the fort's outer walls. These heavy blocks were mined by native laborers on Anastasia Island and then rafted across the Matanzas River. Adult male Indians were taken from the missions and made to work in St. Augustine for periods as long as six months at a time.

A tour of the barracks shows that most of the fish, game, and cornmeal that sustained the fort's soldiers, as well as the Spanish townspeople, were provided by mission Indians. Native people planted, hoed, and harvested corn in fields around St. Augustine, and they did the same at the mission fields, some of which were

The Castillo de San Marcos in St. Augustine, Florida.

more than 200 miles (320 kilometers) from St. Augustine. Mission produce was transported to St. Augustine on the backs of Indians or in ships loaded by Indians.

A tour of the fort makes us realize "colonial might" meant the power to control the bodies of the native people of La Florida. It is no exaggeration to say La Florida, like other European colonies in the Americas, was built atop its native people. As a symbol of colonialism, the Castillo de San Marcos is more than adequate.

The Spaniards made the Indians of La Florida believe that loyalty to the colonial system was in their own best interest. That is why they did not flee St. Augustine, or rebel, or refuse. They labored because that was what mission Indians did in La Florida. It was their duty: a duty instilled in them as children growing up in a mission village; a duty that came with being a loyal Catholic subject of the Spanish monarch. The Spaniards were quick to realize that contributing labor as a duty and a sign of allegiance had a long tradition among the native people. Before Europeans came to La Florida, Indian villagers had provided labor on behalf of their village chiefs. Villagers worked to construct communal buildings, and they tended agricultural fields whose produce was controlled by their chiefs. Some Indians, especially in the Guale and Apalachee territories, also built mounds on which important buildings were erected. The use of labor was a traditional prerogative of the chiefs whose titles, ranks, and powers were inherited. Providing the labor was the duty of the people. It was the way things were.

As we shall see in chapters 5 and 6, the Spaniards essentially co-opted the native chiefs, working through them to obtain the labor to support the colony. Chiefs were given gifts by Spanish officials, and their chiefly status was recognized and reinforced. Special attention was also paid to the religious upbringing of the children who one day would inherit the office of chief.

Loyal Christian chiefs assured the Spaniards of loyal villagers: control the chiefs and you control the people. It was a very clever way to use the indigenous social and political systems for colonial aims. Beliefs, in combination with the threat of force and tied to economic rewards (or sanctions), are strong motivators. Beliefs that are an integral part of lifeways are especially powerful. So it was with the native people of La Florida during the colonial period.

In order to make the La Florida Indians believe that loyalty to the colonial system was in their own best interest, the Spaniards made them into faithful Catholic subjects through missions. When we think of Spanish missions most of us envision buildings constructed of adobe or stone (like those in New Mexico or California), something we might see in an *Adventures of Zorro* television rerun. An excellent example is the Nuestra Señora de la Leche shrine in St. Augustine just north of the Castillo de San Marcos. Built in the twentieth century, the masonry shrine is thought to have been built on the same site occupied by its eighteenth-century Spanish colonial namesake.

But if you were to search for stone, adobe, or even masonry ruins of colonial Spanish missions in the southeastern United States, you would not find a single one. There are none. The churches and other buildings of the southeastern missions were built of wood. They had packed earthen or clay floors, thatched roofs, and, at times, wattle and daub walls. In appearance and construction they were quite different from the better-known California and New Mexico missions and certainly nothing like the modern Nuestra Señora de la Leche shrine.

Many, perhaps most, of the La Florida missions came to fiery ends—burned to the ground. Even the missions that were not destroyed by fire have long since disappeared. The climate of La Florida is not kind to relatively fragile structures built of wood, earth, and palmetto fronds. To put it bluntly, the missions of Spanish Florida have long since rotted away.

Because there are no above-ground ruins of the 150 or so mission churches built in the two centuries following the founding of St. Augustine in 1565, the locations of most have been lost. Joint efforts by archaeologists and historians to find them have been under way for more than half a century.

Historians and archaeologists did not always fraternize. The era of modern archaeology in the United States did not begin until the mid-1930s during the Great Depression, a decade after historians had begun to focus on La Florida's missions. One of President Franklin Roosevelt's initiatives to put Americans back to work included an archaeology program, which hired out-of-work men and women to assist in excavating archaeological sites. One archaeologist and a few assistants could keep a relatively large number of people busy doing productive work. Though historians had a decade-long head start in the search for Spanish Florida's missions, their results were not always pretty.

FALSE STARTS

Scholarly historical interest in the Spanish missions of La Florida can be traced to the 1925 publication of two books. *Arredondo's Historical Proof of Spain's Title to Georgia: A Contribution to the History of the Spanish Borderlands* was edited by Herbert E. Bolton, who only four years earlier had made Spanish colonialism in the United States a legitimate avenue of historical enquiry. Bolton's (1921) concept of the Spanish borderlands—the northern rim of Spain's American empire, the region from California east to Georgia and Florida—continues to guide scholarly thought today. The second 1925 volume, *The Debatable Land,* authored by Bolton and Mary Ross, focused on the eighteenth-century conflicts between Britain and Spain over control and ownership of the Georgia coast.

The influence of these two books should not be underestimated. Historian Ellis Merton Coulter would opine that prior to 1925 and the publication of *Arredondo's Historical Proof* and *The Debatable Land,* "it was not generally known that the Spaniards had occupied Georgia" (1937, v).

One has only to look at the two-volume 1883 classic, *The History of Georgia* by Charles C. Jones, to realize that prior to 1925 most Georgians thought their history began with the colony of Col. James Oglethorpe in the eighteenth century. Volume One of Jones's influential study gives only lip service to the early sixteenth-century expedition of Hernando de Soto, then jumps to Oglethorpe. For Jones, Spanish missions, indeed the whole seventeenth century, did not exist.

Even Bolton's 1921 seminal study, *The Spanish Borderlands,* largely ignored the Franciscan missions of La Florida, although it provides an introduction to the Franciscan missions of California, New Mexico, and Texas. Those of Florida, said to be "little known," received only one paragraph.

Modern scholars owe Bolton and Ross an enormous debt for their contributions. Also deserving of accolades is John Tate Lanning, who published *The Spanish Missions of Georgia* in 1935. Though the works by these three scholars laid the groundwork for all future historical studies of La Florida, they sowed some misinformation that future mission historians would have to dispute and correct. Scholars from the foundling field of archaeology would also be invited into the debate, leading to the first applications of archaeology to the study of the southeastern missions.

One example of this erroneous information can be found in an article by Mary Ross. Ross, a native of Georgia writing from Berkeley, California, was no doubt quite familiar with the ruins of the eighteenth- and nineteenth-century Franciscan missions on the West Coast. In a 1926 *Georgia Historical Quarterly* article, Ross concluded that the tabby (incorporating a mixture of lime, crushed shells, and water in building walls) ruins still visible on the Georgia coast in several places—Sapelo Island, the mainland near Darien, Elizafield Plantation, St. Simons Island, and near St. Marys River—were the ruins of Franciscan missions, the East Coast equivalent of the California missions.

Mary Ross was not alone in her contention that the tabby ruins of coastal Georgia were the remnants of Spanish missions. John Tate Lanning wrote, in *The Spanish Missions of Georgia,* "Almost a score of such mission-type ruins, however, have actually been located from Port Royal to St. Marys, but no more than half a dozen have thus far been authenticated on any authority" (1935, 1).

Not everyone agreed that the tabby ruins dated from the time of the Spanish missions. Reviewing oral tradition and family memories, some individuals argued that the ruins were from the nineteenth century. As Lanning noted in his book, there was sharp disagreement among the historians and literati of the day.

One of the leaders of the opposition camp was Ellis Merton Coulter. In 1937, funded by the Colonial Dames, he edited a volume that should have put the controversy to rest. His *Georgia's Disputed Ruins* included a nearly 200-page study penned by Marmaduke Floyd that systematically debunked the myth that the ruins were from the Spanish mission era. In that volume Coulter pointed out that through the 1880s and 1890s everyone knew exactly what the ruins were, but "romance and tradition" had taken over in the twentieth century, a time when Georgia was searching for its Spanish past.

Floyd's investigations were published with a thirty-page report authored by James A. Ford, a young archaeologist who would earn his trowel in the federal relief archaeology programs of the Depression and go on to become a leader in American archaeology. Ford did something no one else had done to date: he excavated one of the disputed ruins, Elizafield Plantation. Although one can always argue the finer points of archaeological interpretations, Ford's data were emphatic: construction techniques, architecture, artifacts, even measurements used

Ruins of a tabby building on St. Simons Island, Georgia. Tabby is a mixture of lime (from shells), crushed shells, and water. These walls, like others on the Georgia coast, once belonged to a nineteenth-century plantation.

in construction all pointed to American planters, not Spanish friars. Georgia's missions were the ruins of nineteenth-century sugar houses and other plantation buildings.

While Georgia seemingly was losing missions, Florida was trying to find its. In 1925, the year Bolton's and Ross's books were published, A. H. Phinney, writing in the *Florida Historical Quarterly,* sought to make readers aware that not only did Florida have Spanish missions, but the site of one was well documented. Knowledge of mission San Luís de Talimali's location, then 2 miles (3.2 kilometers) west of downtown Tallahassee, had never been lost. Phinney cited a newspaper story written a century before in the April 11, 1825, issue of the *Pensacola Gazette,* stating that at that time the brick outlines—foundations—of two San Luís de Talimali buildings could be seen. One building was said to measure 40 ft. × 60 ft. (12.2 m × 18.3 m), the other 20 ft. × 30 ft. (6.1 m × 9.1 m). Phinney noted that a cannon found in the ruins had been removed, loaded, and actually fired in downtown Tallahassee early in 1925.

The "brick" ruins mentioned in the newspaper may have been the remnants of wattle-and-daub mission buildings, perhaps the church and *convento* (friar's residence), or they may have been associated with the moated and palisaded strong house that was built by the Spaniards at San Luís de Talimali. In 1948 Florida Park Service archaeologist John W. Griffin would initiate excavations at San Luís de Talimali.

Finding more of Florida's Spanish missions would not be as easy. The romantic appeal that Bolton's and Ross's books had stimulated in Georgia resulted in misidentifications south of the St. Marys River as well. And, as in Georgia, it was tabby ruins—sometimes misidentified as coquina stone—that drew the attention of those eager to find concrete evidence of the Spanish colonial past.

For instance, Phinney himself in his 1925 article cited a bronze candlestick found at New Smyrna on Florida's east coast as having been associated with mission ruins. Almost certainly those were the tabby ruins later identified as a post-mission period sugar house. In 1926 the Florida State Historical Society and the Florida Daughters of the American Revolution unveiled a bronze plaque for those ruins, commemorating them as a "mission built . . . by Franciscan friars about the year 1696."

The presence of the plaque was too much for one former local resident, Captain Charles H. Coe, a journalist who had founded the New Smyrna newspaper in 1877 and who was well acquainted with the history of the region. In 1941, having retired to Washington, D.C., Coe published a well-documented and -illustrated authoritative pamphlet, *Debunking the So-called Spanish Mission near New Smyrna Beach, Volusia County, Florida.* Coe concluded that the information on the plaque was "too preposterous for the serious consideration of intelligent men" (1941, 27).

Residents also believed that another set of Volusia County tabby ruins—the Addison Blockhouse—represented a Spanish fort, and a tabby wall at Kingsley Plantation on Ft. George Island just north of the mouth of the St. Johns River was said to be part of a mission building. In the early 1950s archaeologist John W. Griffin would set the record straight both in print and in presentations with titles like "Missions and Mills" that he delivered to historical societies around the state.

One substantial artifact displayed as evidence of Florida's Spanish missions has been exhibited in various Florida museums for several decades, but its authenticity is questionable. The object, a heavy bronze bell nearly 2 feet (.6 meters) high, is said to have been found in the nineteenth century in a pond 45 miles (72 kilometers) east of Tallahassee. Cast on the bell is "1758 Santa Maria Ora Probonis." The bell, later donated to the Florida Historical Society (its present owner), was described in a 1927 article written by Emma Rochelle Williams in the society's journal. The problem with the bell is that by 1758 the missions in interior northern Florida had been gone for half a century. The bell could not have come from a mission unless it were from Nombre de Dios or Tolomato in St. Augustine, the only La Florida missions in existence in 1758. It is more likely that the story surrounding the bell is a hoax.

Ultimately neither Georgians nor Floridians would need hoaxes, plantation period tabby ruins, or romantic notions about the past. Archaeologists and historians would provide evidence of Spanish missions.

EARLY DISCOVERIES

John W. Griffin, a native Floridian and a University of Chicago–trained archaeologist, was hired by the Florida Park Service in 1946 to investigate that state's archaeological sites and to incorporate some of them into the park system, where they could be enjoyed by the public. Griffin, aided by Hale G. Smith, another young archaeologist and a classmate from Chicago, and historian Mark F. Boyd, set out to do just that. They, however, were not the first Florida Park Service employees to investigate missions. In 1934 and 1935 Florida Park Service workers had excavated in what we now think was a church associated with the Nombre de Dios mission in St. Augustine. At that site more than one hundred human burials were uncovered and a number of them were left on display as a tourist attraction. It was not until 1993 that this grisly exhibit was removed and the burials reinterred during a ceremony presided over by Catholic priests, one of them of American Indian descent.

In the late 1940s Griffin and his team made a concerted effort to learn more about Florida's Spanish missions. They moved on three fronts: disproving the notion that the tabby ruins were of Spanish origin; investigating the known mission site of San Luís de Talimali near Tallahassee; and locating and investigating other missions. These initiatives were built upon documentary research and even some field reconnaissances carried out by Boyd a decade earlier.

The results of Griffin's 1948 excavations at San Luís de Talimali were published three years later as section 2 of *Here They Once Stood,* jointly authored with Boyd and Smith. Nearly half a century later, that book remains a mainstay of mission studies.

Somewhat amazingly, although early nineteenth-century visitors to the site of San Luís de Talimali could actually see the remnants of the old Spanish fort and pick up hardware and even cannons, by the time Griffin began his investigations, plowing and other agricultural activities made it "no longer possible to trace the fort outlines on the ground" (Boyd, Smith, and Griffin 1952, 141). The site was not lost, but time certainly had hidden much of it.

Griffin excavated portions of the wooden-walled San Luís de Talimali fort, recovering a host of Spanish and Apalachee Indian artifacts. Although the excavations were limited, Griffin's foresight regarding the potential of mission studies was not. In the conclusion to his report he wrote:

> In one sense, the problem of the Spanish missions of Florida is related to the larger problem of Spanish missions in the hemisphere, and particularly to those in North America. When enough data are available from the various regions to which Spanish missions activity was extended, it will be possible to study the varying reactions and adjustments of divergent aboriginal populations to a similar impact. In this connection, however, one should not assume that the impact was identical in the different geographical areas involved. Matters of colonial policy, location in relation to international affairs, isolation, and environment, as well as the personalities of the individuals involved, will combine to complicate the problem.
>
> So far as the Spanish missions of Apalachee are concerned . . . [t]he picture which emerges is not one of cloistered gardens, tolling bells, and peaceful idyllic communities. Rather it is one of crude structures and few tools, of poverty and discord, of war and martyrdom; but is a picture of greater interest than one painted with the brush of romance, for it is related to reality. (Boyd, Smith, and Griffin 1952, 157–58)

These are powerful words. With them, Griffin laid down a challenge to all future scholars studying the Spanish missions of the Americas and provided a framework for our present-day studies.

San Luís de Talimali was too important a site not to warrant additional investigations. Charles Fairbanks, an archaeologist on the faculty of Florida State University, would return to the mission in 1956 and 1957. And, as we shall see later in this chapter, investigations once again are under way under the auspices of the Florida Bureau of Archaeological Research. Visitors can tour the state-owned site, and some of the excavated mission buildings were being reconstructed even during the writing of this book. A museum and interpretive exhibits document the story of San Luís de Talimali and the mission system. Southeastern mission studies are coming of age.

The year prior to Griffin's 1948 work at San Luís de Talimali, his assistant and colleague, Hale G. Smith, carried out excavations at the Scott Miller site, another seventeenth-century Apalachee Indian–Franciscan mission. This site, 23 miles (37 kilometers) southeast of Tallahassee in Jefferson County, had first been found in the 1930s by a resident who had plowed up five intact Spanish storage jars. An archaeologist working with the Florida Geological Survey, J. Clarence Simpson, heard about the discovery and visited the area shortly after. Later, also in the 1930s, Mark F. Boyd would reconnoiter the site and carry out excavations.

Smith published an extensive report on the Scott Miller site in *Here They Once Stood* with Griffin's San Luís de Talimali paper. Armed with documentary information provided by Boyd, Smith tentatively identified the site as San Francisco de Oconee, although today it is believed by some that this Jefferson County mission is more likely La Concepción de Ayubale. Smith's excavations revealed two mission buildings and thousands of artifacts that he compared to those from San Luís de Talimali. He concluded:

The excavated mission was one of a chain that had a tremendous influence on the aboriginal culture. Through the missionary work of the Franciscan Fathers there was a partial, if not a total, replacement of aboriginal ceremonial and mental attitudes that undoubtedly were reflected in the social and material culture of the Indians. The economy was changed by the importation of various European materials which would speed up and make for more intensive agricultural activities. (Boyd, Smith, and Griffin 1952, 134)

Smith and Boyd located several other mission sites in northwest Florida, aided by the knowledge gained from Scott Miller and San Luís de Talimali, which had taught them what mission artifact assemblages should look like. Griffin and Ripley P. Bullen, another Florida Park Service archaeologist, also found a mission site on Amelia Island on Florida's east coast.

At the same time that Griffin, Boyd, and Smith were investigating Spanish missions in northwest Florida (from the Aucilla River drainage west), John M. Goggin, a young Yale-educated archaeologist recently employed at the University of Florida, was finding Spanish-Indian sites in northern Florida, the mission province called Timucua by the seventeenth-century Spaniards. Between 1949 and 1952 he and his students recovered hundreds of mission artifacts from around a spring head that flowed into the Ichetucknee River. The mission was thought to be Santa Catalina de Ajohica, although today, based on more evidence, it has been identified as San Martín de Ayacuto. Goggin discovered other Spanish mission sites in northern and eastern Florida, including mission San Francisco de Potano.

Goggin also excavated at the Zetrouer site, possibly a Spanish ranch or mission north of Paynes Prairie east of Gainesville, and he excavated in the Indian village associated with the Nombre de Dios mission in St. Augustine. By the mid-1950s much had been learned about the Spanish missions and Indians all across northern Florida, from St. Augustine west to Tallahassee.

While the Florida work was under way, archaeologists Sheila K. Caldwell and Lewis H. Larson Jr. were finding and excavating Spanish-Indian sites in coastal Georgia. At the Ft. King George site near Darien in McIntosh County, Caldwell uncovered several mission-period buildings. Larson's 1952 surveys, carried out for the Georgia Historical Commission, which also sponsored Caldwell's work, pin-pointed a number of sites, including some potential missions, mainly in McIntosh and Liberty counties, but also in Chatham and Glynn.

By the early 1950s archaeologists had been successful in finding a double hand-ful of southeastern missions in La Florida. Discovering a mission site is one thing, but correctly correlating the site with a specific mission is another.

NAMING NAMES AND COUNTING LEAGUES

When it came to naming missions, the Franciscan friars had no problem. It was the custom to name a mission after the saint on whose feast day mass was first said. Thus, San Francisco de Potano was named for Saint Francis of Assisi whose feast day is October 4. Although most missions were named for saints, some took their names from other aspects of Catholic doctrine, such as Santa Cruz (Holy Cross). In some other cases missions were given a particular name to honor an-other individual. Thus, San Damián de Cupaica in Apalachee honored not only Saint Damian but also the then governor of Spanish Florida, Damián de Vega Castro y Pardo.

Almost always a place-name was taken from an Indian town or group and added to the Spanish-Catholic name to further identify the mission and to differ-entiate it from others that might share the same saint's appellation. Thus, because San Francisco was in the region of the Potano Indians, that mission became San Francisco de Potano (San Francisco in Potano), and Santa Cruz in the Timucuan town of Tarihica became Santa Cruz de Tarihica.

Place-names sometimes offer modern researchers clues to mission locations. San Antonio de Enecape tells us that the mission was at the town of Enecape known to be on the St. Johns River, Santiago de Ocone was among the Ocone In-dians in southeast Georgia, and so forth.

Unfortunately, place-names often do not offer clues to precise mission locations on the modern landscape, but our knowledge of the geography of Spanish Florida is improving. And in a few cases mission names remain on the landscape today. For instance, St. Catherines Island, Georgia, is named for mission Santa Catalina de Guale, situated there for a century. The St. Marys River derives its name from Santa María on Amelia Island, while San Juan de Guacara gave its name—San Juan-ee—to the Suwannee River.

In their attempts to find and identify missions, Florida archaeologists and his-torians working in Florida appeared to have had an advantage over their col-leagues in Georgia. Boyd, Griffin, Goggin, and other Florida investigators were aided in their search by two important documents. The first was a report written by a Cuban bishop, Gabriel Díaz Vara Calderón, who visited the La Florida missions in 1674–75 to see firsthand what the Franciscan missionary friars had accomplished. His report on the months he spent in La Florida, translated into English by Lucy L. Wenhold and published in 1936, lists the missions along the main mission trail across north Florida.

That trail, the *camino real* (royal road), ran more than 200 miles (322 kilometers) from St. Augustine west to the province of Apalachee in modern Leon and Jefferson counties. Parts of it remain visible today. The bishop's account not only provides the names of twenty-four missions along the camino real, listing them in the order he arrived at each, but it also records the distances between them. For instance, Calderón's report contains the following passage regarding the missions in Timucua province between the St. Johns and Aucilla Rivers:

> Ten leagues [one league is 3.46 miles] from the city of Saint Augustine, on the bank of the river Corrientes (the St. Johns), is the village and mission of San Diego de Salamototo. It (the river) is very turbulent and almost a league and a half in width. From there to the village and mission of Santa Fe there are some 20 uninhabited leagues. Santa Fe is the principal mission of this province. Off to the side [from Santa Fe] toward the southern border, at a distance of 3 leagues, is the deserted mission and village of San Francisco. Twelve leagues from Santa Fe is the mission of Santa Catalina, with Ajohica 3 leagues away and Santa Cruz de Tarihica 2. Seven leagues away, on the bank of the large river Guacara [the Suwannee River], is the mission of San Juan of the same name. Ten (further on) is that of San Pedro de Potohiriba, 2, that of Santa Helena de Machaba, 4, that of San Matheo, 2, that of San Miguel de Asyle, last in this . . . province. (Wenhold 1936, 8)

What made this mission guide even more valuable was the 1938 discovery and publication of the Stuart-Purcell map of the camino real drawn by a British surveyor, Joseph Purcell, in 1778, when Britain controlled La Florida and occupied St. Augustine. The map was made for John Stuart, Colonial Britain's superintendent of Indian affairs. The road was still the major east-west route across northern Florida and ruins of the abandoned Spanish missions were apparent; some of their names are noted on the map. Armed with these two sources and additional documentary information, archaeologists and historians seemingly could correctly identify the mission sites they were finding in northern Florida along the camino real.

The geography of northern Florida missions has proved, however, to be much more complex than was ever envisioned in the 1950s. As a consequence, during the 1970s and 1980s a new generation of scholars would question some of these earlier mission identifications.

A NEW GENERATION: RESEARCH IN THE 1970s

My own entry into mission archaeology was serendipitous. In 1976 two University of Florida undergraduates, Art Rountree and Tom DesJean, were looking for archaeological sites in southern Suwannee County, just north of the Suwannee River. Driving down a country road, they noticed a tract of land recently cleared for pine-tree cultivation. Thinking that the disturbance might have uncovered evidence of an archaeological site, they stopped to take a look.

As luck would have it, the paved road on which they had been driving was probably built on top or near the old camino real; even better, there had been a Spanish mission close to the road. In a newly cleared pine field beside a small spring-fed sinkhole prophetically named Baptizing Spring, Rountree and DesJean not only collected mission-period Spanish and Indian pottery, they also found a large patch of burned clay, which turned out to be of a daubed wall or floor, once part of a mission building.

I had already planned to teach an archaeological field course the next semester, and I could easily fit in several weeks of excavation at the Baptizing Spring site. Long-time patron of Florida archaeology William Goza provided funding from the Wentworth Foundation, and we were off.

My student field crew quickly uncovered the burned remains of a small wooden building that had had clay daubed walls. Adjacent was an equally small, earthen-floored building with a central hearth, also with wattle-and-daub walls. These two structures were probably a small church or chapel and a convento built early in the seventeenth century by Timucuan-speaking Indians. A number of daub-processing pits were in evidence, and nearby was a much larger depression, perhaps where clay was mined. The clay was mixed with water in the smaller processing pits and used to coat the lathing (wattles) of the walls. After drying, the adobelike daub with its wooden framework inside made a reasonably substantial wall.

The buildings we uncovered were across a small plaza from a larger, crescent-shaped Timucua Indian village. Tests in the village revealed Spanish artifacts and a number of small smudge pits filled with burned corncobs. The charred cobs represent spent fuel. Potsherds of Spanish majolica, a type of tin-glazed earthenware, found in and around the buildings were from the early seventeenth century, a temporal context later confirmed by two radiocarbon dates. We dug up wrought-iron hardware, including spikes and nails, used in the construction of the probable church, as well as Indian pottery with crosslike decorations and ceramics made in the shape of Spanish bowls—Indian-made pottery archaeologists call colono-ware.

Interestingly, the same ceramic anomaly that John M. Goggin and Charles H. Fairbanks had earlier observed at Timucuan missions was also seen at Baptizing

Spring; most of the pottery from the Indian village was not the type made by the local Timucuan people prior to the arrival of the Franciscan friars in the early seventeenth century. Instead, the assemblage of village pottery consisted largely of new types, ceramics not previously seen in northern Florida before the mission period.

Baptizing Spring was an exciting discovery. But there were two puzzling aspects. One, the same question faced by Goggin and Fairbanks, was why were nonlocal types of pottery found at Timucua missions? The second, just as vexing, was what mission had just been excavated? The location of the Baptizing Spring site on the camino real did not fit with any of the locations documented in Bishop Calderón's account. The mission was too far east to be mission San Juan de Guacara, known to have been located on the banks of the Suwannee River. B. Calvin Jones, an archaeologist with the Florida Division of Archives, History, and Records Management (FDAHRM, today the Division of Historical Resources), had already found that site 5 miles (8 kilometers) west of Baptizing Spring.

According to Calderón, the distance to the next mission east of San Juan de Guacara, mission Santa Cruz de Tarihica, was 7 leagues, about 24 miles (39 kilometers). That meant Santa Cruz de Tarihica was 19 miles (31 kilometers) east of Baptizing Spring, and it could not have been the mission we had found.

Something was not right. Things accepted as concrete fact, such as Calderón's account of Timucuan missions, might not be as solid as they seemed. A University of Florida graduate student, Lana Jill Loucks, would return to Baptizing Spring to carry out more excavations. But Loucks's work, reported in her 1979 dissertation, could not answer the questions posed by the initial archaeological discoveries. Loucks and I bickered over the Baptizing Spring site identification with no adequate resolution. Ultimately I opted to take the easy way out and simply not think about Baptizing Spring for the next decade while involved in other research.

Thankfully, while I was trying to ignore Spanish missions, my colleagues were not. The 1970s saw a real resurgence in mission archaeology, especially in northwest Florida's Apalachee province. FDAHRM archaeologists L. Ross Morrell and B. Calvin Jones had begun a systematic field survey to find and study the missions of the Apalachee and western Timucua provinces. Using Calderón's account and the Stuart-Purcell map, Jones accurately traced the camino real across the landscape, actually walking many portions of the ancient trail while looking for mission sites. Jones, who had an uncanny ability to find archaeological sites, discovered and identified perhaps a dozen missions, including some in Timucuan province east of the Aucilla River. With more detailed understanding of mission locations, several erroneous identifications made two decades earlier by archaeologists were corrected.

Portions of nine mission sites were excavated by FDAHRM crews, including the Pine Tufts site in Apalachee, which Morrell and Jones reidentified as mission San Juan de Aspalaga. The results of the San Juan de Aspalaga excavations were published in 1972; Jones reported his other investigations in FDAHRM newsletters from 1970 to 1973. The results of this flurry of archaeological activity constitute one of the most important sources of data on the missions, and from them a much fuller picture of mission architecture began to emerge.

Documents, many found and interpreted by Mark F. Boyd decades earlier, suggested that at any one mission the buildings present would include a church, convento, *campo santo* (burial area), enclosing walls, and a plaza. We would also expect to find native houses in a village surrounding or near the religious complex of buildings. By the mid-1970s, thanks largely to Morrell and Jones and the earlier work of Hale G. Smith, excavations had produced examples of all of these mission features. Such information allowed us to tentatively identify the buildings we had found at the Baptizing Spring site.

In five short decades, from the 1920s to the 1970s, study of the Spanish missions of La Florida had evolved from an art to a science, from romantic misconceptions about plantation period tabby ruins to facts about the La Florida missions. All of this knowledge would pale beside what was to come. Work done in the 1980s and 1990s at mission sites in Georgia and Florida have provided wheelbarrow loads of new information about the Spanish missions. And not all the discoveries were by archaeologists. Historians and anthropologists have made exciting breakthroughs in archives in Spain and the Americas. We can now answer the questions about unidentifiable ceramics and missions posed two decades ago and confidently describe the mission system in detail, including the interactions between the Spaniards and native people who labored together in the mission fields of La Florida.

LOST AND FOUND: THE 1980s AND 1990s

Archaeologists love to visit one another's field projects. Protocol requires that visitors get the royal tour of ongoing research and as extravagant accommodations as can be managed. My experiences in the latter have ranged from a pup tent and camp fire to a field house with electricity, an ice machine, and all the other amenities of home.

Site visitations are not only social occasions, they are also educational endeavors. Hosts consult with visitors about field interpretations and artifact identifications: "Have you ever seen one of these?" And visitors get a crash course in a totally new field situation, something that always pays dividends down the road. Site visits, like archaeology itself, are fun and instructive.

Santa Catalina de Guale on St. Catherines Island

When I visited David Hurst Thomas's excavations at the site of mission Santa Catalina de Guale on St. Catherines Island, Georgia, two things immediately made lasting impressions. The first was that the food and my sleeping quarters were spectacular. Thomas's field project is the only one I have ever seen or heard of that had five varieties of mustard in the refrigerator. Though the room and board were great, the site was even better. The archaeological remains of Santa Catalina de Guale were extraordinarily well-preserved, and Thomas and his American Museum of Natural History field crews were giving them the meticulous care they deserved as they removed the nearly three centuries of earth covering the mission.

That a Spanish mission was once located on St. Catherines Island on the coast of Georgia has always been known—the island takes its name from the mission. The name Guale is derived from the Guale Indians who once inhabited the Georgia coast from Sapelo Island north to just north of St. Catherines Island (see chapter 2).

Though known to be somewhere on the island, the exact location of mission Santa Catalina de Guale had been lost. Finding the mission on a largely wooded island roughly the size of Manhattan would be no easy task. But there were some hints. Other archaeologists had visited St. Catherines Island in the past. Test excavations, by Lewis H. Larson in the 1950s and Joseph R. Caldwell of the University of Georgia in 1969–71, indicated that mission-age artifacts could be found near Wamassee Creek on the inland side of the island.

To find the mission as well as other archaeological sites, Thomas first devised a pedestrian field survey. In 1977 the island was gridded, and field crews systematically walked select areas, digging test holes and looking for artifacts and other evidence. Twenty percent of the island was sampled, resulting in the identification of 135 sites.

The Wamassee Creek area came up as the most likely location for the mission, because the greatest concentration of mission-period artifacts were found there. To further pinpoint the mission, Thomas switched to a program of random test-pitting in the area where mission artifacts had been found. Based on the mission excavations previously done in Florida, Thomas knew that nothing of the seventeenth-century buildings would be visible from the ground surface; digging was needed. Subsequently 200-person days were spent digging 3.3 ft. × 3.3 ft. (1 m × 1 m) test pits. However, not a single mission building was located. Random test pitting was a bust.

Thomas next instituted augering, using a gas-engine-powered bit to dig small posthole-size tests on a systematic grid across the Wamassee Creek site. My colleague at the Florida Museum of Natural History, Kathleen A. Deagan, had previously successfully used augering to interpret the below-ground layout of colonial St. Augustine. The small auger bit can reach several feet into the ground and bring up soil, burned clay, artifacts, and other pieces of data that can be plotted systematically on maps. When Thomas analyzed the Wamassee Creek auger data, it was clear that a 328 ft. X 328 ft. (100 m X 100 m) section of forest, roughly the size of two football fields, most likely held mission Santa Catalina de Guale. (As a result of Deagan's and Thomas's success, augering has now become a standard preliminary valuative technique not only for mission sites, but other archaeological sites as well.)

Digging holes in the ground is an expensive and time-consuming process. I wish archaeologists had Superman's X-ray vision, which would allow us to peer beneath the surface of the earth. Archaeologists, unfortunately, are not gifted with X-ray vision. But we do have high-tech devices that can provide a fair amount of information concerning what lies underground, especially when we are looking for evidence of old buildings. Clay floors, metal hardware, packed shell, and filled-in wells—all of these features would be expected to be present in a mission site, and all can be remotely sensed using various devices. Remote sensing is just that, a way to "see" what is beneath the surface by sticking sensors into the ground, pulling them over it, or even flying over them to record data. The sensing devices create images; their operation is based on the tendency of soils and objects to differentially retain heat or moisture, transmit electrical impulses, or conduct a magnetic field. A filled-in mission well will yield an image quite different from the soil around it.

At Santa Catalina de Guale David Hurst Thomas employed three different remote sensing tools to help him find and interpret specific mission buildings and features. A proton magnetometer was used along with a soil resistivity survey and ground penetrating radar. All provided some degree of success in pinpointing mission features. The remote sensing surveys indicated the size and exact locations and orientations of buildings whose general locations were suspected. To his surprise, he was able to locate what turned out to be the mission convento, the presence of which had not been suspected.

Knowing where to excavate and knowing approximately what you are going to encounter give a tremendous advantage. An archaeologist can excavate a specific feature—whether a building or a well—without digging random holes that might destroy something you do not even realize is there. Thomas likens the advantage to modern surgery. In the old days, a large incision was made to repair knee cartilage damage. Today, the use of MRI's and other such sensing devices allow a surgeon to make a small incision, sparing the patient's good tissue.

One reason that remote sensing worked so effectively at Santa Catalina de

David Hurst Thomas's excavations in Santa Catalina de Guale's cocina (kitchen). The dark humic stain inside the structure is a section of a seventeenth-century clay floor with two broken Spanish earthenware jars on it. This floor was laid down atop several earlier ones, evidence the cocina had been rebuilt more than once. (Reproduced with the permission of the American Museum of Natural History)

Guale was because the site was so well preserved, though nothing—not a single building, not even a well—could be seen from the ground surface. The site had never been plowed. No subsequent houses had been built atop it, and no sewer lines had been run through it. Time had been good to the mission abandoned three centuries ago. Other than disturbances by natural processes such as root action and animal burrowing, the remains of the mission had simply rotted away.

Just as important to the site's preservation was the fact that portions of some of the buildings had been burned. Charred wood and clay floors and clay-daubed walls partially hardened by fire leave far greater evidence of their presence than wood or clay that is not burned. Ironically the very fires that destroyed many of the mission buildings in La Florida helped to preserve their remains for archaeologists.

From 1981, when he first identified the Santa Catalina de Guale mission, to the present David Hurst Thomas has been excavating the mission's buildings and other features and interpreting what he has found. Under his careful hands and those of several generations of student assistants, field crews, and laboratory helpers, Santa Catalina de Guale has been brought back to life. We now know what the mission church, convento, kitchen, plaza, walls, and well looked like, and we have detailed information on the diets of the Guale Indians and the Spaniards who lived there.

At Santa Catalina de Guale we can see evidence of the 1597 rebellion by the mission Indians of Guale province that destroyed some of the mission buildings, and we can see the rebuilding that occurred in 1604. Clark Spencer Larsen, a biological anthropologist formerly at Northern Illinois University and now at the University of North Carolina, has been able to provide unprecedented insights into the health and everyday habits of the Guale Indians who lived at the mission for five generations. The excavations have also given members of the Franciscan order living in the United States today a view of their own history. Those same excavations have given all of us a privileged look at our nation's heritage.

Archaeology is an extraordinary discipline, one that can uncover and help us understand the past. And nowhere does it meet with greater success than when it is combined with archival research. In researching Santa Catalina de Guale, Thomas followed the team approach employed by archaeologists John W. Griffin and Hale G. Smith and historian Mark F. Boyd several decades earlier. Many of Thomas's interpretations were informed by documentary information provided by anthropologist Grant D. Jones and historian Amy Turner Bushnell. As we shall see in subsequent chapters, the alliance between archaeologist, historian, and anthropologist forged in mission studies in the 1940s and 1950s continues to pay huge intellectual dividends. But before we turn to that, let us take a brief look at several other recent projects investigating Spanish missions in La Florida.

Santa Catalina de Guale on Amelia Island

At the same time David Hurst Thomas was leading the American Museum of Natural History's expedition on St. Catherines Island, Georgia, two residents of Jacksonville, Florida, George and Dottie Dorian, were planning to build a house on three lots they had recently purchased on the inland side of Amelia Island. During the preliminary site work, a palm tree was removed for transplanting elsewhere. What happened next resulted in investigations that would stretch from Florida to the Archive of the Indies in Spain and eventually involve a host of scholars, Franciscan friars, and even the Santa Catalina de Guale mission on St. Catherines Island.

In 1680 Santa Catalina de Guale on the Georgia coast was abandoned. Four years later the mission was reestablished on Amelia Island, called Santa María by the Spaniards. The Dorian's palm tree had been growing almost in the center of what would turn out to be the 1684 Santa Catalina de Guale church, and the resting place for the remains of Guale Indian villagers interred in its floor. Another lost mission had been found.

Like its Georgia coast namesake, this Florida Santa Catalina de Guale was located on the inland side of a barrier island near the salt marsh and a creek, Harrison Creek, large enough to be navigable by boats. The presence of this Amelia Island mission had always also been known, though the exact location of the mission buildings had never been pinpointed, at least by archaeologists.

As it turns out, in the 1790s while the island was under Spanish domination—during the Second Spanish Period, 1783–1819—an American family, the Harrisons, established a plantation on the site of the mission. The plantation's main house, which was burned to the ground during the Civil War and was then rebuilt, had been almost exactly atop the Santa Catalina de Guale church. The Harrison family always knew a mission had been there and that it had been destroyed in the first few years of the eighteenth century by English raiders. In the 1970s a Harrison descendant wrote a letter in which she described how, as a child, it was a family evening tradition to stand near the salt marsh to listen for the ghostly cries of Indian children and the breaking of crockery, echoes of the 1702 raid that destroyed the mission (see chapter 7).

In 1951, John W. Griffin and Ripley P. Bullen had surveyed Amelia Island and visited the Harrison site, noting that it most likely was the general location of a Spanish mission. A local resident later sent Bullen a letter telling him that human remains were eroding out of a storm-cut bluff in back of the old Harrison house. A drawing included with the letter depicted burials arranged linearly in the bluff.

In the early 1970s, E. Thomas Hemmings, an archaeologist with the Florida Museum of Natural History, and Kathleen A. Deagan, then a University of Florida graduate student, carried out excavations several hundred yards south of the old Harrison house. They surmised that aboriginal and Spanish artifacts from the large site suggested the presence of a Spanish mission. But until the Dorians began their construction project, no one knew for certain where the mission was within the large site. The situation was similar to that initially encountered by David Hurst Thomas on St. Catherines Island.

Confronted with palm tree roots filled with human bones the Dorians contacted Piper Archaeology/Janus Research, an archaeological consulting firm. Kenneth Hardin, from Piper Archaeology/Janus Research, visited the site and did some tests to discover the extent of what appeared to be mission burials. A single large "augering hole" (the palm tree excavation) had found what had eluded archaeologists in the past.

Kenneth Hardin arranged for Clark Spencer Larsen, who had worked at Santa Catalina de Guale on the Georgia coast, to oversee the Harrison-site excavation of the burials and collection of the data. When it became apparent that a long-term project was needed to adequately study the site, Kathleen A. Deagan and myself were consulted. As a result, beginning in the mid-1980s the Florida Museum of Natural History conducted several field seasons of excavations at the Harrison site, renamed for the Dorians. Rebecca Saunders, a University of Florida graduate student, supervised the field excavations and Clark Spenser Larsen again served as biological anthropologist. Historical research was provided by Amy Turner Bushnell. In a continuation of the historical ties between the Georgia and Florida Santa Catalina de Guale missions, some of the same field crew members who worked with David Hurst Thomas also worked with Rebecca Saunders. Thomas also visited the site.

Our excavations soon spread from the Dorian's three lots to those of nearby residents. In the end, not one but two mission churches were discovered. One was the relocated 1684 Santa Catalina de Guale mission, while the other was probably Santa María de Yamasee built in the late 1660s to serve Yamasee Indians and abandoned in 1683.

Unlike Santa Catalina de Guale in Georgia, the Amelia Island Santa Catalina de Guale had not aged well. Between the 1790s and the 1950s the Harrison family had lived on the land and operated a productive farm. Unfortunately, many of the farming activities that took place on the mission site unintentionally intruded into and, at times, actually destroyed archaeological evidence.

The Harrisons dug trenches for pipes used to run water from a well to the house, and newer underground utility lines were installed. Over the years the Harrisons had constructed buildings, rebuilt buildings, buried garbage in pits, set posts, planted trees, and dug up trees. All of this activity impacted the site in many ways. At times it was almost impossible to separate mission features from plantation and farm disturbances.

Santa María de Yamasee fared even worse. A nineteenth-century privy intruded into the northern end of the church building, nearly half of which had been eroded away into the salt marsh. In truth, we first found the Santa María de Yamasee church building only when a Harrison descendant visited the site and asked if we had seen the human remains eroding out of the bluff. Once shown the exact spot, we soon realized that we had human burials that had been interred in the floor of the Santa María de Yamasee church. The situation exactly reflected the 1950s drawing sent to Ripley P. Bullen. In the bluff we could also see deep, shell-filled postholes that once had anchored support posts for the wooden Santa María de Yamasee mission.

A third, earlier mission, also called Santa María, was probably located somewhere in the vicinity, but we did not find it. Aerial photographs from the 1940s suggest that that mission may have been southeast of the Santa María de Yamasee church and the Santa Catalina de Guale complex, or it may have been to the north.

Saunders's excavations uncovered the Santa Catalina de Guale convento and what was possibly the kitchen building. She also excavated the church from which the palm tree had been taken. More than one hundred human interments were found below the church floor.

Our excavations on Amelia Island demonstrated the relatively impoverished state of the 1684–1702 Santa Catalina de Guale mission relative to that of its parental mission on St. Catherines Island. The church, rather than being a wattle-and-daub floor structure, as was true of its Santa Catalina de Guale namesake on the Georgia coast, was an open, pavilion-like building with an earth floor. As we shall see in the following chapters, Santa Catalina de Guale and Santa María de Ya-masee, two tattered Amelia Island missions, are apt testimony to the fate of the missions and the people they served.

In de Soto's Footsteps

In 1983 I became interested in reconstructing the Florida portion of the route of the sixteenth-century Spanish conquistador Hernando de Soto. A colleague at the University of Georgia, Charles Hudson, and his associates had been working on the route north of Florida. He convinced me that reconstructing the de Soto expedition could help us better understand the native societies of colonial Florida.

De Soto landed at Bahía Honda (modern Tampa Bay) in late May 1539, and marched northward through peninsular Florida toward modern Lake City, then turned west and marched to an Apalachee Indian town (in present-day Tallahassee), where his army spent the winter of 1539–40 before heading northward into Georgia and beyond (see chapter 3). If I could accurately trace de Soto's route, I could use the descriptive narratives penned by members of the expedition to better understand the Indian groups he encountered in Florida. After a few years of research I wisely joined forces with Hudson, and we coauthored *Hernando de Soto and the Indians of Florida*.

In the course of the de Soto research I had a field team headed by Kenneth W. Johnson, then a University of Florida graduate student, perform field surveys to locate and assess de Soto–era archaeological sites. This was no easy task. In this search, however, Johnson was aided by the discoveries of previous archaeologists whose collected data were curated in the Florida Museum of Natural History and the Florida State Archaeological Site File, kept by the Florida Bureau of Archaeological Research (BAR). Johnson also did a great deal of research to find the old trails that de Soto and his army might have traveled. He learned that for a portion of the trek across northern Florida, de Soto followed what would later become the camino real of the mission period.

Johnson also demonstrated that trails led to places, from one Indian town to another and then to another. This simple truth would prove to be a revelation to me. I figured that if I trace the trails, we could find the Indian villages described in the de Soto accounts.

Still another observation that arose from Johnson's research was that archaeological sites in northern Florida, the area later known as the mission province of Timucua, tended to occur in clusters. It appeared to us that over time, as a village's population increased and it became difficult to provide food for everyone, some Indians left and founded a new village nearby. Villages might also be moved when local wood supplies were used up or for other reasons. The result was groups of abandoned villages and villages occupied by historically related people. Johnson correctly concluded that these site clusters correspond to the Timucuan groups mentioned in historical documents.

Johnson found within each cluster both sixteenth-century and pre-Columbian villages. What was very interesting was the presence also of mission-related sites. The seventeenth century was right there on top and beside the sixteenth century. Trails used in 1539 continued to be used in 1639; villages at the time of de Soto were also localities where people lived when Franciscan missionaries entered the region. De Soto led us to the Timucuan missions.

That was the good news. The bad was that the information on missions we were collecting did not fit with Bishop Calderón's 1675 account, the same account used by Goggin and others in identifying the missions of northern Florida. Significantly, Johnson found one mission site, possibly two, well north of the camino real.

Our excitement grew as we correlated the archaeological evidence with new information derived from documents provided to us by John E. Worth, a University of Florida graduate student, and John H. Hann, a BAR historian (both of whom have recently authored books stemming from their research). Working in the Spanish archives in Seville, Worth found documents describing the events surrounding the Timucua Rebellion of 1656, an attempt by the people of interior northern Florida to rid themselves of the Spanish military government. The rebellion provided the governor of Spanish Florida, Diego de Rebolledo, with an excuse to reorganize the mission system of that region (see chapter 7). That reorganization saw the abandonment of some missions, the relocation of others, and the founding of new ones. These machinations were all part of an attempt to redistribute the Timucua Indians, who had been severely reduced in number due to diseases, along the camino real, between St. Augustine and Apalachee.

As a result, the rebellion changed the geography of the Timucuan missions. Calderón's well-known account described the post-1656 alignment of Timucuan missions, not the many missions that had existed earlier, some of which were on the camino real and some well off of it on side trails. Johnson's missions were two of the pre-1656 missions.

With this new information we could begin to answer questions posed in the 1970s. For instance, the Baptizing Spring site I had worked on in 1976 was the pre-1656 San Juan de Guacara mission that had been moved west to the Suwannee River at Charles Spring after the rebellion. B. Calvin Jones had located that later mission, one visited by Bishop Calderón. Another mission, one found by Kenneth W. Johnson, and later investigated by he and Samuel Chapman, could now be identified as pre-1656 Santa Cruz de Tarihica, located far north of the camino real. After the rebellion Santa Cruz de Tarihica was moved southwest of that trail to southern Suwannee County, Florida.

The knowledge that Timucuan mission geography was more complicated than anyone had ever suspected has also led to reidentification of mission sites discovered years ago. Thanks to archival sleuthing by John H. Hann, the site of Fig Springs on the Ichetucknee River that John M. Goggin had thought was the post-1656 mission of Santa Catalina de Ajohica is now correctly identified as San Martín de Ayacuto. On Christmas Eve 1986, Johnson, while excavating near the spring head where Goggin had found mission period pottery thirty-five years before, had found a part of the clay floor of one of San Martín de Ayacuto's mission buildings. That discovery would be the focus of several archaeological field seasons directed by BAR archaeologist Brent R. Weisman and later by myself, Rebecca Saunders, and Lisa M. Hoshower.

During the de Soto surveys, Johnson had also found a mission within a cluster of sites in northwestern Alachua County, Florida, not far from the Santa Fe River. His subsequent excavations uncovered what may have been portions of the church, convento, and other buildings, all associated with the mission identified as Santa Fé de Teleco.

As our understanding of the Florida Timucuan missions was being remolded, we also became aware of Timucuan missions in south-central and southeastern Georgia, previously almost a terra incognita. Once again thanks to John E. Worth's archival discoveries, we learned that prior to the 1656 rebellion Spanish missions extended well into Georgia (though the northern extent of the mission province of Timucua itself reached to about present-day Valdosta, Georgia). For instance, Santa Maria de los Angeles de Arapaha served the Arapaha Indians, a Timucuan group who lived on the modern Alapaha River 10 or 15 miles (16 or 24 kilometers) north of the modern Florida-Georgia state line. Santa Isabel de Utinahica at the intersection of the Ocmulgee and Oconee Rivers was even farther north of the Arapaha Indians, though its exact location has not been pinpointed.

Mission San Lorenzo de Ibihica ministered to the Ibi Indians, a Timucuan group, who lived east of the Okefenokee Swamp between the Satilla and the St. Marys Rivers. Numerous sites have been found in that locality by Christopher Trowell of South Georgia College and recently one that may actually be San

Lorenzo de Ibihica has been discovered. Another mission, Santiago de Ocone, was west of San Lorenzo de Ibihica.

West of the Okefenokee Swamp near modern Valdosta, Georgia, there is a cluster of sites, where Spanish and Indian artifacts have been found. Not far from Interstate 75, those sites probably include the northernmost mission of Timucua province, Santa Cruz de Cachipile. That site is being studied by Marvin T. Smith and his students from Valdosta State University.

Just as research is ongoing in the mission provinces of Guale and Timucua and missions to the north in Georgia, so are archaeologists and historians continuing to investigate missions in Apalachee, west of the Aucilla River. In the last half of the seventeenth century San Luís de Talimali was the largest Spanish settlement in La Florida outside of St. Augustine. Consequently, it was not only a mission, but San Luís de Talimali was where a contingent of Spaniards called home. As such, it can tell us much about the Apalachee missions and the importance of Apalachee province to La Florida.

San Luís de Talimali

"Step through the doorway here, but be careful of the base of that baptismal font." A tour of San Luís de Talimali led by Bonnie E. McEwan is an extraordinary experience, but then San Luís de Talimali is an extraordinary archaeological site. Building on the early work of John W. Griffin and Charles H. Fairbanks, BAR archaeologists and historians have been working at the site since the 1980s.

Like Santa Catalina de Guale on the Georgia coast, San Luís de Talimali is extremely well-preserved. While Santa Catalina de Guale owes its pristine condition to its relative isolation, San Luís de Talimali owes its preservation to a succession of custodial landowners, of which the latest is the State of Florida.

Its ready access—one can practically walk to the site from the Florida State University campus—has opened San Luís de Talimali to quite a number of people. Perhaps more than any other La Florida mission, this site provides visitors with a firsthand look at La Florida's Indian and Spanish past.

The initial BAR excavations at the site were directed by Gary Shapiro, a University of Florida–educated archaeologist. His auger survey of the site identified the fortified strong house and fort previously excavated in part by John W. Griffin. Shapiro's survey also pinpointed Spanish mission buildings, a burial area, and the Spanish quarter nearby. None of these features, as Griffin had noted many years earlier, could be discerned from the ground surface.

One of the more spectacular discoveries was the remains of a huge Apalachee Indian council house, portions of which Shapiro later excavated. The round, wooden, and thatched building was 120 feet (37 meters) in diameter with two in-

Excavating at San Luís de Talimali, Bonnie G. McEwan cleans the base of a limestone baptismal font, preparing it for conservation. In back of her, covered with plastic, is the floor of the church nave. (Reproduced with the permission of the Florida Division of Historical Resources)

ner rows of benches and a central fire around which was a dance area 65 feet (20 meters) across.

In pre-Columbian times, as well as during the mission period, council houses functioned as the village chief's office and the place where the village's business was conducted, including (later) meetings between mission Indians and Spanish officials. Council houses also served as men's lodges and as housing for visitors. Similar council houses were present in missions throughout La Florida.

After Gary Shapiro's tragic death in 1988 Bonnie G. McEwan, another former University of Florida graduate student, was appointed director of the San Luís de Talimali project. Under her expert guidance the site is yielding many surprises. What was thought to have been a cemetery or campo santo has been shown to have been the burial area within the nave of a large church. The friar's convento and an Apalachee chief's house, along with other mission features, have also been found.

McEwan's investigations in the Spanish quarter have shown that the Spaniards living at the mission, including members of the Floréncia family who owned ranches in Apalachee, were living in high style compared to the townspeople in St. Augustine. Money was to be made from the export of corn, wheat, cattle, and other livestock, as well as the products from those animals—ham, tallow, and hides. Living relatively close to the Gulf coast, the Floréncias and other Apalachee Spanish residents could export their products directly to Cuba from a port on the St. Marks River to the south (see chapter 6).

San Luís de Talimali was established in its present location following the 1656 Timucua Rebellion. After that rebellion Apalachee essentially served as a bread-basket of the La Florida colony. The missions of Timucua to the east along the camino real, decimated by epidemics, became little more than way stations along that trail leading to St. Augustine. Although ranches continued to operate in Timucua and east of the St. Johns River, Apalachee and its central town, San Luís de Talimali, would be the colony's chief source of food.

All of the archaeological work at San Luís de Talimali has been enhanced by the historical research of John H. Hann. Hann's work on San Luís de Talimali and the other missions of Apalachee and La Florida has filled a small library.

This chapter highlighted just a few of the recent mission discoveries that have been made. There are other projects I could have mentioned, like Florida State University archaeologist Rochelle A. Marrinan's excavations at two Apalachee missions or B. Calvin Jones's discovery of San Antonio de Enecape on the middle reaches of the St. Johns River. Likewise, I have not given all the historical discoveries their due. For example, several years ago John H. Hann and Eugene Lyon, the latter a historian with the Historical St. Augustine Foundation, found documents in Cuba listing the names of the eighty-nine Indians who were evacuated from St. Augustine in 1763 when La Florida was taken over by the British. Reading those names is a moving experience, one which personalizes 200 years of mission history.

2

A PORTRAIT OF THE LAND AND ITS PEOPLE

G uale, Timucua, Apalachee—these are some of the names of the Indians who inhabited a large region in the southeastern United States at the time of the Spanish missions. It was among these groups that the Franciscan friars would expend their greatest efforts. But missionaries, first Jesuits and later Franciscans, were sent to minister to other Indians as well. At various times they served missions among the Tocobaga and Calusa Indians on Florida's Gulf coast, the Tequesta Indians near modern Miami, groups south of the Timucua Indians in the interior of La Florida, and groups north of the Guale along the Atlantic coast as far north as Chesapeake Bay.

Franciscan missions also served Indians who moved to the Georgia coast and northern Florida from interior Georgia and South Carolina. The relocation of native people into Spanish Florida began during the last third of the seventeenth century, a time when new Indian ethnic groups, people such as the Yamasee Indians, were coalescing all across the southeastern United States. The remnants of once much larger groups banded together because of shrinking populations caused by epidemics, the presence of competing European colonial powers, and the threat of Indian slavers.

All of these southeastern Indians shared cultural similarities. Their ancestors had lived in close proximity to one another for hundreds, even thousands, of years before the missions. Even so, each group had developed certain distinctive habits and cultural patterns, adaptations to their specific natural and social environments. These adaptations in turn influenced the nature of their interactions with the Spaniards.

Missionaries met with few successes among native groups who were not agriculturists. Missions never lasted more than a few years in south Florida, where the Indians lived by fishing, gathering, and hunting wild foods. Nor were missions successful in regions far removed from St. Augustine. The logistical problems of supplying them were too great.

As a consequence, Franciscan missions were considered but never attempted among the densely populated ancestors of the Creek peoples living in the Georgia piedmont. They were just too distant from St. Augustine and its military power. Successful missions and the incorporation of native villagers into the Spanish colony depended in part on the threat implicit in that Spanish town. Spanish officials also desired missions close enough to St. Augustine to provide laborers. In addition they sought farming populations who could grow corn and other food for the colony and transport those products to St. Augustine.

Missions were put on or near trails, such as on the camino real in northern Florida, or in areas that could be reached by water, such as the Florida and Georgia coasts north of St. Augustine. Missions were most successful when they were within relatively easy grasp of St. Augustine.

The presence of European colonies in the eastern United States brought great changes to the native societies. Most if not all declined in number. Others moved out of their traditional territories to take advantage of new trading opportunities or to raid other groups. The market for Indian slaves created by the presence of plantations in the Carolinas and the Caribbean introduced another lucrative economic opportunity, one which stimulated the rise of native slavers quick to take advantage of the situation.

As noted above, new groups were formed as the remnants of once numerous groups met and coalesced. People like the Yamasee Indians who did not exist in the early 1600s became major players in the events of the early 1700s. Changes in economic patterns, geographical territories, and ethnic identity forced many native people to adapt to a world that was constantly being transformed around them.

Let us now travel back to La Florida and draw a sketch of that land as it was before the first Europeans sighted its coasts. Along the way we will place the various Indian groups in their respective regions and briefly describe aspects of their cultures that would become important within the context of the missions. The Guale, Timucua, and Apalachee Indians, the native people who were the focus of Franciscan mission efforts for more than a century, will get a closer look.

THE SETTING OF THE MISSIONS

The southeastern United States that Juan Ponce de León christened La Florida five centuries ago must have been an incredible place by modern ecotourist stan-

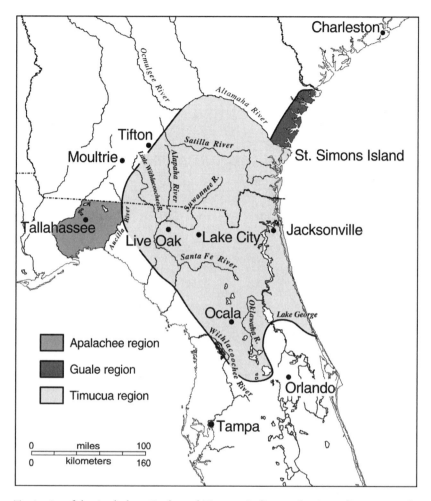

Territories of the Apalachee, Guale, and Timucua Indians at the time of Juan Ponce de León (1513). (Some modern place-names are noted.)

dards. There were gigantic expanses of pine trees, oak and hickory trees, and mixed forests of pine, magnolia, and hardwood trees. Dotting, gashing, and ribboning this veritable sea of green were narrow rivers and streams, placid lakes, small ponds, wet prairies, dark swamps, crystal springs, and huge river highways flowing down to the coast from the piedmont. Surrounding these forests and wetlands were the Atlantic Ocean and the Gulf of Mexico. Where land and saltwater met there were beaches, estuaries, mangrove forests, and salt marshes.

It was home to hundreds of animal species and even more types of plants. La Florida also sheltered hundreds of thousands of American Indians who derived

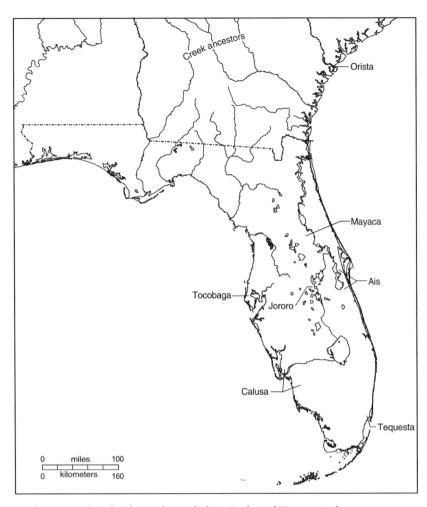

Southeastern Indians bordering the Apalachee, Guale, and Timucua Indians.

their livelihoods from this natural environment. Some of those Indians also grew a portion of their diet. All depended to a large extent on the fish they caught, animals they hunted, and plants they collected.

In the twentieth century only remnants remain of the environments in which the Tequesta, Guale, Timucua, and other southeastern Indians lived. Draining parts of the Florida Everglades at the end of the nineteenth century reduced Lake Okeechobee to nearly half the size it had been when a Jesuit mission was established at the mouth of the Miami River. West of the Guale Indian missions in the coastal plain of Georgia, nineteenth-century agriculture, especially tobacco, obliterated the pine forest that had dominated the region in the early seventeenth century, when Spanish friars and soldiers marched northward from St. Augustine to Tama, a native province in the Georgia piedmont. And in north Florida—Columbia, Suwannee, and Madison counties—the forests that witnessed the 1656 Timucua Rebellion have yielded to pasture and agricultural fields. Not only have the missions and their native villagers disappeared; so have the environments in which they once existed.

La Florida was a land of forests and water, and it can be argued that water actually shaped native cultures. Water was used for transportation, drinking, and washing, and it provided habitats for many animals the Indians used for food. Water also configured the nature of the Spanish colonization. The initial Spanish settlements—St. Augustine and Santa Elena, the latter on modern Parris Island, South Carolina—were on the coast at points easily accessible by sea. So were the first missions, those established by the Jesuits.

Except for the handfuls of Spanish friars and soldiers who traveled among, or lived within, the interior forests of southern Georgia and northern Florida and the Spaniards living at mission San Luís de Talimali (in modern Tallahassee), the Spanish presence in La Florida between 1565 and 1704 was largely restricted to the Atlantic seaboard, mainly St. Augustine. From that vantage point, the Spanish colonists looked not westward into La Florida, but eastward and south toward the sealanes that connected them with Europe and other Spanish colonies, sources of supplies. Even so, without the mission Indians to their west the Spaniards could not have survived.

For a closer look at the land of the missions and the southeastern Indians, let us take an imaginary interstate-highway tour of La Florida. We will start in modern Dade County, Florida, where Interstate 95 (I-95) begins its northerly route to Maine. Today the uncrowned capital of an expanding Latin America, Dade County was once home to the Tequesta Indians, who lived in villages along the Miami River and the bays and coastline nearby. Archaeologists have excavated a number of sites in the region and found evidence that large numbers of native Americans, most likely the ancestors of the Tequesta, had lived in the region for 2,000 years. Smaller numbers of people have been there even longer, some as long as 10,000 years.

The Tequesta Indians were one of the first native groups in La Florida to come in contact with Europeans. In 1513 Juan Ponce de León stopped at the Tequesta's main village while on his voyage of discovery, which took him down the Florida Atlantic coast and around the Gulf of Mexico side near Ft. Myers. Later, in 1566, a group of Spaniards who had mutinied in St. Augustine and were trying to make their way to the Caribbean by boat were abandoned in the Tequesta region by their comrades. Found by other Spaniards still loyal to Pedro Menéndez de Avilés,

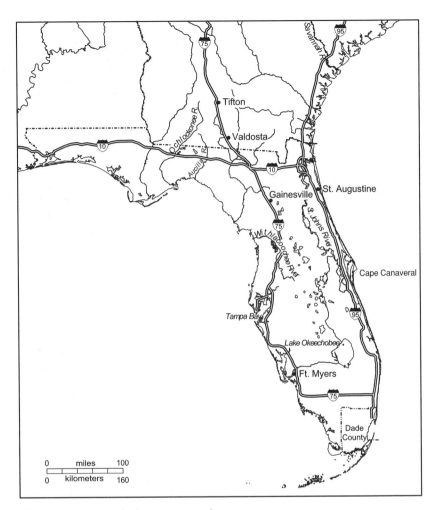

Modern-day interstate highways 10, 75, and 95.

governor of La Florida, the castaways were ordered to build a settlement there, at the mouth of the Miami River. The next year a Jesuit mission was placed at the settlement to minister to the Tequesta, but it lasted only a short time (see chapter 4).

Nearly 180 years later a second Jesuit mission, Santa María de Loreto, was founded near the mouth of the Miami River, intended to serve the remnants of the South Florida Indians who had fled there to escape raids by native slavers (see chapter 8). But it, too, was short-lived.

The Tequesta and southeast Florida would always remain outside the main sphere of the Spanish missions. There were several reasons for this. First, it is 275 miles (445 kilometers) from Miami to St. Augustine, about the same distance from St. Augustine north to modern Myrtle Beach, South Carolina. After the initial missionary efforts of the Jesuits, the Spaniards never put missions in isolated locations. Instead, nearly all missions would be located where they were easily accessible from St. Augustine, most often along land or water trails.

Rarely was a mission more than a day's travel from another. Consequently, a Franciscan friar or a Spanish soldier traveling from the farthest mission in the interior of La Florida back to St. Augustine would always find a safe place to overnight. This was the ideal; in reality, because missions came and went, the actual distribution of missions was not this regimented.

Two groups or chains of mission clusters were established early in the seventeenth century. One, the more linear, led north from St. Augustine along the northeast Florida and Georgia coasts, paralleling I-95, from the area of the Timucua Indians in Mocama through Guale Indian territory. The most remote mission in that chain was about 150 miles (240 kilometers) from St. Augustine. The chainlike nature of these missions was owing to the lineality of the coastline and the barrier islands where the missions were situated. Along that coast, the sea itself and the inland waterway were an important trail connecting the missions.

The second group of missions extended west and northwest from St. Augustine, roughly following I-10 through Timucua Indian territory in northern Florida and southern Georgia into the province of the Apalachee Indians in northwest Florida. Within this group, which had a much less linear arrangement, the westernmost missions were about 220 miles (355 kilometers) from St. Augustine.

That no chain of missions was ever established along I-95 down the coast from St. Augustine toward the Tequesta Indians near Miami is largely due to the nature of the native populations and their environments. The Tequesta Indians and their neighbors, the Hobe, Jeaga, and other groups northward on the Florida Gold Coast to Vero Beach, were not large in number. More important, they were not agriculturists, but lived by fishing, hunting, and gathering wild foods. Consequently, they did not grow produce easily transported to St. Augustine that could sustain the Spanish colonists.

The same was true of the Ais Indians, who lived from about Ft. Pierce north past Cape Canaveral to the Mosquito Lagoon area south of New Smyrna Beach. These native people also lived by fishing, hunting, and gathering, though it is likely that the Ais region was more densely populated than other portions of southeast Florida. In large part this was because of the environment. Looking eastward from I-95 in Brevard County, one cannot help but notice the extensive saltwater marshes. Once they were even more common, especially around Cape Canaveral, which accounts for the name that landmark received from the Spaniards in the sixteenth century: "Cape of Cane Fields." The marshes and estuaries, especially in Brevard County, were rich in shellfish and fish, resources that supported the Ais population. Similar extensive wetlands are not found on the coast south of Ais territory, where populations were smaller and less densely distributed.

The Ais did not escape Spanish attention. Documents indicate that there were plans to establish at least one mission there. But if a mission were established, it only lasted a short time. For missions to be successful, they needed to be connected to St. Augustine by a transportation route, and no such chain of missions ever led to the Ais region. Along I-95 between Miami and St. Augustine there are no known Spanish mission sites.

From Ft. Lauderdale, a short distance north of Miami, I-75 leads westward across the Everglades to near Naples on the Gulf of Mexico coast. There, in the former territory of the Calusa Indians, the highway turns north past Tampa Bay, then to Gainesville, and then into southern Georgia past Valdosta and Tifton on its way to Atlanta and points north.

A trip along I-75 is as instructive as an east coast I-95 tour. The most noticeable feature west of Ft. Lauderdale is the huge expanse of the Everglades. It is hard to imagine that as late as the late nineteenth century, this very wet and flat feature was much more extensive. Even today few roads cross this river of grass; travel off the highways is by airboats or boats. In the past Indian dugout canoes were used.

No missions were ever built in the Everglades either. I am not aware that any Spaniards even traveled through the region in colonial times. But the Calusa Indians on the Gulf coast did attract the Spaniards. Juan Ponce de León anchored off a Calusa town in Estero Bay south of Ft. Myers in 1513. Later, in 1567, a Jesuit mission and Spanish military outpost were established at that same Calusa town, which the Spanish called Calos.

Both the Tequesta and Calusa mission settlements were a part of Pedro Menéndez de Avilés's plan to control La Florida's coasts, a plan he put into effect after the establishment of St. Augustine in 1565 (see chapter 4). But like its counterpart near Miami, the Calusa mission failed after only a few years, as did all Menéndez de Avilés's strategies to use Jesuits to establish settlements in La Florida. By 1572 the Jesuits had withdrawn from La Florida, opening the way for the Franciscan Order to enter the colony.

The sixteenth-century Jesuit mission in Estero Bay was established for both military reasons and to take advantage of the important political position of the Calusa in south Florida. Thanks to the rich, shallow inshore waters found along the southwest Florida coast, the Calusa literally harvested the sea. They were excellent fishers who could sustain a relatively dense population and a complex political structure.

The Calusa chief also received allegiance from other south Florida chiefs, including the chief of the Tequesta Indians. Allegiance, in this case, meant receiving

An Ais Indian priest. (Reproduced with the permission of the
artist, Theodore Morris, Sarasota, Florida)

a share of goods salvaged by south Florida Indians from wrecked Spanish
galleons. By the 1560s the wealth of the Inca, Aztecs, and a host of other native societies in Central and South America was being transported back to Spain by ship.
Fleets of treasure-laden ships sailed on a regular schedule from Veracruz on the
Gulf coast of Mexico. But not all the ships made it to Spain. Storms wrecked some
on the Florida coasts, where their rich cargoes were salvaged by the Tequesta and
other groups, who in turn were forced to provide the Calusa chief his share.

A Spanish presence among the Calusa would have allowed Menéndez de Avilés
to retrieve at least some of this wealth. Menéndez de Avilés also had a personal
reason for placing outposts in south Florida: his son had been shipwrecked somewhere on the shore of La Florida, perhaps along the southwest Florida coast, and

shipwrecked sailors could be ransomed through the missions and military out-posts. The planned Calusa mission and garrison came to naught, however, and the Calusa remained relatively removed from the Spanish sphere of influence.

A third Spanish coastal outpost was established farther north, just west of I-75 among the Tocobaga Indians, whose main town was on Old Tampa Bay not far from the modern town of Safety Harbor west of Tampa. The Tocobaga had con-tact with the Spanish conquistador Pánfilo de Narváez when he landed on the coast west of Tampa Bay in 1528, but they did not maintain peaceful relations. The soldiers who manned the Tocobaga outpost were slain soon after the garrison was established in 1567, and no mission would ever grace the shores of Tampa Bay.

With the failure of his plan for Jesuit missions and military garrisons on the coasts of La Florida, Pedro Menéndez de Avilés advocated a new, harsh solution for controlling the Indians of south Florida: make war on them, capture the sur-vivors, and ship them off to Cuba, Hispaniola, or Puerto Rico as slave labor for Spanish settlements. Writing to the Spanish Crown in 1572 and 1573, he told how his efforts to make peace with the Indians had failed. The Ais and other Indians continued to capture and kill shipwrecked Spaniards. His proposed "war of fire and blood" would eliminate the problem, he argued. Menéndez de Avilés died in 1574, however, and his war of annihilation was not carried out. Central and southern Florida remained a virtual terra incognita throughout the period of the missions.

Late in the mission period, in the 1690s, the Spaniards tried once more to es-tablish a presence among the south and central Florida Indians, principally be-cause they were rapidly running out of Indian labor in northern Florida. The Timucuan missions west of St. Augustine were largely depleted, at least compared to what they had been fifty years earlier, and population levels were insufficient to fill the needs of the colony. Perhaps the Indians living south of the missions could be taught to be farmers and then used as laborers, thought the Spaniards.

Franciscans were therefore sent first to southwest Florida to the Calusa Indians, then to central Florida to the Jororo Indians, who were south of Orlando, and then to the Mayaca Indians in the St. Johns River drainage below Lake George (see chapter 7). But none of these late seventeenth-century efforts succeeded. The Spaniards could not make the Indians live off the land as farmers; the land of south Florida was not fertile enough for agriculture. At the same time, the Calusa and the Jororo were simply too far from St. Augustine. South and central Florida, the realm of the Tequesta, Ais, Calusa, Jororo, Mayaca, and Tocobaga Indians and their many neighbors, would always remain outside the region of the missions.

It would be among the Timucua, Guale, and Apalachee Indians that missions were successful. Returning to our interstate-highway tour will provide insights. First, as noted above, all of these aboriginal provinces were relatively close to St. Augustine. Driving northward up the Atlantic coast on I-95, we reach the southern extreme of Timucua Indian territory around Ponce de Leon Inlet, at the northern range of the Ais territory. For the next 180 miles (290 kilometers), until we reach the Altamaha River in southern coastal Georgia, we are in the land of the Timucua. North of the Altamaha River on I-95 we enter the territory of the Guale Indians, which extended from that river northward along the Georgia coast and its sea islands.

The Atlantic shore from Ponce de Leon Inlet north to St. Augustine is characterized by tourist-enticing sand beaches, narrow barrier islands, and lagoons. But few Timucua Indians lived directly on this coast, because vast expanses of food-producing saltwater marshes like those around Cape Canaveral are not present.

Once we reach St. Augustine the size of the barrier islands and the marsh-estuary systems protected by those islands become vast. On the inland side of Ft. George, Talbot, and Amelia Islands in Florida and Cumberland, St. Simons, Sapelo, St. Catherines, and Ossabaw Islands in Georgia the marshes and the streams that drain them provided plenty of shellfish and fish for the Timucua and the Guale Indians. The same is true of the estuaries at the mouths of the many rivers that drain into this same expanse of coast—St. Johns, Nassau, St. Marys, Satilla, Altamaha, and others.

The Atlantic north of St. Augustine could and did support relatively large native populations. It was those native populations and the bounty of the coast that drew Spanish and French explorers and colonists in the sixteenth century.

Other Timucua Indians lived westward from the coast, on and near the St. Johns River and its tributaries from Lake George north to the river's mouth near modern Jacksonville. Farther west in the interior of northern Florida were still more Timucua. A journey up I-75 north of Tampa would take us into the southwest portion of Timucua territory near the Withlacoochee River and Lake Tsala Apopka. To our east and northeast Timucua Indians once lived around the many freshwater lakes in western Orange County and Lake County. From the Withlacoochee River north past Wildwood, Ocala, Gainesville, and Lake City in Florida and Valdosta, Adel, and Tifton in Georgia, a distance of 275 miles (445 kilometers), I-75 leads through the heartland of western Timucua territory.

For much of that distance, at least until we reach the wiregrass-pine forests of southernmost Georgia, I-75 takes us through what was once a heavily forested region that today is referred to as the Middle Florida Hammock Belt. Mixed hardwood and pine forests harbored plants and animals, and lakes and wetlands held fish and other aquatic animals, all of which sustained the native people.

The Hammock Belt also presented an asset important to the Timucua peoples and one key to the future establishment of missions in the region: fertile soils. Unlike southern and central Florida or even the east coast of Florida south of St. Augustine, the forested regions of northern Florida contain soils well suited to slash-

and-burn agriculture. Fields were prepared by having the vegetation cut—slashed —and then burned.

Cleared fields were sown with corn, beans, squash, pumpkins, and other cultigens. Once harvested, these crops were stored and used to supplement the diet of wild foods and plants. Agricultural pursuits were something with which the Spaniards were very familiar, having come from agrarian areas of Iberia. The colonial overlords expected that cultivated plants would sustain their colony as they did other Spanish colonies elsewhere in the Americas. Indeed, to the Spaniards, farming was an essential ingredient of civilized life.

The Spaniards of St. Augustine relied on the agricultural skills of the native people to provide much of their food. Produce grown in native fields at missions many miles from St. Augustine was transported to that town. And Indians were brought to St. Augustine from the missions to clear, plant, tend, and harvest fields nearby. The colonists came to depend so heavily on corn that it in essence became a colonial currency—one imported, exported, bartered, and eaten by St. Augustine's inhabitants. Without Indian corn there would have been no colony.

Reliance on corn meant that the colony had to maintain close ties with the corn-growing native groups and those who would transport the corn to St. Augustine and work the fields there. The nearest Indians who could do that were the Timucua and the Guale. It is no surprise that early on it was these Indians who were the focus of Franciscan mission activity.

By the time of the arrival of the first Franciscan missions, late in the sixteenth century, the eastern Timucuan populations around St. Augustine and those north and west along the St. Johns River were already heavily decimated by disease. It therefore was the western Timucua, the Timucua in southeastern Georgia, and the Guale who would supply corn and labor to the St. Augustinians in the first third of the seventeenth century.

Yet, the diseases that earlier had hit their neighbors to the east and south eventually had the same effect on the western Timucua and the Guale Indians. Spanish officials were forced to look farther west across north Florida to the Apalachee Indians for more souls to save, more farmers, and more labor.

Their large population, fertile soils, intensive agricultural methods, and centralized political structure allowed the Apalachee to become accomplished farmers. They could offer the colony more food and labor than the Timucua and the Guale. Because of this, the mission frontier pushed west across the Aucilla River between 1633 and 1635.

In the seventeenth century, people traveled from St. Augustine to Apalachee along trails that roughly parallel modern I-10. Food and shelter were found along the way at the missions that dotted the landscape. From the gates of St. Augustine to the St. Johns River, 18 miles (29 kilometers), was a long day's travel. The river was crossed by raft or canoe, and then it was another 180 miles (290 kilometers) to the heart of Apalachee. Total time for the journey on foot was about two weeks. Today one can travel the same distance by car—via I-95 north to I-10 and then west—in less than three-and-a-half hours.

Spain's colony never expanded beyond the region of the mission provinces of Guale, Timucua, and Apalachee and the adjacent region of southern Georgia. But that was no small expanse of territory. At 60,000 square miles (155,390 square kilometers) it was roughly the size of modern Georgia.

GUALE INDIANS OF THE GEORGIA COAST

Remnants of the villages of the Guale Indians who once dominated the Georgia coast north of the Altamaha River still dot the coastal region, and a few Guale place-names remain. For instance, Sapelo Island is a derivative of the Guale town of Sapala, and there is Wally's Leg, a small tidal marsh stream whose name is an anglicized form of Guale.

When first encountered by Spanish and French sailors and colonists in the sixteenth century, the Guale lived in villages on the coastal islands and adjacent mainland of Georgia south of the Ogeechee River. It was long thought that the Guale spoke a Muskhogean language, a language closely related to one spoken by Creek Indian ancestors who lived westward in interior Georgia. But recent research by anthropologist William C. Sturtevant has questioned that notion, and the question of the linguistic affiliation of Guale is unresolved.

Documentation from the early colonial period, the period prior to the appearance of Franciscan missions, suggests that some of the villages of the Orista province near the Spanish town of Santa Elena in South Carolina were Guale, or at least they were affiliated with the Guale. If true, this hypothesis would extend the pre-mission region of the Guale well beyond the Ogeechee River.

Several scholars, notably Grant D. Jones, Lewis H. Larson, and John R. Swanton, have used archival materials to study Guale Indian ethnography. Archaeological excavation of Guale sites has been undertaken as well. But even so, fully describing the Guale as they were prior to contact with the Spaniards and French is no easy task. Most of the documentary material comes from the seventeenth-century missions. However, the nature of the province of Guale during that time was quite different from that present in the sixteenth century. As anthropologist John E. Worth has noted, the mission province of Guale "formed under conditions of Spanish missionization and colonization," and was "a product of the colonial era" (1995, 9).

We do know that the Guale were agriculturists who grew corn, beans, and squash. Those cultivated foods supplemented a diet heavy in wild plants and animals. Prime village locations were near the salt marshes, where fish and shellfish could be collected. Such locations were adjacent to the live oak-magnolia forests that were once plentiful in the region.

Guale villages, centers for social life, were surrounded by agricultural fields. Other fields were in other locations, and crops were rotated at various times to assure soil fertility. The Guale, whose ancestors had lived on the Georgia coast for centuries, would have been extremely knowledgeable about their environment and the resources it offered. They knew when to move into hunting camps to take advantage of the seasonal habits of deer, when it was time for families to move to traditional acorn nutting sites, and when and where certain fish and shellfish could be caught.

These activities left a variety of archaeological sites on the landscape. Some are the remains of villages near where sand mounds were built for burial purposes or as bases for buildings. Shell middens, the remains of pre-Columbian meals, accumulated beside and in the villages. Today, examples of both mounds and middens can still be seen. Other smaller sites represent camps or outlying homesteads where specialized activities related to food collecting, hunting, and farming took place.

The Guale Indians were never united as a single political unit. Instead, the Guale population was divided among a number of individual simple chiefdoms, each consisting of a group of villages. This political system was quite similar to that found among the Timucua Indians and the village clustering observed in north Florida. Each Guale village had a village *mico* (chief) who paid allegiance to the chief of the main village within the chiefdom, the *mico mayor.* The Spaniards referred to this head Indian as the "main chief." Occasionally the Spaniards referred to micos as *caciques,* a name they borrowed from Arawakan-speaking Indians in the Caribbean.

Early in the seventeenth century, one of the governors of Spanish Florida described the role of mico mayor:

> The title of head mico means a kind of king of the land, recognized and respected as such by all the caciques in their towns, and whenever he visits one of them, they all turn out to receive him and feast him, and every year they pay him a certain tribute of pearls and other articles made of shells according to the land. (Swanton 1922, 84)

Documents from the early colonial period indicate to some researchers that the Guale chiefdoms and their mico mayors formed alliances or confederations led by the most powerful chief, whose village became the major village of the alliance. Anthropologist Grant D. Jones has identified two, and possibly three, such chiefly alliances within the northern Guale and Orista regions in the mid-sixteenth century. The exact composition of these political entities changed over time, the result of individual towns and chiefdoms breaking away or of the waxing and waning of chiefly power. Contacts with Europeans and population reductions owing to diseases also influenced the makeup of chiefdoms.

By the late sixteenth century such dynamics had led to a reformulation of chiefdoms in the southerly parts of Guale. These changes may in part have been the result of depopulation around the Spanish settlement of Santa Elena on Parris Island, which had been founded in 1567 and abandoned two decades later, as well as the presence of Spanish missions. Jones has labeled these early mission-period Guale chiefdom confederations the Guale-Tolomato alliance, the Asao-Talaxe alliance, and the Espogache-Tupique alliance, all of whose names are derived from the principal towns.

The population of a single chiefdom was not large. Individual villages were home to 200–300 people, and chiefdoms consisted of as many as ten villages. This suggests the population of each chiefdom was never more than a few thousand individuals. Jones has identified about sixty Guale villages from the time of the first Franciscan missions. We might expect that by then epidemics had already taken a toll and the number of villages was even greater in the pre-Columbian era.

Within each Guale village were several types of structures. Around a central plaza were small houses made of wood and palm thatch for individual families. One account indicates houses were not substantial, but that might have been by European standards. Each chiefdom had a council house—a large structure for community meetings—located in the main village. In 1595 a Franciscan friar described one as

> circular in shape, made of entire pines from which the limbs and bark had all been removed, set up with their lower ends in the earth and the tops all brought together above like a pavilion or like the ribs of a parasol. Three hundred men might be able to live in one; it had within around the entire circumference a continuous bed or bedstead, each well fitted for the repose and sleep of many men, and because there was no bed-clothing other than some straw, the door of the cabin was so small that it was necessary for us to bend in order to enter. (Lewis H. Larson Jr. 1978, 131)

The "bed" was a bench on which participants sat during meetings. Visitors to the village generally were quartered in the council house.

The Guale built temples or charnel houses for storing the bones of their dead. Some of these may have been within the village, while others were said to have been away from villages.

In Guale society each individual belonged to the same lineage or clan as his or her mother. The kin groups of the chiefs were ranked above others. The micos always came from this ranking lineage—the lineage of their mothers and their mothers' brothers. Because people had to marry outside their own lineage, micos never inherited their position from their fathers. Instead they inherited it from one of their mothers' brothers (their uncles). If there was not a suitable male heir, a female could inherit the title of mico and pass it on to her own daughter. This manner of calculating descent and inheritance, which anthropologists call a matrilineal kinship system, was common across the southeastern United States, including among the Timucua and Apalachee Indians.

With the title of mico came powers and obligations. Micos were entitled to certain foods and other goods, paid to them by their subjects. Micos could summon laborers to tend communal fields, which the chief distributed as needed, and require laborers to participate in the construction of communal buildings and earthen mounds. This right of the micos to order villagers to perform labor became a major component of mission period labor conscription.

Among the Timucua, and probably the Guale Indians as well, the chief's duties included performing certain rituals connected to the economy. The mico mayor also presided in the council house where the business of the chiefdom was discussed.

Micos did not rule alone. There were other chiefly officials from the highest-ranking lineages as well. An individual called the *mandador* served as an aide to the mico, and there was also an *aliaguita,* whose exact role is uncertain. These and other high- status males constituted a class of citizens called *principales,* the principal men.

The micos and principales, both of whose positions were inherited, governed in the council houses, seated on the benches built around the interior walls. It was also the micos and principales who played a game called *chunkey* (a game also found among the Creek peoples in interior Georgia), in which spears were used to guide a rolled platelike stone object. The game is described by a friar:

> They all went together with their cacique [chief] to a part of the plaza, each one with a rod or piece of sharp pointed antler of the shape and size of a dart. One . . . cacique had a stone in his hand the size and shape of a loaf of a bread cake or a half real, and commending the game, he who had it threw it, rolling it with all his strength, and everyone at one time and without order pursued the stone with their rods. . . . I did not understand the game well, but it seemed to me that he who ran the fastest and arrived first with his rod and the stone, and without stopping a bit the speed of rolling to where they had left [scored]. In the same manner they took it and rolled it [again]. (Lewis H. Larson Jr. 1978, 129)

TIMUCUA INDIANS OF NORTHERN FLORIDA AND SOUTHERN GEORGIA

As previously noted, the Timucua Indians originally occupied the northern one-third of peninsular Florida (not including the Gulf of Mexico coast) and southern and southeastern Georgia as far north as the Altamaha River. This is a large territory, about 19,200 square miles (49,725 square kilometers), of which two-thirds is in Florida and one-third in Georgia.

It is estimated that as many as 200,000 Timucua lived in that region prior to the arrival of the Europeans, a population density of 10.4 people per square mile. That statistic corresponds with density figures for similar native societies. If a similar density were present in the Guale-Orista coastal region, an expanse about 3,000 square miles (7,770 square kilometers), that suggests the aboriginal Guale-Orista population was roughly 31,000.

The Timucua, like their Guale neighbors to the north, were not a single political unit. Rather, when the first Europeans came to La Florida the people we today refer to as the Timucua consisted of 25–30 simple chiefdoms. And as was true of the Guale, each Timucuan chiefdom encompassed two to ten villages, each with a chief.

Among the Timucua the chief was called *holata,* although the Spaniards most often referred to them as caciques. Within each chiefdom was a main village whose holata was paid homage by the vassal chiefs. These higher-level chiefs were possibly the individuals called *utina* (or *outina*) or *paracusi.* Like the Guale, the Timucuan chiefs inherited their positions through their matrilineage. Lineages or clans were ranked, and chiefs were members of the highest-ranking kin group. Other similarities with Guale social and political organization existed, this despite the fact that the Timucua and the Guale apparently spoke different languages. Timucua, of which perhaps a dozen dialects were spoken, appears to be unrelated to the languages spoken by the Guale, Apalachee, and other native people bordering the Timucuan region on the north and northwest.

Other cultural similarities between the Guale and Timucua include the presence within each chiefdom of a hierarchy of chiefly officials. One such official, the *inija,* was from the same kin group as the chief and may have been a close relative. This individual may have had the same duties as the Guale mandador, giving orders on behalf of the chief. At times the Spaniards did refer to the inija as mandador. There were other chiefly officials responsible for specific duties and tasks. They may have been the individuals known as *anacotima, second anacotima,* and *afetema,* each probably coming from specific lineages.

Chiefly officials were usually village elders and other high-status individuals whom the Spaniards referred to as principales. As among the Guale, the Timucua chiefs, chiefly officials, and other principales were assigned specific seats in their council house, their relative positions reflecting their inherited social status.

The highest-ranking Timucua lineage or clan, the one from which chiefs normally came, was the White Deer clan. Other Timucuan clans were Panther, Bear, Fish, Earth, Buzzard, and Quail. Documentary evidence suggests that the system of clan rankings differed among some of the Timucuan chiefdoms, including the Potano Indians and the Timucuan chiefdoms along the St. Johns River north of Lake George.

Some Timucuan chiefs were women, called *cacicas* by the Spaniards. As with the Guale Indians, women may have inherited the position when there was no suitable male in the chiefly lineage. There are hints that some villages regularly had women chiefs. When a cacica presided in the council house, that was the only time other women sat in attendance.

In several instances, Timucuan chiefdoms also formed alliances or confederacies, each led by the strongest chief. Documentation shows that at least five such Timucuan chiefly alliances existed in the sixteenth century.

Father Francisco Alonso de Jesus, a Franciscan friar, described the system of Timucuan chiefs:

> They have their natural lords among them. . . . These govern their republics as head with the assistance of counsellors, who are such by birth and inheritance. [The chief] determines and reaches decisions on everything that is appropriate for the village and the common good with their accord and counsels, except in the matters of favor. That the cacique alone is free and absolute master of these, and he acts accordingly; thus, he creates and places other particular lords, who obey and recognize the one who created and gave them the status and command that they hold. (Hann 1993a, 95–96)

Utinas, paracusis, holatas, and their assistants acted as civil officials, guiding and governing the villagers within each chiefdom except in times of war. Like the later Creek peoples of the Southeast, the Timucua also had a hierarchy of war chiefs and officials. The war chief was called *uriutina* or *irriparacusi;* the prefixes *irri-* and *uri-* are Timucuan for "war." Like their civil counterparts, the war chiefs apparently had aides and counselors. These may be the officials called *ibitano, toponole, bichara, amalachini,* and *itorimitono.*

Creek Indian towns were organized in a dual system with some designated white (civil or peace) and some red (war). Civil chiefs and officials traditionally came from the white towns and war chiefs from the red. This same system could have existed among the Timucua in the sixteenth century, but went unrecognized by the Europeans. It may have been that the utinas, paracusis, uriutinas, and irri-paracusis were all war chiefs from red towns. Lewis H. Larson Jr. has suggested it likely that this system of dual towns and war chiefs was present among the Guale.

Within Timucua society were other officials who were important in the mission period. One was *isucu* (curer) and the other *yaba* (or *jara*) (shaman or native priest). Curers were essentially native doctors who used various herbs, while shamans performed rituals associated with gathering food, portending the future, finding lost items, and many more activities. Shamans also used magic to cure or curse someone. To the Franciscan friars, many of the rites and spells invoked by the curers and shamans were idolatrous and were actively discouraged. The Catholic friars would work diligently to replace the native priests with themselves and substitute new beliefs and religious practices for traditional ones, even while maintaining and supporting the Timucuan chiefs.

Timucuan Chiefdoms

It is likely that the first Timucuan chiefdom to come in contact with Spanish sailors, in 1525, was Guadalquini on St. Simons Island, Georgia. Later in the sixteenth century the Guadalquini may have been part of an alliance headed by Chief Tacatacuru, who lived on Cumberland Island. The Spaniards later called the coastal region encompassing this alliance—from Ft. George Island, Florida, to St. Simons Island, Georgia—Mocama, at times using that same name to refer to the chiefdom on Cumberland Island whose chief led the alliance. There were other Mocama towns on Amelia Island, including the major town of Napuica.

Inland from the coastal sea island region of Mocama in southeastern Georgia were three chiefdoms: Icafui, Yufera, and Ibihica. The Icafui, closest to the coast, lived in eight or nine villages. Slightly farther inland were the Yufera, and still farther west were the Ibihica. The Ibihica, whose name means "water people" in Timucua, were just east of the Okefenokee Swamp between the St. Marys and Satilla Rivers.

Immediately to the south along the coast and on that portion of the St. Johns River from present-day Jacksonville, Florida, east to the river's mouth was an alliance of chiefdoms headed by Chief Saturiwa. His main village, on the south bank of the St. Johns River just inland from its mouth, was described in the 1560s:

> One enters the harbor [the river mouth] . . . , and on the left hand there is a pueblo of 25 large houses, where in each one live eight or nine Indians with their wives and children, because [those of] one lineage live together. (Solís de Merás 1964, 159)

The Saturiwa alliance was said to include thirty chiefs, only a few of whose villages are known. They include Caravay on Little Talbot Island and Alimacani on Ft. George Island north of Saturiwa's own village; west of Saturiwa's village, all on the St. Johns River, were Casti, Malica, and Omoloa.

South of Chief Saturiwa's alliance in the St. Johns River drainage was another large confederation, one led by Chief Outina. Outina's main village was west of the river on a major trail leading into the interior of northern Florida. (During the mission period, that trail would become the camino real running from St. Augustine across Timucuan territory to Apalachee and beyond.) Chief Outina's alliance, which was at war with Saturiwa's, included forty chiefs and villages. Not all the names of the villages are known, but they included Coya, near the mouth of Etoniah Creek on the St. Johns River; the nearby Molona; and Onachaquara, Omittagua, and Astina, all away from the St. Johns River proper. Farther south on the river were Patica, Chilili, and Enecape. Enecape is the archaeological site today known as Mt. Royal just north of Lake George. The Outina alliance stretched for many miles along the St. Johns River, from north of modern Palatka, all the way to Lake George.

Early in the mission period, by 1616, the chief of Enecape had gained control of the Outina alliance. This power shift was probably a result of disease-related population decimation in the northern sector of the alliance, that portion closest to the sixteenth-century European settlements at St. Augustine and Ft. Caroline. The Indians of the Saturiwa-Enecape alliance sometimes were called the *Agua Dulce* (Freshwater) Indians by the Spaniards.

Another Timucuan chiefdom, one led by Chief Seloy, was located at St. Augustine. It was in Chief Seloy's main village that Pedro Menéndez de Avilés established his first La Florida colonial settlement in 1565.

West of the St. Johns River on the Oklawaha River was the chiefdom of the Acuera Indians, who at least for a time were members of Saturiwa's alliance. It is uncertain how far south of the Acuera Indians the Timucuan territory extended. Documents from the 1539 Hernando de Soto expedition suggest that Timucua Indians lived as far south as the lake district in Orange and Lake counties. To the west of those lakes, probably in Sumter and Marion counties near the Withlacoochee River in central Florida, were the Ocale Indians, another Timucuan chiefdom.

North of the Ocale and Acuera in northern peninsula Florida was Timucua, the heartland of the mission province. One of these chiefdoms, the one headed by Chief Potano, may not have coalesced until after the de Soto expedition passed through the region. Potano towns included Itaraholata, Potano (the main town where Chief Potano lived), Utinamocharra, and Malapaz. In the 1560s Chief Potano's alliance was at war with that of Chief Outina.

North of the Potano Indians in north Florida were several Timucuan chief-doms, which modern scholars at times refer to as the northern Utina (distinguishing them from the Outina) and were commonly called Timucua by the Spaniards in the mission period. When de Soto's army marched through the region—modern Columbia, Suwannee, Hamilton, Madison, and northernmost Alachua counties in Florida north to Valdosta, Georgia—the Spaniards stayed at villages associated with several Timucuan chiefdoms, all of which were confederated under Chief Aguacaleyquen. Those towns, a few of many, included Cholupaha, Aguacaleyquen, Uriutina, and Napituca.

West of the alliance led by Chief Aguacaleyquen were the Yustaga Indians, another alliance of Timucuan chiefdoms. The Yustaga, whose territory lay between the Suwannee and Aucilla Rivers and extended up the Withlacoochee River drainage into south-central Georgia, were the most densely populated of the Timucuan groups.

In 1539 the Yustaga alliance and the alliances among the Timucua to their west were linked in some fashion. Perhaps the native leaders found it in their best interest to cooperate with one another, especially for military defensive purposes. The powerful Apalachee Indians controlled the land west of the Aucilla River and were traditional enemies of the Yustaga. The threat posed by the Apalachee may in part have been the stimulus for the Yustaga-Timucua alliances.

Northeast of the Yustaga and north of the neighboring Timucuan chiefdoms in north Florida were other Timucuan chiefdoms, those of south-central Georgia west of the Okefenokee Swamp. The Arapaha lived on the modern Alapaha River. Farther north near the confluence of the Ocmulgee and Oconee Rivers was still another Timucuan chiefdom, one whose main town was Utinahica.

Southeast of Utinahica, apparently in the Okefenokee Swamp, were the Ocone Indians, still another chiefdom. Immediately to their east, just east of the swamp, were the Ibihica and other southeast Georgia chiefdoms mentioned above.

There were probably other chiefdoms, especially in the lake district of central Florida near the southern end of Timucuan territory. We do, however, know all the Timucuan chiefdoms that received missions, and we have a very good idea where they were located. The reason we have this information is because the Spanish and French colonists and explorers who interacted with the Timucuan chiefdoms documented those encounters. Unfortunately, where contact was most intense, such as near the mouth of the St. Johns River (where the French founded Ft. Caroline and lived for about a year and a half) and around St. Augustine (settled by the Spaniards), the opportunities for the introduction of diseases were maximized. Disease epidemics increased proportionally to the intensity of European interactions. More contact meant greater chances of infection.

As a result, the overall distribution of Timucuan chiefdoms by the end of the sixteenth century was quite different from what it had been a century earlier. Most of the chiefdoms of the Saturiwa alliance had disappeared by the early part of the seventeenth century. The same is true for the chiefdoms of the Outina alliance, most of the Freshwater Timucua living in the St. Johns River drainage north of Lake George. Contact with the French and Spanish exploring the river took its toll.

The Spanish presence in St. Augustine was just as devastating. Epidemics created almost a no-man's-land of Indians from St. Augustine north to the mouth of the St. Johns River and west and southwest to the St. Johns River. The Timucuan chiefdoms well west of St. Augustine in interior north Florida and in southern Georgia escaped, at least for a time, the almost total decimation that occurred nearer St. Augustine. The same was true of the Guale Indians on the Georgia coast and the Timucua in southern Georgia. As a consequence, the first Franciscan missions, other than Nombre de Dios, were established away from St. Augustine. By that time there were no native people left near St. Augustine to missionize other than those brought there as laborers.

APALACHEE INDIANS OF NORTHWEST FLORIDA

Farthest removed from the late sixteenth-century colonial intrusions along the Atlantic coast were the Apalachee Indians of the Florida panhandle. Having endured the presence of the Narváez (1528) and de Soto (1539–40) expeditions, the Apalachee Indians remained outside the main sphere of Spanish colonization until the 1630s. When Franciscan friars first established missions in their territory in 1633, the native population was relatively large and densely distributed, especially when compared to the Timucua and Guale. A friar who visited the province in 1608 said there were 107 towns in Apalachee, a very large number (Hann 1988b, 27).

There are several reasons for the large and dense Apalachee population in the early sixteenth century. The most obvious is that the Apalachee group was much denser to start with. John H. Hann, the premier scholar of the Apalachee Indians, estimates there were 50,000 Apalachee at the time of first contact with Spaniards. Living in what is today Leon and Jefferson counties the Apalachee Indians occupied about 1,285 square miles (3,330 square kilometers) and thus would have enjoyed a population density roughly four times that of the Guale and Timucua, about 39 people per square mile. (By comparison, the density of modern Leon County, home of Florida State University, is 305 people per square mile.)

Economically and politically, the Apalachee had a more complex system than the Guale and Timucua, which promoted larger populations. Both archaeological evidence and Spanish documentation leave little doubt that the Apalachee were a Mississippian culture, as were the late pre-Columbian native societies who lived elsewhere in the interior of the Southeast, people who were responsible for the massive mound and village sites like Moundville in Alabama and Etowah in northern Georgia.

Mississippian cultures, so named because they were first recognized in the Mississippi River Valley, are characterized by their complex chiefdoms, each with a paramount chief who ruled over many subchiefs, village chiefs, and their people. Mississippian populations were large and densely distributed, and they had complex political and economic systems.

The political structure of each Mississippian chiefdom was reflected in a hierarchial settlement system. Each society had a capital town with civic and ceremonial buildings built atop large truncated pyramidal mounds arranged around plazas. Capital towns were home to the paramount chief, his family, and the other religious and political officials who governed the chiefdom. Ruling by virtue of birth, in essence they were royal officials.

There were regional town centers, each governed by a high-ranking chief who was a vassal of the paramount chief. Each of these chiefs in turn controlled outlying small villages or hamlets and farming homesteads scattered across the landscape. The occupants of those hamlets and homesteads constituted lower tiers of society below the elites. Complex political and settlement structures, as well as the state religion, were ways to organize large and dense populations and assure the people's well-being. Such institutions were intimately entwined with religious beliefs and agricultural pursuits. The state religion, aspects of which were controlled by the societal elites, provided the belief system that rationalized and explained the social and political systems and the society's place within the cosmos.

It was farming, especially the intensive cultivation of corn, beans, and squash that provided the economic basis for Mississippian societies. Because a significant portion of their diet was grown, Mississippian societies could support large, densely distributed populations. It is therefore not surprising that the Apalachee population was denser than those of the Guale and Timucua Indians. Nor is it surprising that the Apalachee and their successful farming enterprises would become the mainstay for La Florida's Spanish population.

By co-opting the Apalachee paramount chief and other chiefs, the Spaniards could essentially control the entire province, including the people who lived at the many farmsteads providing the bulk of the agricultural produce. Working through the existing chiefly structure, the Spaniards would be able to place nearly a dozen missions among the Apalachee in only two years.

Archaeologists have noted four types of settlements within the Apalachee territory in the late pre-Columbian period that correspond to the settlement hierarchies found in other Mississippian chiefdoms. At the top was the Apalachee capital town, the Lake Jackson site in Leon County northwest of modern Tallahassee, probably the largest town ever to have existed in pre-Columbian Florida. An imposing center, Lake Jackson served as a locus of political and religious life and the heart of the Apalachee realm.

By any standards Lake Jackson was an impressive capital. Six of its seven mounds are arranged in pairs in two rows separated by a small stream; the seventh mound is farther north. Ornate temples, centers for religious activities, and residences for the paramount chief and his family were built on these mounds, the largest of which measures nearly 90 yds. X 100 yds. (82 m X 91 m) at its base and rises 36 feet (11 meters) high. That mound, shaped as a truncated pyramid, had a ramp built on its east side. At times such mounds were rebuilt and enlarged, and the structures on them replaced.

Members of the Apalachee populace came to their capital on special occasions to pay homage to the elite rulers and to participate in community-wide activities. Some of those who came were the chiefs of the regional towns, the second rung of the social ladder, represented among the Apalachee by smaller town sites (relative to Lake Jackson), which feature only a single pyramidal mound.

In the Apalachee hierarchy of towns there were still smaller hamlets composed of five to ten houses and a larger building that probably served as a place for communal religious and governmental activities. The community of people associated with each hamlet included the residents living there and the families who lived nearby in small farmsteads. At one time, farmsteads, each composed of one or two houses, covered the landscape of Leon and Jefferson counties. It is likely that the bulk of the Apalachee population actually lived on farmsteads or hamlets, at the bottom of the social hierarchy. It was these farmers in the countryside who produced the food that supported the Apalachee political system and their rulers living at the regional towns and the Lake Jackson site.

The Apalachee paramount chief and his associates controlled the redistribution of goods and resources within the society. Tribute—corn and other cultigens, rabbit furs, bear hides, feather cloaks, and other items—was paid to the paramount chief by the regional town chiefs, who collected goods from the people under their control. Other tribute items were obtained through trade. The common people also provided labor for chiefly projects, such as building the mounds and repairing structures, and they served as warriors for the chiefs.

The status of individuals in life was reflected in the treatment afforded them after death. The farmers at the lowest end of the social scale might only receive interment in a shallow grave in the floor of their small, thatched house. At the other end of the social spectrum, the paramount chief and his family received truly opulent burials in tombs dug into the tops of the platform mounds.

An Apalachee man wearing a bearskin robe. (Reproduced with the permission of the artist, Theodore Morris, Sarasota, Florida)

B. Calvin Jones's excavation of tombs in one Lake Jackson mound provides some idea of the Apalachee burial traditions of the elite. After death, an individual's body was laid on a litter in a rectangular tomb 3 to 6 feet (1 to 2 meters) deep and roofed with split logs. (In life elite individuals were carried on litters, hoisted on the shoulders of their subjects.) Within tombs Jones found further reflections of opulence: fragments of woven cane mats, plant-fiber cloth, leather clothing and wrappings, and other items.

The outermost layer was usually the wooden tomb covering. The next layer included leather wrappings or coverings over cane matting . . . followed by woven cloth coverings, wrappings, or clothing over the body. The body usually lay on leather. When copper plates were present over the body, cloth—usually several layers in thickness—was found between the plates and the body, probably indicating that the plates were wrapped. (Jones 1982, 11–12)

The grandeur and value of the paraphernalia that accompanied the elite interments were immense. Many of the items were made from raw materials not native to Florida, including copper, lead, mica, anthracite, graphite, steatite, and greenstone. These artifacts were placed in the tombs with shark teeth, pearls, artifacts crafted from shells and bone, and elaborate ceramic vessels. The Apalachee participated in Mississippian trade networks that stretched across the eastern United States.

The elite Lake Jackson individuals were buried wearing large and small shell beads, shell gorgets (from headdresses), shell pendants, and bone hairpins with copper inlay. Shark-teeth bangles decorated clothing, and one individual was found with a belt clasp of galena. Copper and stone celts accompanied some of the elites, as did copper hair and headdress ornaments and copper pendants. Among the other extraordinary objects found at the site were three engraved shell gorgets and an assortment of repoussé copper plates, all exhibiting iconography like that found with other Mississippian elite individuals from elsewhere in the Southeast. These symbols provide strong evidence that pre-Columbian Apalachee society was organized in the same rigidly stratified system found in other Mississippian chiefdoms.

Agriculture played a major role in supporting the political and social complexity of the Apalachee chiefdom. With their cleared-field, row-farming techniques the Apalachee could outproduce the Timucua and Guale Indians. It is no surprise that de Soto chose to winter among the Apalachee in 1539, the first Mississippian farming society he found in La Florida.

3

A CLASH OF CULTURES

On September 4, 1565, Spanish voices sounded across the water to French sailors in the distance, asking questions to which answers were already known: "Who is your captain and what are you doing here?" "We are captained by Jean Ribault and are here on orders of the king of France," the response came back.

It was a moment in history. Over the next month and a half Pedro Menéndez de Avilés, Spain's most accomplished naval captain in the Americas, would oust the French from Ft. Caroline, their small settlement near the mouth of the St. Johns River, and reclaim La Florida for his sovereign, Philip II. France's colonial initiative would be obliterated. In the process, Ribault and several hundred of his men would be executed, even though they had laid down their arms and surrendered—a black incident that to this day remains controversial.

Two days after his September encounter with Ribault, Menéndez de Avilés landed supplies, soldiers, colonists—men, women, and children—and slaves at an Indian village about 36 miles (58 kilometers) south of the St. Johns River and set up camp. That modest encampment, first reconnoitered on St. Augustine's Feast Day, would grow into the capital of La Florida. For the next two centuries St. Augustine would remain in Spanish hands as a modest coastal outpost on the northern fringe of Spain's American empire.

Menéndez de Avilés's attempt to establish a settlement in La Florida would be a success. But it was by no means the first such venture. It followed on the heels of four decades of failures sanctioned by the monarchs of both Spain and France. Let us briefly review those attempts to settle La Florida in an effort to understand how they contributed to European knowledge of this region and its people, especially the Indians who would be incorporated into the colonies through Spanish missions.

CROSS AND SWORD

The European invasion of the Americas may have began by sea, but it quickly led to overland expeditions intended to explore the interior lands and discover resources that could be exploited. The driving force behind these initiatives was a desire for wealth: precious stones or metals, fertile lands suitable for productive plantations, human populations to be sold into slavery, and animals and plants that could be hunted or harvested and exported.

Spanish monarchs were quick to endorse expeditions in exchange for a portion of any profits. Typically such agreements or contracts spelled out the region to be explored, the tasks to be accomplished (especially the establishment of forts and settlements), the time frame for the expedition, and the division of the spoils. Monarchs not only wanted wealth that could be wrested from the land and people and taken back to Spain; they wanted the land and people themselves. The Americas offered opportunities to expand their realms.

The kings and queens of Castile and Aragon were Catholic monarchs. They had sworn not only to uphold the monarchy, but to support the Catholic church. To be a loyal subject of the Crown was to be a loyal subject of the church. If new lands and populations were brought under control of the Crown, then they should be made Christian lands and Catholic people. Royal charters typically required the building of settlements, which obligated the conquistadors to provide for the conversion of the native people to the Catholic faith. It was indeed God, gold, and glory that drove the colonization of the Americas.

The provisions of royal contracts and the desires of monarchs at times gave way to the realities of the clashes that erupted as conquistadors and entrepreneurs sought profits by usurping lands held for a dozen millennia by American Indians. Blanket stipulations calling for the humane treatment of native people became points of contention and negotiation when Indians were seen as refusing to display loyalty to Spanish officials. The result was often military action intended to punish Indians for what was viewed as disloyal behavior. The 1572–73 plan by Menéndez de Avilés to destroy the south Florida coastal Indians (cited in the previous chapter) was one such example. The colonization of the Americas was accomplished by both cross and sword.

EARLY COASTAL EXPLORATIONS
AND SETTLEMENTS

The initial voyage of discovery to La Florida that claimed the land for Spain appears on the surface to have been an accident. But we do not have to dig deeply before suspecting that it was not entirely serendipitous.

In 1512 a royal contract was awarded to Juan Ponce de León charging him to sail northward from Puerto Rico in search of an island called Bimini, thought to lie beyond the Bahamas. Ponce de León was a former governor of Puerto Rico, usually called San Juan, whose financial fortunes were declining. He was eager to invest in an expedition to discover new lands—and wealth—north of the Bahamas, islands reasonably well known to Spanish sailors of the time. It was already twenty years after Christopher Columbus's first voyage, and Spanish ships were venturing well away from the port towns established in the Greater Antilles.

That some type of land, perhaps more islands like those already charted in the Bahamas and Caribbean, lay farther to the north was known to Europeans even before Ponce de León's voyage. Basque fishermen regularly exploited the cod fisheries off the Canadian maritime provinces, and fifteen years earlier John Cabot, sailing under the English flag, had made landfall on that same Canadian coast before sailing southward down the Atlantic seaboard for an unknown distance. It is also likely that clandestine Spanish voyages—ones not sanctioned by the Crown—had reached La Florida prior to 1512.

In early March 1513 Juan Ponce de León's fleet of three ships lifted anchor in San Juan harbor and took a northwesterly course through the Bahamas past the Caicos, the Inaguas, Mayaguana, and then Guanahani (probably modern San Salvador, where Columbus had first landed in 1492). Passing modern Great Abaco Island, the ships knowingly took a more westerly heading that brought them to what Ponce de León thought was a very large island, which would turn out to be the Atlantic coast of Florida.

Because it was *Semana Santa* (Holy Week) preceding Easter and the time of the *Pascua Florida* (Feast of Flowers), Ponce de León christened the land La Florida and claimed it for his sovereign. The best interpretations of Ponce de León's route suggest his landfall was just north of Cape Canaveral at the northern end of Ais Indian territory.

A later account of the voyage penned by a Spanish historian based on Ponce de León's log and Conte Ottomanno Freducci's 1514–15 map, which incorporates information from the voyage, allow us to trace Ponce de León's route along the Florida coast. Sailing southward past Cape Canaveral and Ais territory, the Spaniards came to the Biscayne Bay–Miami area where, either then or on their return voyage, they sailed into Biscayne Bay, encountering the Tequesta Indians, probably landing at their main town at the mouth of the Miami River. From Tequesta, Ponce de León's fleet sailed southward around the Florida Keys and then headed north up the Gulf coast of Florida to the Ft. Myers area, land of the Calusa Indians, where they remained for more than three weeks.

Both the Calusa and the Spaniards were interested in learning about one another and trading. Even so, several skirmishes took place before the Spaniards lifted anchors and returned to Puerto Rico.

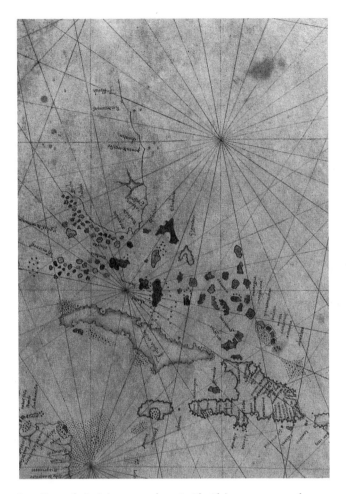

Juan Ponce de León's voyage along La Florida's coast apparently
provided geographical information depicted in Conte Ottomanno
Freducci's world map, drawn about 1514–15 (True 1944). Place-names
on the coast of the "Island of La Florida," include *chequiche*
(Tequesta on the lower Atlantic coast) and *stababa*, the Calusa
Indian name for the town of Calos, on the lower Gulf coast south of
modern Ft. Myers. The Ten Thousand Islands along the Gulf coast
are shown, as are the Florida Keys, the Bahamas, Cuba, Hispaniola,
Puerto Rico, Jamaica, and the Yucatán.

By the time Juan Ponce de León returned to Calusa territory eight years later,
other Spanish voyages had established that La Florida was not an island but a
peninsula attached to a large body of land of unknown size. In addition, navigators had mapped the entire Gulf of Mexico coast from Florida to the Yucatán and

charted the locations of Charlotte Harbor, Tampa Bay, and the mouth of the Mississippi River. Spanish sailors had also sailed up the Atlantic coast at least as far north as the Carolinas.

Some of these early voyages were for capturing southeastern Indians who could be taken to the Caribbean as slaves. Already the native population of the Bahamas and the Caribbean Island was greatly reduced in number, the result of diseases and maltreatment associated with forced labor.

Juan Ponce de León's 1521 voyage to La Florida was a colonizing expedition contracted by the Spanish Crown. He had with him two ships, 200 men, Catholic priests, 50 horses, and livestock, including cows, sheep, and goats. But Ponce de León and his colonists were poorly prepared for life in a new land. Nor did the Spaniards do anything to endear themselves to their hosts, the Calusa Indians. In a battle with Calusa warriors the Spaniards suffered a number of fatalities and Ponce de León was wounded. Facing failure, the Spaniards retreated to Cuba, where Juan Ponce de León died from an arrow wound.

Ponce de León's voyages and those of other sailors made the Spanish aware of the Tequesta and Calusa Indians and probably other coastal native groups, such as the Ais. Those voyages also would have made the Spanish aware that great wealth was not to be found on the coasts, among the hunting, gathering, or fishing populations. If La Florida held any riches, it was most likely farther up the Atlantic coast or in the interior of the country.

The same year Ponce de León made his second voyage to La Florida, in 1521, Pedro de Quejo and Francisco Gordillo, intent on slaving, sailed into Winyah Bay just north of the mouth of the South Santee River in South Carolina. Luring Indians aboard their ships with trinkets, they captured five dozen people and took them back to Santo Domingo.

The stories told by the slavers and their Indian captives, especially one boy whom the Spaniards named Francisco and who was later taken to Spain, gave rise to what historian Paul C. Hoffman has called the "Chicora legend," the belief that somewhere in the interior of modern South Carolina there was a rich native land of natural bounty and mineral wealth. Chicora would bring fortunes to its discoverers and their sovereigns. It only had to be found. The myth of Chicora would draw Spanish, French, and English colonists to the middle Atlantic region throughout the sixteenth century and after.

One of the first to attempt a settlement in that region was Lucas Vázquez de Ayllón, a Santo Domingo judge. Ayllón secured a royal charter to explore and colonize the Atlantic coastal region north of Ponce de León's discoveries. In 1525 he sent Pedro de Quejo to that coast to lay the groundwork for a colonizing expedition. The two ships commanded by Quejo reached the mouth of the Savannah River in early May before sailing north to Winyah Bay and then Cape Fear on the coast of modern North Carolina. Quejo next turned south, exploring the coast-

Shot in the right front leg by a musket, this dog must have suffered greatly before succumbing to infection and being buried in a small grave in an Indian village on the northern end of St. Simons Island, Georgia.

line all the way to St. Simons Island, Georgia, looking for a harbor where Ayllón could plant his colony. Along the way he must have encountered Orista and Guale Indians.

From St. Simons, Quejo continued on to the north end of Amelia Island, passing by Timucua territory. The Florida coast below that point was apparently already well known to Spanish navigators, so Quejo reversed course and sailed north all the way to the Delmarva Peninsula and into Chesapeake Bay before returning to port in Hispaniola. That voyage provided the information that would open the Atlantic coast not only to Ayllón, but to other Spaniards as well.

SAN MIGUEL DE GUALDAPE

Following Quejo's return, Ayllón readied his expedition. His royal contract, like most issued at the time, stated that he was to establish settlements and bring Christianity to the native inhabitants. He was also permitted to take slaves from among the Indians. That stipulation was rationalized by the belief that the Indi-

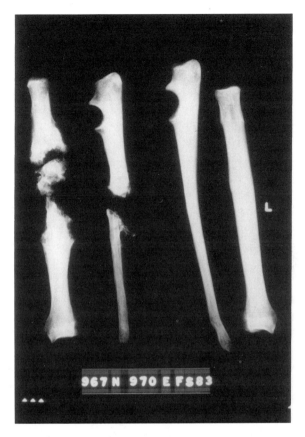

X-rays of the dog's legs reveal the damage done by the musket ball. Archaeologists believe the dog was killed by crew members of Pedro de Quejo, who were in the vicinity in advance of the 1526 Lucas Vázquez de Ayllón expedition.

ans themselves kept slaves; Ayllón would only be capturing people already enslaved.

Ayllón's expedition of 600 people aboard six ships sailed from Puerto Plata on the north coast of Hispaniola in mid-July 1526. The colonists included 100–150 sailors, women, children, African slaves, Dominican friars, and doctors. They were reasonably well supplied with corn, olive oil, serge cloth, and bread made from manioc flour. The cattle included pigs, goats—used for food and breeding stock—and 100 horses. But like Ponce de León five years earlier, Ayllón would find that establishing a colony in La Florida was not as easy as it appeared.

The ships sailed directly to Winyah Bay, where one ship ran aground and lost its cargo. A young Indian man taken from that region who was to serve as translator and guide jumped ship and headed for home as soon as an opportunity presented itself. (He had been captured by the 1521 Quejo-Gordillo slaving expedition and taken to Spain in 1523.) With supplies running low, Ayllón sent a party ashore to reconnoiter. The men reported that the Indian population was not large, so Ayllón decided to find a better location for his colony. Ships were sent to scout the coast; one sailed southward as far as modern Ponce de Leon Inlet just north of Cape Canaveral and on its return explored the St. Simons locality. Another ship sailed south to Port Royal Sound and the Broad River (near modern Charleston) and then on to Amelia Island. Along the way, the point of land that is modern Tybee Island, by Parris Island, was christened Santa Elena (Pedro Menéndez de Avilés would later return to that same location). A third ship sailed southward to Amelia Island. Based on information gathered by these scout ships, Ayllón opted to move his colonists to Sapelo Sound in Guale Indian territory. In late September the settlement of San Miguel de Gualdape, a church and houses, was christened.

San Miguel de Gualdape's colonists suffered from disease, hunger, and cold. They enjoyed few successes in securing food from the Guale. As a result of the hardships, a number of people died, including Ayllón. The situation grew worse. Some colonists broke away and moved to a nearby Indian village, where they were slain after only a few days. Raids by Indians continued to take their toll, and fire destroyed buildings. After two months the defeated colonists abandoned San Miguel de Gauldape and sailed for the Caribbean, probably abandoning the African slaves they had brought with them. Only 150 people survived. San Miguel de Gualdape, like Juan Ponce de León's ventures, was an abject failure. Neither colony had been a match for the land and its people.

PÁNFILO DE NARVÁEZ

Although Spain had failed to place a settlement in La Florida by 1526, a great deal of information had been gathered about the North American coasts themselves. La Florida occupied a strategic position relative to Mexico, Central America, the Caribbean, and the shipping lanes that connected those regions with Spain. To protect those shipping lanes and the expanding Spanish empire in the Caribbean and Mexico, La Florida had to be put under Spanish control. A logical step toward that end was to extend Spanish hegemony northward from the new Gulf settlements on the east coast of Mexico, tying La Florida to New Spain.

To accomplish this task the Crown awarded a contract to a seasoned conquistador of Caribbean and Mexico campaigns, noted for his cruelty toward native people in the conquest of Cuba. The lengthy contract given Pánfilo de Narváez by Charles V was signed December 1526. At the time neither was aware of the failure of the Ayllón expedition. The document stated that Narváez was to build three forts and colonize the region with Catholics, people who could bring Christianity to the Indians. Narváez, like Ayllón, was permitted to take any Indian slaves already being held by other Indians.

Charles V was well aware of the mistreatment of Indians that had taken place elsewhere in the Americas. He inserted in Narváez's contract a document that spelled out some of these past depredations and the need to treat the Indians humanely and convert them to Christians. This document, the *Requerimiento,* was to be included in all contracts awarded for American colonization. It required that two friars or priests accompany each expedition to see that the Indians received proper treatment. They were also to explain to the Indians, through interpreters, that the king had

> sent them to teach the Indians in good ways, and lead them from sin and cannibalism, and educate them in Our Holy Faith, and preach it to them so that they may be saved, and bring them into Our Realms, so that they should be better treated than they are. (Quinn 1979, 8)

Narváez's expedition—5 ships, 80 horses, and 600 people, including 10 women and African servants—sailed from Spain June 1527. At the time no one could have dreamed that they would meet with even greater tragedy than Ponce de León and Ayllón. The ships first made landfall at Santo Domingo, where horses were loaded and additional arrangements made. One hundred forty members of the expedition used the occasion to desert. From Hispaniola Narváez next sailed to Santiago, Cuba, where more supplies were to be loaded. Next the ships were sent to various other Cuban ports for supplies. While in port, two ships were destroyed by a late-season hurricane. As a result, sixty hands and twenty horses were lost—a third of the expedition. Faced with these misfortunes Narváez remained in port in Cuba for the winter.

In February 1528 the remaining 400 soldiers and colonists and eighty horses prepared to sail along the Cuban coast to Havana in four ships and a brigantine. The intent was to resupply and sail up the west coast of Florida to their goal, the northwestern Gulf of Mexico coast. But the small fleet ran hard aground; for fifteen days the ships remained stuck, waiting for a higher-than-normal tide to free them. Then two storms struck, delaying them several more days. Finally, the fleet neared the harbor at Havana, only to have a storm blow them toward Florida. Though low on supplies, Narváez opted to continue the voyage without resupplying, the first of several crucial mistakes. On Thursday of Holy Week, April 12, the fleet sighted land. It was fifteen years after the expedition of Ponce de León had made a similar Holy Week landfall in La Florida.

The fleet anchored off the upper Pinellas Peninsula north of modern St. Petersburg and a party was sent ashore. The horses needed to be walked; half of the eighty already had died on the voyage. Narváez formally took possession of the land on behalf of his sovereign and had himself acknowledged governor. Presumably, when the first Indians were encountered the friars read the *Requerimiento,* informing the Indians they now had the opportunity to become members of the Spanish empire. An account of the landing notes that the Indians made signs that seemed to indicate they wanted the Spaniards to leave.

Narváez ordered the ships to be off-loaded. A scout party went inland to explore and within a single day came to an arm of Bahía Honda, modern-day Tampa Bay. It was decided that the bay they had found was not Bahía Honda, which their charts indicated was farther north along the coast. As it turned out, their charts were wrong, an error that sealed the fate of the expedition. Their incorrect charts showed Bahía Honda to be a degree and a half of latitude farther north, about 90 miles (145 kilometers). Because it was known to be an excellent harbor, Narváez decided to mount his expedition from there. A ship was sent to locate the harbor with orders to sail to Havana, pick up supplies, and then return to the Pinellas Peninsula camp if the harbor was not found.

That ship of course did not find the harbor, and so it sailed to Havana as ordered. When it returned to the Pinellas Peninsula camp several months later, there was no trace of the expedition. Four men were put ashore to gather information but were captured by Indians. Their shipmates, unwilling to attempt a rescue, departed. One of the four captives, Juan Ortiz, would live among the Indians for eleven years until rescued by de Soto.

Meanwhile, after having sent the scout ship north, Narváez took some of his men and returned to the bay his first scouting party had found. The Spaniards followed the shoreline, taking several Indians captive and extracting information from them. The Indians were forced to guide Narváez to their village, probably at or near the town of Tocobaga near the head of Old Tampa Bay, a northerly arm of Tampa Bay. In that town there was corn, though not yet ripe. To Narváez the corn signaled agriculture, which meant that he could march overland to find Bahía Honda, feeding his crew with corn taken from Indian towns along the way.

Along with the corn, the Spaniards saw other interesting things. Wooden shipping crates salvaged from a wrecked Spanish ship had been reused as boxes for storing bodies. The Spaniards, horrified, burned the boxes and the remains in them, each body wrapped in a painted deer hide. They also found linen and wool cloth, as well as feather work from Mexico. (The salvaged ship had probably been on its way from Veracruz back to Spain when it had been lost on the Florida Gulf coast.)

Of even greater interest to the Spaniards were small bits of gold, most likely also salvaged from the wrecked ship. When pressed for information on where these items had come from, the Indians led the Spaniards to believe they were from Apalachee, a province where there was an abundance of gold and other valuables. This was not total misinformation; Apalachee was indeed a prosperous province and there was a precious metal there, although it was copper, not gold, and it was acquired by trade, not mining. But the Spaniards only heard what they wanted to hear.

Narváez took Indians as guides and traveled roughly 36–43 miles (58–70 kilometers), north of Tampa Bay to another town around which were cornfields. He now had confirmation that his army could live off the land if it marched north to Apalachee.

Narváez returned to his coastal camp and set about making plans for the trek north. Against the wishes of some of his officers, he ordered the remaining ships to sail north along the coast to the harbor thought to lie in that direction; there, they were to wait. The ships never found the harbor. Narváez and the remainder of the expedition—300 men, including two friars and three priests—set out overland, staying near the coast and exploring. They thought they could not miss the harbor, which charts said extended inland for 41.5 miles (67 kilometers). With them would be the forty remaining horses and daily rations, about two pounds (.9 kilograms) of biscuit and half a pound (.2 kilograms) of bacon per person. The expedition set out on May 5, 1528.

Narváez marched north for two weeks, paralleling the coast. Travel was rough. They were trekking through the little-occupied, swampy region just inland from the Gulf, and they came to no Indian villages and found no food.

Finally, Narváez's expedition came to and crossed the Withlacoochee River by swimming and building rafts. On the far side in modern Levy County the Spaniards met about 200 Indians from a nearby village. Narváez captured five or six and forced them to lead the Spaniards to their village, where stored corn was found. Thinking that the river they had crossed might flow into Bahía Honda, Narváez sent men to reconnoiter. No harbor was found.

After a week of rest at the Indian village they had invaded, Narváez, using captive Indians as guides, resumed his northerly march. His goal was still Apalachee.

Somewhere in Dixie County, the Spaniards came face-to-face with a Timucuan chief whose name they recorded as Dulchanchellin. The chief arrived in a litter with a great deal of pomp. People with him announced his presence by playing reed flutes. The Spaniards gave him small metal bells and glass beads; in return the chief presented a painted deer hide he had been wearing.

After learning that the army was in search of Apalachee, the chief saw an opportunity to turn the situation to his own benefit. He invited the Spaniards back

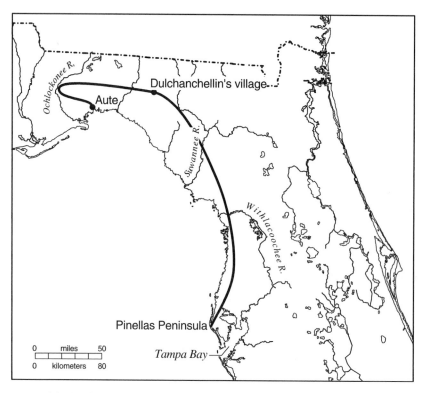

Route of the Pánfilo de Narváez expedition from northern Tampa Bay through Florida.

to his village and said that he would like to join them in an attack on the Apalachee Indians, who were his enemies. I believe that from this point on, Chief Dulchanchellin, and then the Apalachee Indians themselves, manipulated Narváez's expedition, deliberately misleading the Spaniards and steering them away from the more populous localities. The journey north to the chief's village took the Spanish-Timucuan expedition, which crossed the Suwannee River, about three days. Once at the chief's town they were fed corn. The village was in Madison County, and Dulchanchellin was leader of a Yustaga Indian chiefly alliance.

Relations between Chief Dulchanchellin and his guests quickly soured. The Indians abandoned their village and the Spaniards. Narváez departed and set out for Apalachee, capturing several Indians who were members of a raiding party and forcing them to lead the army to his goal, now known to be due west.

The Indians' revenge was complete. Instead of leading Narváez along the dryland trails to the Aucilla River, they took the Spaniards through San Pedro Bay and other lowland, often swampy forests in southern Madison, Jefferson, and Leon counties south of the Apalachee heartland. Downed trees and other hindrances made travel extremely difficult. Having walked through portions of this territory myself, I can only marvel at the ingenuity and determination of the Indians. Traveling with 300 men and forty horses through the region would have been tremendously arduous.

At last the army arrived at an Apalachee village of forty houses. They had hoped to find food and gold, but there was little of the former and none of the latter. Exactly where in Apalachee territory they were at that time is a matter of contention. I believe Narváez had been led all the way to the Ocklockonee River—which they named the River of Magdalena—at the western boundary of Apalachee territory.

During the three and a half weeks the Spaniards stayed in the town, they explored the countryside, encountering agricultural farmsteads and at least one small village or hamlet. They described the countryside as thinly populated, which suggests either that their scouting excursions were inept or that their Indian guides, taken from the village in which they were camped, continued to lead them astray.

While at the town the Spaniards endured numerous raids by the Apalachee Indians. Knowing they could not stay long at that location, Narváez sought information from his captive Indians. They convinced him that near the coast, eight or nine days' travel away, was a town called Aute where the Spaniards would find adequate food. The Spaniards must have wanted to believe it was true, for they set out in search of Aute. Once again the Indians were probably deceiving the invaders; from anywhere in Apalachee, the Gulf coast was much closer than eight or nine days.

The nine-day trip toward the coast was arduous and along the way the army was harassed by native archers. At Aute, believed to be on the St. Marks River near the coast, there was a little food, and the town itself had been burned and its villagers had fled.

Men were sent farther south to find and reconnoiter the coast, a day away. They returned to report the coast was marshy with many streams and inlets. Reaching the open waters of the Gulf or trying to travel through the marshes to Mexico would be difficult at best. Narváez's men came under attack by Indians and many in the army had fallen ill; some had deserted. Even so, he ordered the army to the coast.

Narváez and his depleted army eventually reached the coastal marshes, where they opted to build rafts and try to float along the Gulf coast to Spanish settlements on the Mexican coast. A makeshift bellows helped to turn horse tack and weapons into nails and tools. At the end of six weeks, five rafts had been built, caulked with palmetto fiber and pine pitch. During those weeks, the army lived off food raided from Indian villages. The Spaniards also butchered and ate their horses, fashioning ropes from the manes and water bags from the hides. On September 22 the 250 remaining Spaniards floated out of the Bay of Horses—named for their sacrificed mounts.

For a week they followed the marshy coast along the modern St. Marks Wildlife Refuge to Ocklockonee Bay and beyond before finally reaching the open Gulf waters, perhaps near Dog Island. Eventually hunger and thirst, Indian raids, storms, and water-logged rafts wore them down. A few rafts were washed ashore, and others simply disappeared. The survivors scattered: some tried to walk to Mexico, some took up residence in Indian villages, and some were taken captive.

Five years later, four of the survivors were living among Indians in coastal Texas: Cabeza de Vaca, Alonso de Castillo Maldonado, Andrés Dorantes de Carranza, and Esteban, a man from Morocco who was Dorantes de Carranza's servant. Putting a plan they had devised into effect, the four escaped together and headed west. After an incredible two-year odyssey the four were found by Spanish slavers in northern Mexico.

One would think that the failure of Narváez would have dampened enthusiasm for colonizing La Florida. But quite the opposite was true. Stories told by the four survivors about the Indian societies they had seen prompted the 1539 expedition of Father Marcos de Niça, a Franciscan friar, who traveled from northern Mexico into the region of the Pueblo Indians in the American southwest. The stories also contributed to the 1542 expedition of Francisco Vásquez de Coronado into Pueblo territory and beyond.

HERNANDO DE SOTO

These same stories also reached Europe and the planner of another expedition when one of the survivors traveled to Portugal and Spain in 1537. Hernando de Soto, who was in Seville making arrangements for another colonial assault on La Florida, could only have smiled as Cabeza de Vaca, at the Spanish court, portrayed La Florida as a veritable Eden.

Like Narváez, de Soto was a seasoned conquistador, having acquired personal wealth and a reputation as a competent military mind from his slaving campaigns in Central America and his participation in the Pizarro brothers' sacking of the Inca empire in highland South America.

De Soto's royal contract issued in late 1536 superseded all claims that might have arisen from the estates of Ayllón and Narváez, the latter then missing in action for eight years. De Soto was to explore, conquer, and settle La Florida, building forts and settlements. He was also responsible for the just treatment of the Indians and for their conversion to Catholicism, stipulations it appears he ignored. His treatment of the Indians was abysmal. And, as was true of the Ponce de León, Ayllón, and Narváez expeditions, there is no evidence that his attempt at colonization ever resulted in a single native American converting to Christianity.

De Soto's expedition was well planned and well supplied. It would be both a military invasion and a colonization initiative. Among the more than 700 participants were craftsmen needed to help build the forts and settlements. The army would take all the weapons, tools, and hardware needed to accomplish its goals. The state-of-the-art expedition sailed in April 1538 for Cuba, where de Soto was to assume the governorship and make final preparations for the assault on La Florida.

De Soto did not wish to repeat the failures of his predecessors. Ships were sent from Cuba to scout Bahía Honda, whose location was by then correctly charted. On May 18, 1539, de Soto sailed in a fleet of five large and four smaller ships. One week later the fleet dropped anchor just to the south of the mouth of modern-day Tampa Bay. Over the next several days a channel into the harbor was found and the ships unloaded. A camp was established on the north side of Little Manatee River near its mouth in the village of Chief Uzita.

The off-loading must have drawn an awed Indian audience. Moved into the village were two women, tailors, shoemakers, a stocking maker, notary, farrier, trumpeter, servants, friars, priests, cavalry, and infantry, plus war dogs, 220 horses, a drove of pigs, and supplies for eighteen months. De Soto spent six weeks scouting the land and learning about its people before proceeding inland. His ability to communicate with the Uzita and other Tampa Bay native groups, like the Mocoso, was enhanced when his men rescued Juan Ortiz, the Spaniard abandoned while looking for Narváez eleven years earlier.

De Soto, like Narváez before him, intended to take food from the Indians along his route to feed his expedition, and his army used captive Indians as bearers to carry supplies. The bearers probably numbered into the hundreds. Indian women were taken and used as consorts. The Spaniards were also quick to use force—often torture—to break the Indians' will. A common practice was to take hostages, often village chiefs or members of their families, in an effort to coerce the Indians into providing food, information, bearers, or consorts. There is nothing in the narratives to indicate that any of the priests and friars on this expedition objected to any of these practices, though later in the sixteenth century de Soto would be included among the conquistadors of the Americas held responsible for great cruelty.

Having satisfied himself that the army could exploit the Indians sufficiently, de Soto next considered where and when the expedition would spend the winter. He did not know exactly when cold weather would arrive, nor how harsh winter might be. And the longer the army camped, the greater would be the amount of

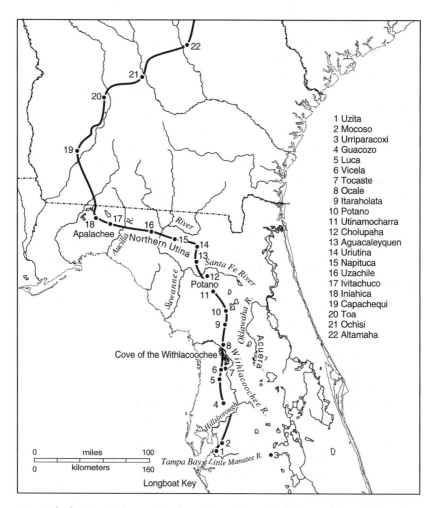

1 Uzita
2 Mocoso
3 Urriparacoxi
4 Guacozo
5 Luca
6 Vicela
7 Tocaste
8 Ocale
9 Itaraholata
10 Potano
11 Utinamocharra
12 Cholupaha
13 Aguacaleyquen
14 Uriutina
15 Napituca
16 Uzachile
17 Ivitachuco
18 Iniahica
19 Capachequi
20 Toa
21 Ochisi
22 Altamaha

Hernando de Soto's 1539–40 march from Tampa Bay to Apalachee and through Georgia, with towns and chiefdoms along the route indicated.

food it would consume. After seemingly working out solutions to these various contingencies, de Soto, about 500 Spaniards—among them two women—and probably an equal number of captive Indian bearers marched out of the Tampa Bay camp. Remaining behind were most of the ships, another one hundred people, and supplies—a reserve force that would await word from de Soto before it moved inland.

The overland expedition's immediate goal was to reach the main town of the Ocale Indians somewhere to the north. The Indians living around Tampa Bay had convinced de Soto he would find large quantities of food there, and he selected it as a potential winter campsite, though it was only early summer when he departed.

Moving 1,000 people, pigs, and supplies was not an easy task, and the expedition was probably quite spread out as it cut a swath through peninsula Florida. From Uzita territory the Spaniards and their native captives marched through the territory of Chief Mocoso on the east side of Tampa Bay. Unlike the Narváez expedition, de Soto's route was well inland along established trails rather than through the swampy coastal lowlands.

South of Lake Tsala Apopka, south and west of the Withlacoochee River, the expedition was reunited with a large scouting party that previously had been sent further inland to check out the realm of Chief Urriparacoxi, an important leader to whom the Tampa Bay Indians had been forced to pay tribute. The chief was probably a Timucua Indian whose territory just west of Orlando was at the southern end of the Timucuan region.

The scouts, who must have used runners or cavalry to stay in communication with the main body of the expedition (they knew exactly where to join them), had found neither wealth nor quantities of food. De Soto pressed on to Ocale, then known to be only a few days' travel ahead on the opposite side of the Cove of the Withlacoochee, a large wetland through which the Withlacoochee River flows.

De Soto was misled by his Indian guides into believing that the only way to Ocale was to cross the cove. In reality, the Spaniards simply could have marched around it. An advance party was sent into the cove to mark a trail, which they did with great difficulty. After crossing the Withlacoochee River, no easy task in itself, the advance party marched through a small village and then into the main Ocale town at the southwestern edge of the Timucuan region.

It took several days for the rest of the expedition to cross, during which many people were forced to forage for roots because they had run out of food. What should have been a happy reunion in Ocale turned to dismay when the Spaniards realized that they had been sold a bill of goods. Ocale was not large, nor did it have huge stores of food. De Soto had difficulty feeding everyone for even a few days—time desperately needed for recuperation.

At this point, de Soto's wisest move would have been to return to Tampa Bay. Perhaps because so much had already been invested in the expedition, he decided to move on to Apalachee, his new choice for a winter camp. To obtain the immediate food he needed, de Soto ordered soldiers on horseback to the Acuera Indians —a day's fast travel to the east. Then de Soto, fifty cavalry, and sixty infantry set out on a forced march northward to scout the land and determine whether the entire expedition could indeed make it to Apalachee. The remaining nearly 400 people stayed at Ocale, raiding the region to sustain themselves. It was early August.

This advance party moved rapidly north, from one Indian town to the next.

Over five days they journeyed from Ocale Indian territory through the land of the Potano Indians, and then across the Santa Fe River to the town of Aguacaleyquen among the north Florida Timucua. Along this 130-mile (210-kilometer) trek, de Soto found himself among farming populations, a turn of events that could only have heartened him.

The Aguacaleyquen's population was much more densely distributed than the native groups previously encountered in Florida. De Soto and his 110 men were badly outnumbered. In an attempt to forestall any hostilities on the part of the Indians, de Soto took the daughter of the chief of the Aguacaleyquen hostage. Eight cavalrymen then were sent back to Ocale with orders for the force left there to reunite at Aguacaleyquen. After they joined the advance party, de Soto led his army north and then west through what would become the heart of the Timucua mission province toward Apalachee. With him went the chief of the Aguacaleyquen, also taken hostage, as added insurance against attacks by the Indians.

Having hostages did not pay off. At the town of Napituca east of the Suwannee River, still in Timucua, two battles were fought with warriors of the Aguacaleyquen alliance. In the end, the Spaniards, with their superior weaponry and tactics, prevailed. To punish the Timucua for their actions, nearly a dozen chiefs and several hundred warriors were cruelly executed. Royal decrees or not, the Spaniards did not tolerate opposition and did not hesitate to administer swift and fatal retaliation.

The massacre at Napituca probably lived forever in the memories of the western Timucua. No Franciscan missions were ever established in that locality. The mistreatment of Indians by the Spaniards had gone too far.

From Napituca the expedition continued west, crossing the Suwannee River and entering the territory of the Yustaga Indians, also called the Uzachile. They marched into the main town, probably the same town where Chief Dulchanchellin had taken Narváez in 1528. Earlier the Uzachile chief had sent emissaries with gifts in an effort to seek peace with the Spaniards. The Indians were well aware that even peaceful overtures might not placate the Spaniards. By the time the latter entered the town, the residents had abandoned it. De Soto pushed on toward Apalachee.

The army traveled through a largely uninhabited forest to the Aucilla River, the western boundary of Apalachee territory. Again, as had happened with the Narváez expedition, Indian guides probably led them on a route through San Pedro Bay that took them south of the many Yustaga villages in central and northern Madison County.

The Apalachee attempted to defend their land against the invaders, launching an attack to prevent the Spaniards from crossing the Aucilla River. But de Soto's soldiers prevailed, and the expedition marched into northwest Florida, reaching the Apalachee town of Ivitachuco. The Apalachee, aware of the Spanish force's reliance on native stores to sustain itself, destroyed the town before the army arrived.

Over the next several days the expedition continued to press westward, moving from town to town despite continued attempts by their guides to mislead them. The passage was also hindered by guerrilla raids by Apalachee archers. In early October 1539 the expedition arrived at Anhaica, the Apalachee capital town. There de Soto would establish his winter camp, amidst the Indians' stored agricultural bounty.

Once encamped, de Soto sent calvary back to the village of Chief Uzita on Tampa Bay with orders for the reserves there to join him at Anhaica. The supplies and some of the people were loaded aboard ships; the remainder of the people would march overland, following the route de Soto had taken five months earlier.

The winter was spent warding off Apalachee attacks. On two occasions parts of Anhaica were burned by Indians, literally over the heads of the Spaniards. Soldiers and colonists could not venture far from town unless well protected, for fear of being picked off by Apalachee warriors.

In the spring de Soto's expedition, once again at full strength, began its exploration of the interior of La Florida. On March 3, 1540, his army broke camp, heading north into southwest Georgia. Ultimately they marched the length of the Mississippian world, the realm of native chiefdoms whose descendants during the later colonial period would be known as the Creek, Cherokee, and Choctaw Indians.

North of Apalachee in the Flint River drainage in southwest Georgia the army arrived first at the Mississippian chiefdom of Capachequi, then Toa, the latter near the Georgia fall line. Continuing diagonally across modern Georgia toward the northeast, the expedition reached Ichisi, a chiefdom whose main town was near contemporary Macon on the Ocmulgee River. Next, in the Oconee River drainage, was still another chiefdom, Ocute. Each of these sixteenth-century societies, like their Apalachee relatives to the south, consisted of large populations, multiple towns with a settlement hierarchy, complex political and social organization, and an economy based on intensive farming, especially of corn, beans, squash, and pumpkins. The river valleys of fall-line and piedmont Georgia and South Carolina, their fertility replenished each year by floods, fostered the plentiful agricultural yields crucial to Mississippian life.

From Ocute, de Soto's army continued northeast, passing through a huge, sparsely occupied land before reaching the town of Hymahi at the meeting of the Congaree and Wateree Rivers below modern-day Columbia, South Carolina. The "desert of Ocute," as one expedition participant referred to the 130-mile-wide (210-kilometer-wide) uninhabited region across the Savannah, Saluda, and Broad

Rivers, seems to have been a vast geographical buffer separating major Mississippian chiefdoms. The expedition would encounter other such buffers in its trek across the southern United States, though none so large.

From Apalachee, de Soto maintained a northeastern heading. Although nowhere in any of the narratives concerning the expedition is it explicitly stated, I believe that de Soto was leading his army in search of the legendary land of Chicora, thought to be somewhere in the interior of the Carolinas. While encamped in Apalachee, de Soto had interviewed a young Indian captured in north Florida who said that he came from a land far away, ruled by a woman chief who received gold and other tributes from her people. His description of how the gold was mined and smelted excited the Spaniards. They wanted to believe such stories were true and probably equated that land, called Yupaha, with the Chicora legend. When de Soto left Apalachee, one chronicler wrote that he went in search of Yupaha.

When the army entered the main town of Cofitachequi near modern Camden, South Carolina, de Soto may have thought he had found his goal. Cofitachequi was ruled by a woman chief and she presented him with a string of pearls. An additional 200 pounds (90 kilograms) of pearls were taken from a Cofitachequi temple. But further wealth would prove elusive.

Because it was early spring—before the harvest—the stored food supplies of Cofitachequi were inadequate to feed the army. Men were sent to a nearby chiefdom, Ilapi, near contemporary Cheraw, South Carolina, to gather more supplies. Even so, some of the expedition's members urged de Soto to colonize Cofitachequi, which the Indians said was two days' journey from the Atlantic coast (perhaps by runner; Camden is more than 100 miles [160 kilometers] from the coast).

De Soto decided to push on. In answer to his inquiries about where to find wealth, the people of Cofitachequi provided the name of Chiaha, a chiefdom subject to the powerful chief of Coosa. Coosa was a huge native province stretching 200 miles (322 kilometers) from eastern Tennessee into Alabama and encompassing a number of individual chiefdoms and towns. Chiaha marked Coosa's eastern boundary, but to get there, the Spaniards would have to cross the Appalachian Mountains north of the Cofitachequi and Ilapi. To accomplish that, they first marched northward to Xuala near modern Marion, North Carolina. Then, turning west, they entered the Blue Ridge Mountains through Swannanoa Gap and followed the Swannanoa River to near modern Asheville, North Carolina. They continued, following a trail along the French Broad River into the Tennessee River Valley and Chiaha. There the army camped while a detachment was sent to Chisca farther northeast in Tennessee, where they hoped to find gold.

From Chiaha the army proceeded southwesterly through Coosa, moving from town to town until they neared the capital town, which was also called Coosa. Coosa, a major Mississippian capital, was fortified with palisaded walls, and its paramount chief was borne in a litter carried by sixty or seventy Indians. The journey through Coosa must have been extraordinary. With its large population, magnificent towns, and powerful chief, Coosa would remain in the minds of the Spaniards and draw the interest of future expeditions.

South of the town of Coosa the army came to Itaba (the archaeological site of Etowah), today a Georgia state park northwest of Atlanta. Next came Ulibahali, then Talisi, near modern Childersburg, Alabama, at the southwestern end of the Coosa province.

After crossing the Tallapoosa River in Alabama, the expedition arrived at the chiefdom of Tuscaluza and two of its towns, Piachi and Mabila, the latter probably near the lower portion of the Cahaba River. The initial encounter with Chief Tuscaluza took place in October 1540, about a year after de Soto had first arrived in Apalachee. Chief Tuscaluza, an imposing leader, was a shrewd general. He lured the Spanish expedition into the walled town of Mabila where hundreds of warriors were hidden. A tremendous, bloody battle took place, and the Spaniards were nearly defeated. They lost many supplies and weapons. In the end the Spaniards' superior tactics and war horses carried them through.

While his men recovered from the battle, de Soto had a tough decision to make. Should he continue exploring La Florida, or should he move the expedition to the southern coast? He knew that in Pensacola Bay at Ochuse ships awaited him with more supplies; he could leave La Florida and return to Cuba. But he choose to push on northwest, to the Indian town of Apafalaya on the Black Warrior River. Next the army crossed into what would someday be Mississippi and reached the chiefdoms of the Chicaça (modern-day Chickasaw) Indians. There the expedition spent the winter of 1540–41, their second in La Florida.

Although de Soto's route through northern Apalachee—Georgia, the Carolinas, Tennessee, and Alabama—was outside the region of the later mission provinces, the Mississippian societies of that huge region would continue to draw Spanish attention. Future expeditions would retrace some of de Soto's steps and visit the same Indian towns. From Mississippi west, however, the remaining territory covered by de Soto was beyond the limits of later Spanish exploratory endeavors.

From the winter camp at Chicaça, the de Soto expedition traveled for more than a week through another unoccupied geographical buffer before entering the chiefdom of Quizquiz in northwest Mississippi, south of Memphis on the Mississippi River itself. It was a heavily populated region. On four large flat-bottomed boats, the Spaniards crossed the river into Arkansas in May 1541, two years after their Tampa Bay landfall.

The entire third year was spent in Arkansas marching from one Mississippian chiefdom to another and searching for wealth. They found none. Finally, the expedition returned to the Mississippi River. De Soto, ill, died June 20, 1542.

Luis de Moscoso de Alvarado took charge and attempted to lead the expedition out of La Florida to Mexico by marching across Arkansas and Texas. After traveling hundreds of miles, perhaps as far as the Trinity River, Texas, the Spaniards concluded that it was futile to continue. Their captive native interpreters could no longer understand the languages of the Indians they encountered. They had long left the territory of Mississippian farming societies, and the Texas Indians did not have enough food to feed an army.

With the prospects for obtaining sufficient food bleak, Moscoso de Alvarado led the expedition all the way back to the Mississippi River, and they spent the winter of 1542–43, its fourth, there. Over six months the Spaniards built six boats large enough to carry them down the river. They set out in early June and three weeks later arrived in the Gulf of Mexico. It then took another two and a half months to reach a Spanish settlement near present-day Tampico, Mexico. Three hundred and eleven people, about half the number who had set out from Tampa Bay, survived what by any standards had been an incredible odyssey.

TRISTÁN DE LUNA Y ARELLANO AND OCHUSE

Ponce de León, Ayllón, Narváez, and de Soto—La Florida's terrain and its people had thwarted all these Spanish attempts at conquest. For a time after de Soto's expedition, the Spanish Crown would look elsewhere, leaving La Florida to its native inhabitants. But the realities of geography—La Florida commanded the northern access to Spain's American empire—and European national interests soon revived Spanish desires to colonize that land. If Spain did not, certainly England or France would.

In the late 1550s another plan for colonization surfaced. Backed by the viceroy of Mexico, Luis de Velasco, and led by Tristán de Luna y Arellano, 1,500 people would set sail from the Gulf of Mexico coast in June 1559 bound for Ochuse territory, modern-day Pensacola Bay, Florida. Thirteen ships carried craftsmen, soldiers, settlers, clergy, and Mexican Indian servants. Some of these men were survivors of the de Soto expedition.

The Luna expedition was part of a lofty plan that had several goals. One was to establish an overland route from northern Mexico across the Gulf coastal plain to Santa Elena on the Atlantic coast, the place associated with Ayllón in 1526. Goods, including silver mined in Mexico, could be transported by land, avoiding the sealanes around peninsular Florida that continued to wreak havoc on ships. From Santa Elena, ships could journey safely across the Atlantic Ocean to Spain.

This overland road would need to pass through Coosa and skirt the Gulf coast at Ochuse. Spanish settlements along this road could protect travelers, and missions, especially along the Gulf coast, could make allies of the Indians. Coastal outposts could help protect victims of Spanish shipwrecks. A Spanish presence in La Florida, it was believed, could give conquistadors and entrepreneurs access to the wealth that must be hidden somewhere in La Florida. Even in the aftermath of the de Soto expedition, the Chicora legend never died.

The Luna fleet experienced problems finding Pensacola Bay, causing them to take more than two months to travel the relatively short distance from Veracruz to reach the harbor. Some would consider this a harbinger of the awful times that followed. When the ships finally sailed into Pensacola Bay in early August, it was renamed Bahía Filipina del Puerto de Santa María, usually shortened to Bahía de Santa María. The colonists also referred to their settlement as Polonza, possibly related to the name Pensacola. Less than a week after anchoring, a hurricane struck Ochuse, sinking nine of the expedition's ships and destroying many supplies. If they were to survive, the colonists needed an adequate food supply for 1,500.

Two expeditions were therefore sent to scout the territory around Polonza. One traveled 30 miles (48 kilometers) on land, possibly along the bay, but was unable to locate any Indian towns from which food could be taken. The second party sailed in a small boat up the Escambia River into the interior and did not fare any better. There were too few Indians or they had withdrawn. It was decided that the expedition would have to go farther afield.

Men who had been with de Soto suggested that Piachi, one of Chief Tuscaluza's towns that they had marched through two decades earlier, would have food. In response Luna sent a detachment of 150–200 people to find Piachi. The men marched more than 100 miles (160 kilometers) west-northwest, and came to the Alabama River. They failed to find Piachi, but they did come to several other towns, the largest of which, with eighty houses, was Nanipacani. Desperate, the rest of the colony was ordered to Nanipacani. One group of colonists traveled there in two small boats along the coast to Mobile Bay and then up the Alabama River. The rest of the people, except for fifty left at Ochuse, traveled overland.

There was not sufficient food in Nanipacani to feed the expedition. The Indians of the region, victims of de Soto's excesses fifteen years earlier, had abandoned their villages, taking stored corn and other food with them. They also burned their fields, denying that food to the Spaniards as well. The Spaniards soon learned that adjacent towns up and down the Alabama River had done the same. Even on the nearby Tombigbee River, Indian villages were abandoned, making the food shortage critical. A detachment was sent by boat farther north up the Alabama River, but again no suitable place to house the expedition was found.

In April 1560, eight months after landing at Ochuse and near starvation, 140 cavalry and infantry were sent overland to the interior native province of Coosa. Those men ultimately did reach the Tennessee River and the heart of Coosa in

Tennessee and northwest Georgia, but they were outwitted by the Indians, who allowed them nothing.

Unable to feed themselves, the expedition members left behind at Nanipacani went back to Ochuse, where they were eventually joined by the returning Coosa detachment. The expedition fell to squabbling. Some members tried to oust Luna so they could leave La Florida. At last, in April 1561, ships arrived with orders from the viceroy of Mexico to move the colony to Santa Elena on the Atlantic coast. The starving colonists, reduced to eating shellfish and grass, were only too glad to leave. On the way to Santa Elena they made port at Havana so those people wishing not to go on could disembark. Then the rest, led by Angel de Villafañe, sailed on to the Atlantic coast, exploring from Santa Elena to near Cape Hatteras, looking for a suitable site to settle. At the cape a storm struck, sinking some of the ships. Thwarted, the expedition gave up and sailed for the Caribbean.

Nearly half a century had passed since Juan Ponce de León's 1513 landfall on the Atlantic coast of La Florida, and Spain had yet to plant a successful colony. This failure left eastern North America open to initiatives by other European powers who wished to exercise their own land claims.

France was Spain's main rival for La Florida. The Florentine explorer Giovanni da Verrazzano had sailed under the French flag in 1524, when scouting the Atlantic coast from La Florida to Cape Breton, Nova Scotia. By late 1561, rumors that France was planning a colonization expedition to La Florida reached Spain. That news prompted plans for a Spanish settlement on Chesapeake Bay, the Bahía de Santa María. It would be led by Lucas Vázquez de Ayllón, son of the leader of the 1526 San Miguel de Gualdape colony expedition.

Ayllón, who had considerable trouble getting his expedition organized, did not sail from Spain until October 1563, and his ships sailed no farther than Santo Domingo. Unhappy colonists and financial problems caught up with Ayllón, who fled in the middle of the night, reportedly for Peru.

CHARLESFORT AND FT. CAROLINE

The French dispatched a colonial expedition to La Florida in early 1562. Jean Ribault and 150 people made landfall on the Atlantic coast of peninsular Florida near St. Augustine and then sailed north to the mouth of the St. Johns River. There Ribault christened the River of Mai (May) and erected a stone marker inscribed with the arms of France, claiming the land for his sovereign.

Sailing farther north, the French explored the coast as far as Santa Elena, which was renamed Port Royal. Another stone marker was raised, demarcating the northern extent of exploration. Work began on Charlesfort, a fortified settlement. Ribault left thirty soldiers to hold the fort and sailed for France with the remainder.

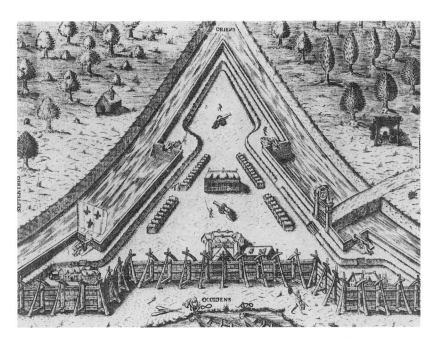

Ft. Caroline (engraved by Theodore de Bry in 1591).

After returning to Europe, Ribault would travel to London, where his stories of La Florida would influence future efforts in the 1580s by England and Sir Walter Raleigh to colonize the coast of modern North Carolina, the land the English called Virginia. The first English colony, at Roanoke, included one hundred people, but it was withdrawn in less than a year. The second attempt, which resulted in the infamous lost colony of Roanoke, was never heard from again.

The thirty Frenchmen left at Charlesfort fared a little better. But when it became obvious that they would not survive—the rigors of the land and Indian raids being too much to overcome—they sailed back to France in a small boat. Poorly supplied for the journey, the soldiers are alleged to have resorted to cannibalism to survive.

News of the French fort reached Spain. In the summer of 1564 a Spanish ship was dispatched to destroy it. Arriving at the already abandoned site, the Spaniards retrieved the stone marker and transported it back to Spain, symbolically obliterating what was viewed as a French intrusion into Spanish-claimed lands.

Even while the Spanish were planning and carrying out their reprisal against Charlesfort, a second French expedition to colonize La Florida was in the works. In April 1564 René Goulaine de Laudonnière and 300 soldiers and settlers sailed in three ships for the southeastern Atlantic coast. Laudonnière had been Ribault's second in command on the 1562 voyage to Santa Elena. Laudonnière and his expedition, which included women, children, sheep, and chickens, made landfall on the Atlantic coast of Florida in July 1564, then sailed to the mouth of the St. Johns River, where they found the first stone marker Ribault had raised two years earlier. The ships sailed up the St. Johns about 11 miles (18 kilometers), to St. Johns Bluff and landed to search for a site to build a settlement. They then sailed northward along the coast past Guale Indian territory before opting to return to the St. Johns River. In late July work began on Ft. Caroline, an earthen and log-walled fort with storage sheds, houses, and other buildings.

The problems of feeding a colony, which had vexed Ayllón and Luna, also plagued the French. By November the hardships had caused some of the soldiers to steal a boat and desert the colony for the Caribbean and the promise of plunder. There also was a mutiny, and for a short time Laudonnière was imprisoned. In December sixty additional men deserted, taking two boats.

The French were forced to trade with local Timucua Indians for food. The main village of Chief Saturiwa, who headed the large lower St. Johns–region alliance, was only a short distance from Ft. Caroline. But the Timucua of northeast Florida were not extensive agriculturists and did not have large supplies of stored corn and other foods.

The next year brought no relief for the French. The Timucua did not plant until spring, and the harvest was in the summer; as a result the winter and spring 1565 were lean times for the colonists. They survived by trading iron tools, trinkets, and even clothing to the Indians for small amounts of corn, beans, acorns, fish, deer, turkey, and other wild food. The Indians traveled great distances and struck hard bargains with the hungry French.

Expeditions were sent by boat up (south) the St. Johns River as far as Lake George—the entire range of eastern Timucua territory. Smaller expeditions were sent overland across northern Florida through Timucuan territory as far as the Yustaga Indians. Twice the French were convinced by Chief Outina, head of the Timucuan alliance north of Lake George, to aid him in attacks on the Potano Indians in north-central Florida.

In late summer 1565 a small fleet of four ships captained by John Hawkins, an Englishman, made landfall at Ft. Caroline. From Hawkins the colonists received flour, beans, salt, oil, vinegar, olives, rice, biscuit (hardtack), candle wax, shoes, and even one of his ships in exchange for arms and artillery. Resupplied and with a second ship at their disposal, the French immediately made plans to return home in mid-August. Laudonnière intended to take captive Indians back to France, educate them in European ways, and then return them to La Florida, where they could serve as ambassadors for French interests.

All these plans and preparations would ultimately go for naught. On August 28, as favorable tides and winds made departure imminent, a small fleet of ships was sighted in the distance. It was Jean Ribault returning with orders giving him control of the colony. Laudonnière's return to France was put on hold. Less than a week after Ribault, a second naval force sailed into view: that of Pedro Menéndez de Avilés.

Spanish spies in the court of France had brought back news of the French attempts to found a colony in La Florida. Marauding in the Caribbean by the French deserters from Ft. Caroline had also drawn the attention of Philip II, king of Spain. To counter these French intrusions, the Crown had dispatched Menéndez de Avilés, commander of Spain's Caribbean fleet.

4

BLACK-ROBED FRIARS AND MILITARY OUTPOSTS

News of the French attempt to place a colony in La Florida reached Philip II of Spain in 1563, after Jean Ribault had built Charlesfort. At first, it appeared that the French threat would be dealt with in a timely fashion. Pedro Menéndez de Avilés was already preparing to return to Seville in 1563, when summoned by his king. As soon as he landed in Spain, Menéndez de Avilés ran into problems. Powerful commercial officials and merchants brought charges of smuggling against him, initiating proceedings that would delay him for more than a year.

Menéndez de Avilés was held under house arrest while the allegations were investigated. The dispute kept him confined through 1564. In February 1565 claims against him were settled, and he was free to proceed to negotiate a royal contract to found a colony in La Florida. The contract, dated March 15, 1565, was quickly confirmed, and Menéndez de Avilés set about planning and supplying an expedition whose goals would involve both military actions and colonial endeavors.

Three months later, in late June, Menéndez de Avilés sailed for La Florida. He commanded a large expeditionary force of more than 1,500 soldiers, colonists, and crafts persons, along with supplies, including food, ammunition, and armaments, all loaded aboard nineteen ships. But not all the ships sailed at once. The plan called for one group of ships to rendezvous in the Canary Islands and then sail to the Caribbean before advancing on La Florida. A second, smaller fleet with another 1,000 people would follow later.

Unfortunately, all did not go as planned. Only eight ships made the first Canary Islands rendezvous. Near the Windward Islands, Menéndez de Avilés's small fleet was hit by a hurricane. Cannons and millstones were tossed overboard to lighten one vessel, and several of the other ships sustained damage and sprang leaks. One

Pedro Menéndez de Avilés, first governor of Spanish Florida,
portrayed in a sixteenth-century painting.

caravel with more than one hundred soldiers and supplies was blown well off course
and captured by French corsairs. Limping into the harbor at San Juan, Puerto Rico,
Menéndez de Avilés set about regrouping his forces and making repairs.

On August 15 Menéndez de Avilés's remaining ships set sail from San Juan for
La Florida. Originally the fleet was to stop at Havana for reinforcements before
going on, but before leaving Spain, Menéndez de Avilés had received intelligence
that Ribault's fleet was about to depart France. Wanting to arrive at Ft. Caroline
before Ribault's reinforcements reached the French settlement, Menéndez de
Avilés decided to skip Cuba and sail through the Bahamas. French prisoners had
previously given the Spaniards the approximate location of the fort.

The Spanish fleet successfully made its way to Cape Canaveral in late August,
on the same day Ribault dropped anchor in the St. Johns River. Ribault, however,
had left France in May, a month before Menéndez de Avilés. The Spanish ships
sailed northward up the coast, and near modern Ponce de Leon Inlet, Menéndez

de Avilés went ashore to gather information from the Indians, probably the Timucua. He learned that indeed the French fort was to the north. Two days later he sailed to the mouth of the St. Johns River.

Ribault's ships were at anchor, some near the fort itself and four others outside the mouth of the river. Still in the process of unloading, the ships were sitting ducks for a Spanish attack. As Menéndez de Avilés maneuvered to board one of the ships, the French sailors at the river's mouth quickly cut their anchor ropes and took to the sea. The Spanish fleet pursued, shooting cannons. After an all-night chase, it was clear that the partially repaired Spanish ships could not catch the faster French vessels.

Menéndez de Avilés gave up and sailed back to the St. Johns River, intending to take control of the river's mouth. However, the three French ships that had been nearest the fort were now blocking the mouth, and French soldiers lined the shore. The Spaniards withdrew.

Menéndez de Avilés sailed south to a harbor he had passed by a few days earlier. There, after a formal ceremony to take possession of the land, the Spaniards began to set up camp at the landing they named Nombre de Dios. The settlement itself was named St. Augustine, after the saint on whose feast day the fleet had first sighted La Florida. Menéndez de Avilés ordered the site—a Timucua-Seloy Indian village—fortified, and soldiers, settlers, and African slaves began work. Ribault's ships later would sail by and spy the colonists unloading supplies and infantry.

The Seloy Indians continued to report the Spanish activities to Ft. Caroline. Ribault decided to mount an offensive with sailors from his fleet's crews and soldiers who had been serving under Laudonnière. On September 10, 1565, about 600 Frenchmen sailed for St. Augustine. When the fleet reached the open waters of the Atlantic, they were greeted by a huge summer tropical storm, perhaps a hurricane, which scattered the French ships. Four of Ribault's vessels were blown ashore, three near Ponce de Leon Inlet. The fourth, the *Trinité*, Ribault's flagship, heavily armed with bronze cannon, was wrecked near Cape Canaveral.

Meanwhile, Menéndez de Avilés had decided to attack Ft. Caroline, whose complement of fighting men had been greatly reduced by Ribault's departure. The Spanish would not attack by sea, as the French expected, but by land. On September 18, Menéndez de Avilés and 500 arquebuses marched north. Two days later at dawn and under cover of a driving summer rainstorm, the Spaniards attacked Ft. Caroline. The battle was a short one. In the foul weather the French lookouts foolishly had been ordered to step down. By the time the French realized their fort was under attack, Menéndez de Avilés and his men were practically inside.

One hundred thirty-two French men, some still in their nightclothes, were killed, and fifty women and children were captured. Laudonnière and forty people managed to escape and make their way to the three French ships anchored in the St. Johns River. One ship was scuttled and the other two, with partial crews, sailed for France.

Ft. Caroline, devastated, was commandeered by the Spaniards and renamed San Mateo. The victors rounded up those French who had fled into the woods. Capturing these escapees was made easier by paying bounties to the former Indian allies of the French.

While Ft. Caroline was being taken by Spaniards, the survivors of Ribault's ships, unaware of what had occured, were marching northward from Ponce de Leon Inlet to reunite with their fellow colonists. By late September they had made their way to a point 18 miles (30 kilometers) south of St. Augustine, where their progress was temporarily stymied by an inlet. They were observed by Timucua Indians who told Menéndez de Avilés what they had seen. He and a company of men confronted the French soldiers on the morning of September 29. Hungry, tired, and outnumbered, the French agreed to surrender if their lives would be spared. But Menéndez de Avilés would offer no such assurances to the French, whom the Spaniards labeled outlaws for having tried to usurp Spanish-claimed lands, and heretics for having embraced the Protestant faith.

In accordance with his own beliefs and duties, Menéndez de Avilés swore "to pursue them with a fire and blood war to extermination" (Lyon 1976, 125). Numbering as many as 200, the French had their hands bound, were taken behind a nearby dune, and slain. A dozen or so individuals were spared because they professed to be Catholics. The small inlet where the executions took place would be named Matanzas for the massacre. Today, it still bears the infamous name.

Two weeks later on October 11, a second group of French shipwreck victims, including Jean Ribault, arrived at the same inlet. Again Menéndez de Avilés and his soldiers confronted the French soldiers and sailors. About half agreed to surrender and put themselves at the mercy of the Spaniards. The others opted to return south. Like their compatriots, all the French who surrendered, Ribault among them, were killed.

Later in October, Menéndez de Avilés was brought information about a third group of shipwrecked French encamped at Cape Canaveral, close to where the *Trinité* had been blown ashore. These survivors had built a sand-and-wood-walled fort and armed it with six bronze cannons salvaged from the ship. Thought to number between seventy and eighty, they may have included men who had refused to surrender to Menéndez de Avilés at Matanzas at the time of the second massacre. Reports indicated the French were building a boat in which they hoped to escape La Florida.

Menéndez de Avilés set about finishing off the French in early November. One hundred fifty infantry marched overland to face the French, while three armed vessels with another one hundred Spaniards anchored offshore. Under the cover of darkness, Menéndez de Avilés moved his army into place for a dawn attack. The French discovered the plan and abandoned the fort, along with the unfinished boat, both of which Menéndez de Avilés destroyed. With no supplies, the French soon surrendered. A few, however, refused and fled. Menéndez de Avilés, perhaps having second thoughts about the Matanzas massacres, spared the lives of these captives.

MENÉNDEZ DE AVILÉS'S PLAN

Pedro Menéndez de Avilés had won, and although that hold was tenuous, La Florida was in Spanish hands. Two short months after landing at St. Augustine, he was ready to extend his grasp over the land and its people in accordance with his royal contract.

Part of the royal contract stipulated that he explore a region extending from the Gulf of Mexico, northeast of Mexico to around the Florida peninsula, and up the Atlantic coast to Newfoundland—a huge territory. Menéndez de Avilés was also required to establish and occupy two or three towns and convert the native peoples to Catholicism.

From letters written during his first several months at St. Augustine, it is clear Menéndez de Avilés had a plan, albeit one based on faulty geographical knowledge. First, he intended to establish a series of garrisoned coastal settlements to protect La Florida and its shipping lanes against future attempts by other European powers who might want to duplicate France's short-lived efforts. Menéndez de Avilés already had two such settlements: St. Augustine and San Mateo.

Coastal garrisons would not only help to counter England and France, they would also offer succor to shipwrecked Spaniards, some of whom were already known to have been living among coastal Indians, at times as captives. Initially, outposts were to be spaced along La Florida's coasts from the Gulf of Mexico to Chesapeake Bay, which the Spaniards called Bahía de Santa María. He also intended to have his colony's capital not at St. Augustine, but farther north on the Atlantic coast at Santa Elena, the same place Ribault had build Charlesfort in 1562. Santa Elena had a better harbor and was closer to the wealth that Menéndez de Avilés expected to find in interior La Florida.

Another part of Menéndez de Avilés's plan was to tie the coastal settlements together using the inland rivers of peninsular Florida and the coastal waterways, such as the Indian River. As he explored the coasts and gathered information from the Indians, Menéndez de Avilés had come to believe that the various rivers of peninsular Florida—St. Johns, Caloosahatchee, Miami, and perhaps the Hillsborough—were all interconnected with one another. For instance, he thought the

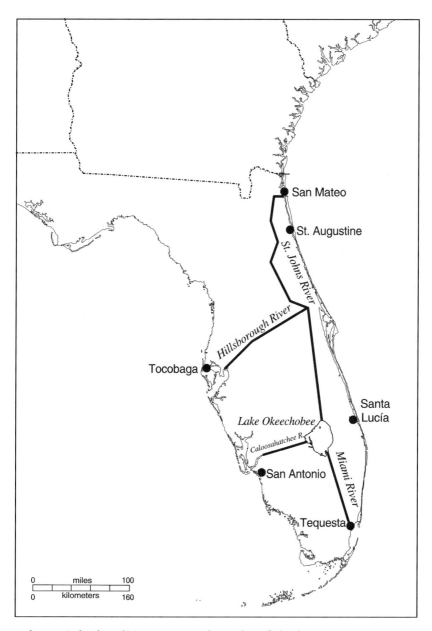

Pedro Menéndez de Avilés's erroneous understanding of Florida's rivers.

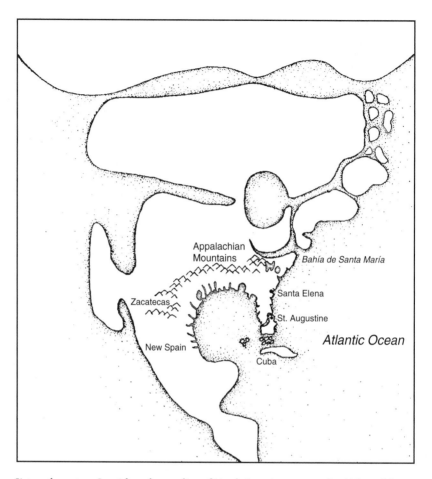

Sixteenth-century Spanish understanding of North American geography. (Adapted from Lewis and Loomie 1953)

Caloosahatchee River was a tributary of the St. Johns River. So one could sail from San Mateo south on the St. Johns River and then southwest on the Caloosahatchee River to the land of the Calusa Indians, where Juan Ponce de León had been. Menéndez de Avilés intended to place coastal settlements and garrisons at the mouths of these rivers and combine them with missions. Small boats could travel without exposing themselves to the storms and sandbars of the Gulf of Mexico and the Atlantic.

It was also thought by Menéndez de Avilés and other Spaniards that an arm of the Pacific Ocean extended well east, close to the Atlantic coast. This was believed to be the fabled Northwest Passage, which could provide European powers access to the riches of the Orient by sailing across the Atlantic Ocean, through the passage, and into the Pacific. The most likely access to that passage was considered to be via the Bahía de Santa María, Chesapeake Bay. By gaining control of that bay and the Atlantic coast, Spain, and Menéndez de Avilés could gain untold wealth; Santa Elena could become a major port, transshipping goods from the Orient to Spain, and vice versa.

Another part of Menéndez de Avilés's plan involved the establishment of an overland route from northern New Spain and the silver mines of Zacatecas, Mexico, across La Florida to a port in Santa Elena. The Spaniards believed the Atlantic coast was much closer to northern Mexico than it actually is. Menéndez de Avilés related in letters to his sovereign that the Appalachian Mountains extended to Mexico. A road to Mexico paralleling those mountains across the coastal plain would pass through the impressive Indian provinces where de Soto had marched twenty years earlier. Spanish settlements and missions would be used to protect the route and make allies of the Indians.

Missions to convert the native peoples of La Florida and subject them to Spanish rule were implicit in Menéndez de Avilés's plan. He even intended to have a Jesuit school founded in Havana, where heirs of chiefs could be sent to learn to be Christians: when they returned to La Florida to assume their chiefly offices, these individuals would be loyal Spanish subjects.

In March 1565 Menéndez de Avilés had first written to the leader of the Jesuits, Father Francisco Borgia, about the possibility of providing missionary priests to serve the native people of La Florida. The Society of Jesus, a new order founded in 1540 and dedicated to missionary work, had yet to send missionaries to a Spanish colony, though their missionaries were serving Portuguese colonies in Africa, Japan, India, and Brazil. If a passage to the Orient was established, the order would be well situated to expand its efforts to those far eastern lands, extending their good works around the globe.

THE REALITY

Menéndez de Avilés was quick to try implementing his plans, taking advantage of new opportunities and challenges as they arose. Immediately, he faced the same supply problems that every previous European attempt to colonize La Florida had confronted. Despite all his advance planning, the storm and other difficulties had destroyed needed supplies or apparently delayed or diverted reinforcements. And although he had captured the Ribault's supplies at Ft. Caroline, the damp climate had caused widespread spoilage. The amount of food available to the new Spanish colony was much less than anticipated.

There was another food-related crisis: feeding the seventy French prisoners taken at Cape Canaveral. If they returned with Menéndez de Avilés to St. Augustine, it would only mean more mouths to feed. Perhaps seeing it as an opportunity to establish one of his planned coastal settlements and reduce the pressure on St. Augustine, Menéndez de Avilés moved the French prisoners and a small army of 250 soldiers and sailors 52 miles (84 kilometers) down the coast from Cape Canaveral. There, by an Ais Indian village next to a small inlet, probably modern Sebastian inlet, the Spaniards set up a camp, intending to live off the land and supplies that would be delivered later.

The Ais were given gifts of scissors, mirrors, and knives, and at first, things went well. It was decided that 200 of his men and one boat would remain at the camp, and Menéndez de Avilés would take the remaining fifty men and some of the French prisoners in the two other boats and sail to Havana, where he hoped to find missing components of his colonial flotilla and garner supplies for his beleaguered colony. In Havana, Menéndez de Avilés found 325 more colonists from several recently arrived ships. He also learned that other ships had turned back en route or were still lost. After purchasing needed supplies two ships were loaded and sent to St. Augustine; another ship with supplies was sent to the men at Ais.

In Cuba Menéndez de Avilés also received word that 1,800 colonists were planning to sail from Spain to join his colony. They, too, would need to be fed, so he dispatched a boat to Campeche, Mexico, for additional supplies. He also witnessed the arrival of another of his lost ships, but there was little to cheer about; one hundred fifty of his men took the opportunity to desert. Apparently the real or imagined rigors of La Florida were too bleak, and the men opted instead for life in the Caribbean.

Meanwhile, the supply ships sent to La Florida returned with grim news. It seems that discontent had surfaced only days after Menéndez de Avilés had departed to oust the French from Cape Canaveral in November. More than one hundred of the colonists in St. Augustine and San Mateo had died. Others were openly fomenting rebellion and threatening to leave. The settlement left at Ais was in worse condition. Starving, the men were forced to forage for food, probably raiding Ais villages. The Ais had retaliated, and the Spaniards and the French prisoners had been forced to retreat farther down the coast to a second inlet about 70 miles (110 kilometers) south of Cape Canaveral, modern St. Lucie Inlet. There they had built a fort christened Santa Lucía.

After resupplying his colony, Menéndez de Avilés set about implementing more of his plan for coastal settlement. In February 1566 he set sail from Cuba for southwest Florida and the Calusa Indians. He wanted to befriend the Calusa and place a garrison near the mouth of the Caloosahatchee River.

At Calos, the Calusa capital town on Mound Key south of modern Ft. Myers, Florida, Menéndez de Avilés and his men found five Spanish men, five mestizo women from Peru, and an African woman, all survivors of a 1545 shipwreck along the coast. Originally there had been more, but the Calusa had killed forty-two other survivors. One of the five male survivors, Hernando d'Escalante Fontaneda, would later write an informative account of what he had seen. At least two of these survivors would choose to remain among the Calusa, where they had lived for more than two decades.

The Spaniards wanted the Calusa Indians to know they were powerful allies. Most likely similar to the La Florida governor's entrances into other Indian villages, Menéndez de Avilés's entry into Calos was intended to display the religious and military might of the Spaniards. With weapons drawn and 200 arquebuses primed for firing, the Spaniards marched into the Calusa town to the accompaniment of fifes, drums, and trumpets under unfurled banners. The pomp included the playing of a harp, violin, and psaltery and a dwarf who sang and danced. Even the most passive observer would have been impressed.

The Calusa chief, whom the Spaniards called Carlos, sought to cement the friendship of this powerful new ally by offering Menéndez de Avilés one of his own sisters in matrimony; apparently such an exchange to unite a chiefly alliance was a common native practice. Menéndez de Avilés, already married to a Spanish woman, saw the utility of accepting the offer. The woman was christened Doña Antonia, and a wedding was held. When Menéndez de Avilés departed for Havana he took Doña Antonia and seven of her companions with him.

Later in 1566 Menéndez de Avilés would send a second expedition to the Calusa village with orders to establish a garrison and a small settlement. The garrison would be named San Antonio. Because Jesuit missionaries had not yet arrived in La Florida, Menéndez de Avilés used knowledgeable soldiers to act as Catholic teachers offering religious instruction to the Indians. At each of the coastal settlements he erected large wooden crosses as symbols of Christianity.

While Menéndez de Avilés was among the Calusa in southwest Florida, his three small settlements at San Mateo, St. Augustine, and Santa Lucía continued to suffer. The men at Santa Lucía had been reduced to eating palmettos and chewing on discarded animal bones. Their hastily built wooden fort offered some protection against Indian arrows, but before it was completed fifteen colonists had been killed. Raids on the fort killed eight more people. Continually under attack, the Spaniards and the French prisoners were essentially trapped. Some of the men had deserted on a boat sailing south toward Havana. By chance they were intercepted by Menéndez de Avilés returning to St. Augustine from the Calusa.

In St. Augustine Menéndez de Avilés learned that some of those colonists had also mutinied and deserted. Efforts to escape the hardships of La Florida were rampant. He was able to restore order, but not without losing more of his colonists, several groups of whom departed for the Caribbean.

Menéndez de Avilés next sailed north to Santa Elena, taking about 150 people. Along the way he encountered a few fugitive Frenchmen living on the coast who had escaped his raid on Ft. Caroline the previous year. The voyage took Menéndez de Avilés through the coastal lands of the Guale Indians. He was careful to befriend and pacify them. After all, they occupied the territory between San Mateo and Santa Elena through which future Spanish travelers would pass.

At Easter time 1566 Menéndez de Avilés founded a second Spanish town at Santa Elena. Santa Elena was intended to become La Florida's main town and the port that would anchor both the overland route to Mexico and the shipping lanes between Spain and the Orient. Menéndez de Avilés then returned to Cuba, where there was finally good news. The fleet he had been expecting from Spain—seventeen ships carrying 2,000 people and supplies—had arrived at St. Augustine.

But this encouraging development was tempered by another unsettling incident: back in Santa Elena a supply ship had been seized by deserters who fled south in it toward the Caribbean. Along the way they had stopped at Tequesta to get fresh water. While ashore, about twenty of the men had been abandoned by their companions, who sailed away. The men left behind were found later by another of Menéndez de Avilés ships. To avoid punishment for their original desertion, the twenty agreed to remain at Tequesta and man a small garrison.

Less than a year after having landed in La Florida, Menéndez de Avilés's plan was unfolding. In addition to St. Augustine, garrisons and small settlements had been established among the Calusa, at the mouth of the Miami River, at Santa Lucía, at San Mateo, and at Santa Elena. Later in 1566 Menéndez de Avilés dispatched a small expedition consisting of two Dominican friars, thirty soldiers, and an Indian boy (apparently kidnapped from Virginia in 1561) north to establish still another settlement on the Bahía de Santa María at a place called Jacán—the hoped-for Atlantic entry to the fabled Northwest Passage. That attempt, however, would end in failure. The expedition reached the Delmarva Peninsula, and a storm pushed it back to the outer banks of the Carolinian coast. The Spaniards opted to abandon their mission and sail to Spain.

Next, Menéndez de Avilés wanted to explore the interior of La Florida, both the Florida peninsula and the vast region between Santa Elena and Mexico. He hoped that such explorations would provide access to the interconnected riverine system he believed would tie together his peninsular coastal settlements and establish the long-sought overland route to Mexico.

In the summer of 1566 Menéndez de Avilés therefore led a peninsular exploration, traveling up (south) the St. Johns River. On the voyage he met and gave gifts to a number of Timucua chiefs, many allied with Chief Outina. One goal, as it was with the Calusa, was to befriend the chiefs and impress them with the might of the Spanish. Because the requested Jesuits had not yet arrived in La Florida, Menéndez de Avilés could only lay the groundwork for the establishment of missionary activities. The St. Johns River expedition eventually reached the territory of the Mayaca Indians, which began at Lake George in central Florida. The Spaniards were stymied there, because the narrowness of the river allowed the Mayaca to block further passage up river. Afraid of attacks from shore, Menéndez de Avilés retreated, unable to explore the actual river connections he thought led to Miami, Tampa Bay, and southwest Florida. He would later send men down the coast from St. Augustine to the Mosquito inlet, modern Ponce de Leon Inlet, with orders to march overland (west) to the St. Johns River and Mayaca territory. The expedition, led by Gonzalo Gayón, failed; the trek overland was too difficult.

To explore the interior of La Florida and the route to Mexico, Menéndez de Avilés sent a land expedition headed by Juan Pardo inland from Santa Elena in late 1566. On that journey Pardo and more than one hundred soldiers marched as far as western North Carolina before returning. Pardo's Catholic chaplain, Father Sebastian Montero, a secular priest, chose to stay in the village of Guatari in western North Carolina to provide religious education to the Indians. Several years later Father Montero returned to Santa Elena and then went back to Spain.

In 1567 Pardo left on a second expedition, retracing his path to North Carolina and then continuing across the Appalachian Mountains to the vicinity of modern Newport, Tennessee. Along his route he established a string of five small forts. At each fort he erected a cross and left supplies and soldiers, some of whom were to instruct the Indians in religious matters. None of the forts lasted very long. By May 1568 all had been destroyed, presumably by Indian attacks. One soldier survived and returned to Santa Elena.

At about the same time that Pardo was marching back into Santa Elena at the end of his first journey, Jesuit missionaries were finally landing in La Florida. In July 1566 three Jesuits—Father Juan Rogel, Father Pedro Martínez, and Brother Francisco Villareal—had sailed from Spain on a Flemish ship bound for St. Augustine. Their pilot, inexperienced in navigating the La Florida coastline, could not find St. Augustine; at one point their ship passed right in front of the harbor entrance and was seen by lookouts.

The Flemish ship finally dropped anchor off the Georgia coast, probably near St. Simons Island, where Father Martínez and the sailors went ashore in a small boat to ask the Indians for directions. A storm arose September 14, blowing the Flemish ship away from land and marooning the shore party.

For ten days the party waited to be rescued, but no one came. Finally they boarded their small boat and began to make their way southward along the coastal barrier island. Near the south end of Cumberland Island they landed to take food from some Indian fishermen, villagers of Chief Tacatacuru. More Indians appeared and a skirmish followed. Father Martínez and three of his companions were killed. The other sailors, some wounded, made their way back to the boat and sailed to the mouth of the St. Johns River where they were rescued. The ship with Father Rogel and Brother Villareal, it turns out, had sailed to Havana. There they met a ship sent by Menéndez de Avilés who had learned of Father Martínez's martyrdom.

Just after this incident, in early 1567, Menéndez de Avilés sent orders for an expedition from San Mateo to travel up the St. Johns River to Mayaca, the point his earlier expedition had previously reached. Menéndez de Avilés intended to sail to San Antonio on the southwest Florida coast and then ascend the Caloosahatchee River to the St. Johns River, where he would meet the expedition from San Mateo sent to Mayaca. With him aboard his fleet of seven boats were the two surviving Jesuits and Doña Antonia. Arriving among the Calusa Indians, near the Caloosahatchee River, he had a chapel built in which Father Rogel could administer mass. He also received information from the men he had left there that the Caloosahatchee River could not be used to reach Mayaca. They told him of another river that led to the St. Johns River and emptied into Tampa Bay in Tocobaga Indian territory.

There was nothing to do but sail north to Tampa Bay, where still another garrison would be needed to guard the entrance to that inland riverine passage. Menéndez de Avilés also intended to use the occasion to force peace between the Tocobaga and Calusa Indians who were at war. At Tocobaga he was successful in obtaining a truce. He also learned that a navigable river to Mayaca did not exist. Indians in canoes, using poles and portage, may have been able to reach the St. Johns River or one of its tributaries from Tampa Bay; Spanish boats could never make it. Menéndez de Avilés sailed back to Calos, leaving behind thirty soldiers to man the new Tocobaga garrison.

Menéndez de Avilés next sailed to Tequesta at the mouth of the Miami River and installed Brother Villareal in the settlement there. He also returned home some Tequesta Indians who had been captives of the Calusa. At Tequesta the Spaniards built a blockhouse and erected a cross. Leaving more soldiers there, Menéndez de Avilés headed back to San Mateo, taking with him several Tequesta Indians, who would later accompany him when he returned to Spain.

At San Mateo, Menéndez de Avilés learned that the expedition sent up the St. Johns River to Mayaca had wisely given up and returned to the fort. There was also news of continuing warfare between the Spaniards and the Indians of Chief Saturiwa's alliance near Ft. Caroline. The latter had suffered heavy losses. Relations with the Indians living around St. Augustine were a little better; though on several occasions the town itself had been attacked.

Menéndez de Avilés returned to St. Augustine and in May 1567, sailed for Spain via Santa Elena. With him were three Tequesta Indians and three Timucua Indians, all of whom he took to Madrid. It was less than two years since Menéndez de Avilés had established the settlement at St. Augustine.

In Spain the news of Father Martínez's death had fueled a flood of Jesuit volunteers wanting to minister to the native peoples of La Florida. Menéndez de Avilés's dreams, however, and those of the Jesuits would never become reality. The next two years, 1568 and 1569, saw a string of disappointments and a shift in missionary efforts from southern Florida to the Guale-Orista region along the Atlantic coast south of Santa Elena.

Even before Menéndez de Avilés arrived back in La Florida in mid-1568, things were deteriorating. Juan Pardo had returned to Santa Elena from his second journey, having failed once again to find the route to Mexico. His five forts would prove to be as ephemeral as Menéndez de Avilés's coastal settlements, most of which also were gone by the end of the year. A ship landing in Tocobaga in January 1568 found that all thirty soldiers had been killed. That garrison was no more.

At Tequesta the soldiers had slain a relative of the chief. The Indian retaliation was severe. Some of the soldiers were killed and the others, Brother Villareal included, were holed up in their fort. They were rescued by a Spanish ship that took the survivors to San Antonio among the Calusa. The soldiers stationed at San Antonio had killed Chief Carlos, and supported the installation of a successor, whom the Spaniards had christened Don Felipe. But Don Felipe was as reluctant to embrace Christianity as Chief Carlos had been. By mid-1568 Father Rogel and Brother Villareal were forced to leave for Havana.

Disaster had also struck San Mateo. In retaliation for the slaughters at Matanzas, French soldiers, commanded by Dominique de Gourgues, anchored on the south end of Cumberland Island in late March 1568 and quickly joined forces with local Timucua Indians. Several days later the French and 400 Timucua warriors marched on two Spanish outposts of the fort, capturing and destroying both and killing a number of Spanish soldiers. By the time another attack was mounted, about two weeks later, the Spaniards had fled and the fort was taken without opposition; a few soldiers were captured. Before departing for home, the French hung their captives and burned the fort.

MORE FAILURES

In June 1568 a second group of Jesuits—eleven priests, lay brothers, and novices—arrived at St. Augustine. Led by Father Juan Bautista de Segura, the vice-provincial, they included Gonzalo del Alamo, Antonio Sedeño, Juan de la Cerrera,

Domingo Agustín Báez, Juan Baptista Méndez, Gabriel de Solís, Pedro Ruíz de Salvatierra, Juan Salcedo, Christobál Redondo, and Pedro Mingot de Linares. Father Rogel and Brother Villareal sailed from Cuba to join them. On the way to St. Augustine, Father Rogel apparently scouted Guale territory and traveled to Santa Elena, searching for potential locations for new missions.

Based on Father Rogel's experiences among the Calusa and Brother Villareal's at Tequesta, the Jesuits apparently reached several conclusions. La Florida was going to present many hardships and the native people, at least those in south Florida, were openly antagonistic to the Jesuits and the message they brought. The La Florida colony was poorly supplied and geographically spread out; it would be difficult to support a large missionary effort. The Spanish soldiers at the garrisons often exhibited cruel and vicious behavior toward the Indians, which was detrimental to missionary work. The Jesuits therefore decided to try separating themselves from the military presence.

The resulting tensions between church and state—often played out in disagreements between soldiers and friars at remote missions—would plague the La Florida colony. Menéndez de Avilés, for instance, sought to control the Jesuits, deciding where and when they should establish missions. The Jesuits, however, believed they answered to a higher power and could not be constrained.

Among the Tequesta and Calusa, few if any adults had accepted Christianity. Many of the chiefs and native priests were openly hostile toward the Jesuits, viewing them as threats to the power of the native elites. Conversions would take time, and most initial successes were likely to be among youths.

The Jesuits therefore decided to build a school in Havana, as Menéndez de Avilés had envisioned, that would serve both Spaniards and the children of native leaders, especially the heirs of chiefly positions. Children raised as Christians would be powerful allies who, as chiefs, would help bring Catholicism to their people. The Jesuits also had another weapon at their immediate disposal: the six Indians who had been taken to Spain by Menéndez de Avilés and returned to La Florida with them. At least one, a Tequesta man who was the brother of a chief, had accepted Christianity and been given the name Jacob. He certainly could be used to help secure new conversions.

Father Segura put the Jesuits' plan into motion. They would return to south Florida, and they would break new ground among the Guale and Orista of the Georgia and South Carolina coasts. It had appeared to Father Rogel, on his reconnaissance of that region, that missionary efforts would find fertile minds among the native "tillers of the soil" (translated from Zubillaga 1946, 325).

Fathers Agustín Báez and Ruíz de Salvatierra were sent to minister in Guale and Orista; later Father Sedeño would join them. In Guale, Agustín Báez would compile a grammar of the Indian language, apparently lost now, before dying, probably of malaria, late in 1569. The other Jesuits departed for the school in Havana, initially run by Father Rogel and Brother Villareal.

In 1569 both Father Rogel and Brother Villareal reentered the mission field in La Florida. Brother Villareal and Father Alamo returned to San Antonio among the Calusa, while Father Rogel went to preach in Orista near Santa Elena. Father Alamo, however, did not adapt well to the hardships of the field and soon returned to Spain.

Father Segura and one of the novices, along with the brother of the Tequesta chief, went to Tequesta. The return of their kinsmen led the Tequesta to once again accept the presence of missionaries in their village.

In Havana the Jesuits' school was not proving successful; two of the first three students died. The Jesuits withdrew from Tequesta in 1570, and the Spaniards pulled out of San Antonio and Calos, apparently early the next year. Soldiers again had killed a Calusa chief and fourteen high-ranking men, leading to a rebellion in which the Indians burned their village and fled, leaving the Jesuits and the Spanish garrison with no alternative but to depart.

On the coast north of St. Augustine, things were not much better. A tally showed only seven baptisms—four were of children, and three were adults on their deathbeds. The same epidemics and diseases that killed the Indians infected the Jesuits as well. Although only Father Agustín Báez died, other missionaries suffered, some having to withdraw to Santa Elena to regain their health.

In 1570 Menéndez de Avilés, returning from another voyage to Spain, brought three more Jesuits—Luís de Quirós, Gabriel de Gómez, and Sancho de Cevallos —to Santa Elena. Father Quirós entered the mission field in Guale, at least for a short time. But these reinforcements did little to boost progress. During 1570, bad relations with the Indians, a lack of successful conversions, and ill health led the Jesuits to leave Orista and Guale and move to Santa Elena, where at least some treated sick Spanish colonists. Fathers Rogel and Sedeño returned to the school in Havana, taking with them Indian children.

DON LUÍS DE VELASCO AND JACÁN

With so few missionary successes among the native peoples of South Carolina, Georgia, and Florida, Father Segura decided to make a dramatic move and establish a mission well north of Santa Elena in Jacán on the Bahía de Santa María— the Virginia side of modern Chesapeake Bay. In line with his view that the friars would do better without a military presence, Father Segura took only seven Jesuits with him and a teenage Spanish boy, Alonso de Olmos, son of a Santa Elena colonist and a catechist studying with the Jesuits. With the expedition went a set of church vestments and vessels taken from Santa Elena.

Also accompanying the Jesuit contingent was one of the most intriguing figures among the many people identified in the sixteenth-century documentary record of La Florida: Don Luís de Velasco. Velasco was probably a member of the Kiskiack tribe of the tidewater Virginia area. The son of one of the tribe's elite families and nephew of a chief, he had been taken—most likely kidnapped—from his home in 1561 by the Spaniards when he was about twenty years old.

During his nine years living among the Spaniards, he had been to Cuba, Mexico—where he was christened Don Luís de Velasco, the name of the viceroy of New Spain and his baptismal sponsor—and Spain. In Spain he had had an audience with Philip II, who issued an order charging the Jesuits with educating him. By the time he returned to La Florida in 1566, Velasco could read and write Spanish. Little is known about the six or seven years he spent in Spain, but his experiences were no doubt extraordinary.

When Menéndez de Avilés first sailed for La Florida in 1565, Velasco was probably with him. Velasco, in part, may have been responsible for convincing Menéndez de Avilés that the Northwest Passage could be reached from the Chesapeake Bay and Jacán, the region where he had grown up. It was for that reason that Velasco had been sent by Menéndez de Avilés on the unsuccessful 1566 expedition to establish a settlement on the bay. Now, four years later, Velasco would be a key member of another expedition to that same region. One wonders whether Velasco's tales of a passage to the Pacific were a clever ruse to get him home. It would not be the only occasion Indians manipulated the Spaniards for their own purposes.

The Jesuit expedition sailed from Santa Elena in late summer 1570 and made landfall on the Virginia coast in early September. Following the advice of Velasco, they sailed up the James River near where they intended to build their mission. Two of the Jesuits, Fathers Segura and Quirós, wrote letters recounting what they had found on their arrival.

The Jesuits said the land Velasco left had suffered a famine for six years. There were no corn crops. Many people had died and the population was severely reduced. Although it was not spelled out, at least some deaths were apparently disease-related. The Jesuits had few supplies to take ashore with them, having used much of their stores on the longer-than-expected sea journey from Santa Elena and when they had shared them with the crew. Ashore, the Indians quickly learned not to give food to the Jesuits without receiving goods in return. Though poorly supplied, the Jesuits chose to bid adieu to the sailors and send their letters with them. In their letters they penned detailed instructions on how and where they could be reached with supplies. The letters also told how Velasco's relatives were astounded to see him. They thought that he "had risen from the dead and come down from heaven" (Quinn 1979, 557).

In late spring 1571 the same ship that had transported the expedition the year before returned to the Virginia coast, looking for the smoke signals the Jesuits had specified they would use. None were seen. Instead the crew and Father Salcedo who had accompanied them, saw Indians wearing Jesuit cassocks, an indication that something clearly was wrong. The Indians later attacked the ship, but were repelled. Two Indian men were taken captive, though one dove off the ship. The other, taken to Havana and housed with the Jesuits, told the Spaniards that the boy Alonso de Olmos was alive and living with the Indians. The fates of the Jesuits were not revealed, and the worst was feared.

Just over a year later, in late July 1572, Menéndez de Avilés, accompanied by Father Juan Rogel and two other Jesuits, sailed for Jacán in search of the missing Jesuits and Alonso de Olmos. Using the captive Indian as an interpreter, Menéndez de Avilés first employed negotiations and then used military power to force the Indians to turn over Olmos.

Olmos related all that had taken place after they arrived in 1570. Velasco, he said, had spent the first two nights with the Jesuits. As soon as the ship departed, he had left for his own village, staying there at night and helping the Jesuits during the day. After five days Velasco had abandoned the Jesuits all together. In February 1571 three of the Jesuits had traveled to the village where Velasco was living, hoping to talk with him and to barter for corn. Velasco had killed all three, then had taken a war party to the main encampment and slain the other five. Only Alonso de Olmos had been allowed to live. The vestments and books brought by the Jesuits had been taken. A brother of Velasco was said to have been "going around clothed in the Mass vestments and altar cloths" (Quinn 1979, 561).

It was a terrible loss. By 1572 nine of the Jesuits who had gone to La Florida had been killed at the hands of the very people they had sought to convert to Christianity. The order, only thirty years old, could not afford further sacrifices and the remaining Jesuits were withdrawn that year; some moved on to Mexico. The successes the Jesuits would enjoy in Brazil and elsewhere in the Americas were never duplicated in La Florida.

Velasco continued to live in Jacán. Anthropologist William C. Sturtevant has noted that documentation from the Jamestown colony, founded in 1607 in Virginia, hints that Velasco's knowledge gained in Spain may have been put to good use by the Indians. The head of the famous Powhatan Confederacy was said to be the son of an Indian who had been brought from the West Indies by the Spaniards, perhaps a garbled reference to Velasco. Chief Powhatan's daughter, Pocahontas, herself would travel across the Atlantic in 1616; it is intriguing to think that the granddaughter of Velasco might have also traveled to Europe.

STRANGER IN A STRANGE LAND: FATHER JUAN ROGEL

During a portion of the time Velasco was with the Jesuits in Havana and La Florida, Father Juan Rogel, a native of Pamplona, Spain, was living and traveling among the Indians of La Florida. Many of Father Rogel's experiences—and hardships—during those six years are recorded in a series of letters that have been preserved in Jesuit archives.

His letters provide details about the activities of the Jesuits in La Florida and the nature of the Indians with whom Father Rogel came into contact. They are also poignant testimony to the clash of cultures and beliefs that occurred when Spanish missionary friars and Indians met in the sixteenth century.

Father Rogel wrote that the Indians quickly learned the material benefits—they would demand gifts like trade goods and even food—of attending Jesuit classes. The Jesuits did not always know whether to believe if the Indians were sincerely accepting the tenets of Christianity, or it they were acting in order to receive goods.

Father Rogel, a fierce proponent of his religion, could not tolerate aspects of Indian culture that conflicted with his own, especially spiritual matters. To Father Rogel there could only be one god. The Indians' gods, idols, and spirits could only be the antithesis of the Christian god. At times Father Rogel directly equated the devil with specific native deities. He often sought to build on selected aspects of native beliefs by adding Christian concepts. He also made special efforts to convert native leaders, thinking that chiefs would then bring their people to Christianity.

The Indians expressed a willingness to accept some tenets of Christianity, especially those concepts that did not conflict with their own beliefs. Chief Carlos of the Calusa, for example, clearly recognized the power of the Spaniards and their beliefs. He was willing to experiment with the latter, perhaps trying to make that power his own.

The extracts that follow are freely translated from three of Father Rogel's letters published by Felix Zubillaga (1946). I have modernized sentence constructions, put in proper names as appropriate, and otherwise clarified the text. My translations should not be considered exact. In selecting these vignettes I consulted previous translations of the letters by John H. Hann (1991), David B. Quinn (1979), and William C. Sturtevant (1964).

This first letter was sent by Father Rogel to a fellow Jesuit April 25, 1568. In it Father Rogel describes his efforts to introduce Christianity to the Calusa Indians, the opposition he encountered, and his own doubts.

> Although initially adverse to the idea, Chief Carlos finally consented to learn about being a Christian. I offered to be not only his teacher, but the teacher for his people who also wished to learn.

At the place where classes were to be held we erected a large cross. Every day the chief came, along with his advisers and other important people and women and children. I began to teach them the catechism by first reciting the Our Father in Spanish and then chanting (in Latin) the Hail Mary. I told them these words were used to talk with God and to ask him for the things we needed.

Little by little, through an interpreter, I taught them about the oneness of God, his power, and his creation of the universe and the first man and woman. I also explained the concept of a soul and corrected their own erroneous concepts. The Calusa believe each person has three souls. One is in the pupil of an eye, another in one's shadow, and the third is a person's reflection in a mirror or in still water. When an individual dies, the Calusa believe the latter two souls leave the body, but the soul in the pupil of the eye remains forever.

The Indians go to where the dead are buried and talk with them and ask their advice. I believe it is actually the devil who answers them, because the dead tell them about real events that occurred in far away places and things that actually happen in the future. . . .

The Calusa began to see that the things I taught them made sense, while their own beliefs did not. But they said that their ancestors had lived with their beliefs forever, and they wished to do the same. They told me to leave them alone; they did not want to listen to me. But by treating them with kindness and love and using handouts of corn as bribes, I was able to get them to continue coming to lessons. . . . Though when the corn ran out, they left.

I truly believe that the chief wants to become a Christian because he tells me when he does not believe something I teach him; he also is willing to think about things. For instance, when I asked him if he believes in the immortality of the soul and the resurrection of the dead, he said no. But when I asked him about the oneness of God and his being the creator of the universe, he said he believed that part. He also said that the belief in a supreme deity [and, most likely, the ability to communicate with that being] was something that he and all his chiefly ancestors shared, a secret they kept from the common people. . . . After talking about this and other theological points he became more inclined to accept the immortality of the soul and the resurrection of the dead. But I still saw he was reluctant to believe all of it, because if he truly did accept it, he would be more concerned about his own salvation than he is.

The chief promised that when Menéndez de Avilés returned he would quit his worship of idols and give them to me so they could be burned. He also said he would cut his hair, a great sacrifice. But his deeds conflict with his promises. He is still very involved with his worship of idols and his witchcraft and superstitions. . . . But still, some of the Spaniards and other Indians have told me that sometimes at night they have seen the chief kneeling before the crosses we have in the fort and in his house. He actually told me this himself, without my asking. He is, in his own way, giving himself to God. He makes the same offerings before the crosses that he makes before his idols. . . .

I still have doubts about whether or not the chief really wants to become a Christian because of an incident a few days ago. His daughter, a young girl he loves very much, became sick and was about to die. I went to visit her and I tried to convince her father to baptize her as a Christian. I trusted in God that the baptism would cure her, but if it was God's will that she die after having been baptized, she would go to heaven anyway. If she were not baptized and died, she would go to hell. I tried to convince him that if he loved his daughter so much he would not allow her to go to hell. He ignored me and never answered. Instead, he used witchcraft to cure her. I am puzzled by all this and I hope the Lord sends Menéndez de Avilés back soon so I can see if the chief actually will give up his non-Christian ways.

The second letter was penned by Father Rogel after he had left Orista. Written in Havana on December 9, 1670, the letter tries to explain why Orista seems such a likely place for missionary work, but because of the economic practices of the Indians that require them to move among various food-gathering camps most of the year, it is impossible to instruct them.

After establishing our convento in Santa Elena, the vice-provincial sent me to Orista where I went with great happiness and hopes of making conversions. In the beginning my hopes increased; the Indians' customs were much better than those of the Calusa. I thanked God when I saw each Indian man with only one wife, each cultivating his own field, having his own house, and carefully rearing his own children. The Indians were not contaminated by sins such as incest, cruelty, and thievery. They interacted with one another with truth, peace, and simplicity.

At the end of six months I could speak the language. I taught the Indians those tenets of our religion that can be easily understood. . . . At first they seemed to listen and they asked questions, though naive ones, like, "Does God have a wife?"

This happened in the time of the year when the Indians gathered together, which lasted two and a half months. Then when it was the time of the acorn harvest they all left me, and individual families went to the woods, each to a different place. They only gathered together for festivals every two months, always in different places. I tried to go to the gatherings to preach to them, but they laughed at what I said. Nonetheless, I kept at it, trying to convince them that in the spring they should plant enough crops so they could stay in one place all year. To help them do that I suggested I give them iron hoes and corn seed and that they all plant their fields together at the same place. . . .

But after having promised many times to do that the villagers who had been living in twenty households where we were gathered divided up and moved to twelve or thirteen farms separated from one another by four, six, ten, or twenty leagues. Only two households stayed here and planted. . . .

To make conversions among the people of this province who are unaware of Christianity they must be made to come together, live in settlements, and cultivate enough food so they can live year-round in one place. After they are settled, let the preaching commence. If this is not done, even if missionaries visit them for fifty years, they will have no more success than we have had in that last four years.

Father Rogel would join the 1572 expedition to Jacán led by Menéndez de Avilés to determine what had happened to the Jesuits who had gone there in 1570. On August 28 he wrote a letter to Father Francisco Borgia, head of the order, recounting the tragic end of the Jesuits. After relating all of the bad news, Father Rogel's own faith and optimism in the missionary work of the Jesuits still shone through:

I have observed that in this land the native population is larger than it is anywhere else along the coast explored so far. The Indians are more settled than elsewhere and I think that if the Spaniards establish a settlement here, their presence would scare the belligerent Indians that might threaten us and we could preach the Holy Gospel.

As it turned out, neither the Spaniards nor the Jesuits would settle Virginia. That would be done thirty-five years later by the English. Instead, the Jesuit missionary efforts in La Florida had come to an abrupt end.

5

FRANCISCAN FRIARS AND NATIVE CHIEFS

Pedro Menéndez de Avilés wasted little time finding another religious order to minister to the native people of his still young La Florida colony. Securing missionary friars remained predicated on the same three factors that had led him to invite the Jesuit order to La Florida in 1565: the legal and moral responsibility to see to the conversion of the Indians; the need to assure a labor force; and the protection of the residents of Santa Elena and St. Augustine. Christian Indians would provide his colony the allies needed to succeed.

At the same time the Jesuits were withdrawing from La Florida, the general minister of the Order of the Friars Minor of the Regular Observance of St. Francis of Assisi—the Franciscans—was establishing the office of Commissary General of the Indies. The office, located in Madrid, was to act as an intermediary between the Spanish Crown and the Franciscan Order in matters dealing with much of the Americas.

The Commissary General of the Indies and the Crown moved relatively quickly in response to a request from Menéndez de Avilés for friars. In February 1573, the Crown issued two royal orders directing eighteen Franciscans be sent to La Florida. Sponsored by Menéndez de Avilés, the first Franciscans would arrive by the end of the year. Father Diego Moreno led the first small group of three: himself, another friar, and a lay brother. Soon the three missionaries were in the field among the Guale and Orista Indians, seeking to assure that these native neighbors of Santa Elena did not become a threat to the colonial outpost.

The Franciscans were successful in baptizing the chief and his wife of the main town of Guale. The Spanish colony's lieutenant governor, Diego de Velasco, and his wife, Dona María Menéndez de Avilés—Pedro Menéndez de Avilés's daughter—

served as godparents and gave their names to the newly converted Christians. The assumption of a Spanish name at the time of baptism was common, as was the giving of gifts to elite Indians who were baptized.

Conversion of the Guale chief was a great coup for the Franciscans because he was in line to become the mico of a substantial number of villages. Unfortunately, the success would be short-lived. In 1574 Pedro Menéndez de Avilés and the lieutenant governor were soon disagreeing on the approach to take with the Indians. By fall 1575 the three Franciscans decided it was in their best interest to withdraw and, against Diego de Velasco's wishes, leave for Veracruz. They became lost at sea and never made it to Mexico.

Relations between the Spaniards and the Indians deteriorated. The latter were being harassed by soldiers to provide food for the two Spanish towns. With the abandonment by the Franciscans, the Indians' hope of continued material benefits from Catholicism disappeared. Mistreatment of the Indians, including the execution of one chief's heir in retaliation for the murder of another chief, a Christian, led to further disenchantment. Near the end of 1576, the Orista and Guale Indians openly rebelled.

The rebellion began with the killing of twenty Spanish soldiers who had gone to an Escamacu Indian village just north of Santa Elena. When the heads, or perhaps scalps, of the murdered soldiers were taken to Guale in an effort to build support for the rebellion there, three more soldiers were captured and killed. Still later, another dozen or so soldiers were slain.

It was a time of great uncertainty for both Santa Elena and St. Augustine, the latter also the object of Indian raids. The Indians continued their hostilities at Santa Elena through 1578. A French ship run aground on the coast near Santa Elena was captured, and its 280 passengers were either killed or taken prisoner by the Indians. At one point Indians actually laid siege to the fort at Santa Elena for a month and a half. The Spaniards retreated to St. Augustine, burning the fort and leaving it to the Indians.

The fort was rebuilt, and the Spanish military staged a retaliatory offensive in 1579, intended to punish the Indians and prevent them from waging further raids. Along 155 miles (250 kilometers) of the coast, probably most of Orista and Guale territory, nineteen villages and their stored corn were burned, a tactic the Spaniards used often in La Florida. The Spaniards hoped that without sufficient food the Indians would be forced to break into smaller groups to forage.

The Indians, however, continued to press. In 1580, 2,000 Indians were said to have attacked Santa Elena. Hopes of creating allies of the Guale and Orista were dashed, and the coast between Santa Elena and St. Augustine remained a dangerous place for Spaniards.

It was thought that the Franciscan friars' missionary work might help to quiet the coastal Indians, but it was not until 1584 that the order was able to send more missionaries from Spain. In that year eight friars led by Father Alonso de Reynoso sailed for St. Augustine. Though perhaps an accomplished recruiter of friars, Father Reynoso was less effective as a transoceanic guide. Discontent plagued the group almost from the beginning. One friar was deliberately left behind in the Canary Islands; two opted to remain in Hispaniola when their ship docked there; and a fourth deserted. Shortly after arriving in La Florida a fifth friar left for Havana and then Mexico.

Father Reynoso was accused of using some of the funds entrusted to him to buy beads, hatchets, and knives for the Indians, an action one detractor labeled fraud because the money had been earmarked to support the friars and their work. Father Reynoso was also denounced for excessive card playing. In his wake through the Atlantic and Caribbean, he left a trail of outraged officials and fellow friars. The 1584 effort thus ended almost before it had begun.

Excellent recruiter that he was, Father Reynoso would lead nine additional friars to La Florida in 1587 and twelve in 1590. The La Florida colony was extremely challenging; in 1592 only two priests and one lay brother remained. During that time, the Guale-Orista coast remained largely off-limits. Santa Elena, unable to sustain itself in the face of Indian hostilities, had been abandoned by the Spaniards in 1586.

In 1595, this time led by Father Juan de Silva, another group of twelve friars arrived. They would be the first of more than 270 Franciscan friars sent to La Florida between 1595 and 1695. These twelve also mark the beginning of successful Franciscan missionary efforts among the La Florida Indians. Those efforts, carefully choreographed, would be couched within the context of Spanish colonial enterprise and carried out against a backdrop of native depopulation.

PLEDGES OF ALLEGIANCE

Missionary activities were an integral part of the conquest of the La Florida Indians and their subsequent incorporation into the Spanish colony. That process of conquest and colonization was not as haphazard as it sometimes seems when viewed four centuries later. Though hindered by the paucity of documentation—the archives of the Commissary General of the Indies, for instance, were destroyed in a fire in the nineteenth century—researchers like anthropologist John E. Worth and historians Amy Turner Bushnell and John H. Hann have been able to discern the designs of conquest from the records that do exist.

Thirty years after the founding of St. Augustine, the Spaniards were aware of aspects of the Indian cultures that they could use to their advantage. They were well acquainted with ethnic and linguistic differences, and they understood the power chiefs and elites held over their subjects. The Spaniards did not hesitate to use this information, at times cajoling Indian chiefs or bribing them, and, at other times, playing native groups against one another. For example, in 1598 St. Augustine colonists encouraged an Indian war party to attack the Surruque Indians living just south of modern New Smyrna Beach on the Mosquito lagoon. Because of poor relations with the native people near St. Augustine and along the coast to the north, the Spanish townspeople were in need of Indian laborers. The war party brought back fifty-four Indian men, women, and children who were then distributed among the Spaniards as slaves.

To win the allegiance of an Indian group the Spanish first needed to win over the Indian chief, to make that individual acknowledge the superior status of the Spanish Crown and the Crown's La Florida representatives, the governor of Spanish Florida and his designates. Winning over the chief involved a formal ceremony with a baptism and the bestowing of a Christian name. This ceremony generally took place in St. Augustine, and the governor himself usually sponsored the chief, giving him gifts.

John E. Worth (1998a, 36–39) has written that the Spanish-Indian alliances were reciprocal. Chiefly alliances were well known to the Timucua, the Guale, and other La Florida Indians. As noted in chapter 2, village or local chiefs would pledge allegiance to a more powerful chief in order to gain that chief's favor. Vassal chiefs offered up loyalty and, at times, warriors or tribute. In exchange the vassal chief received status in the form of recognition by the paramount chief, as well as material symbols of that status. Similarly, today allegiance is given to a sports team or an elected political official; received in exchange is a T-shirt with the team logo or a photograph with a senator.

And so it was in the colonial Southeast. Chiefs gave their allegiance to the Spanish Crown by pledging obedience to the governor of Spanish Florida and accepting Christianity. The governor accepted that allegiance and gave back not only material items, but also increased status. The chief was now allied with a very powerful paramount leader (the governor), greatly enhancing his status among other Indian chiefs.

The gifts given to chiefs at these ceremonies included iron tools and wheat flour—a high status item relative to native cornmeal. The most valued gifts, it seems, were outfits of Spanish clothes, colorful and highly visible symbols of the chiefs' new status. Shoes, hats, stockings, doublets, shirts, and other pieces of clothing—a complete Spanish gentleman's outfit—adorned each new Christian chief and important members of his entourage. Returning home, the newly at-

A Timucua Indian chief. (Reproduced with the permission of
the artist, Theodore Morris, Sarasota, Florida)

tired chief exhibited his new status not only to relatives and villagers, but to other
chiefs as well. Those chiefs could not have missed the display of social wealth and
wanted to also render obedience, in essence creating a bandwagon effect.

The practice of rendering of obedience that began during Pedro Menéndez de
Avilés's tenure as governor continued throughout the mission period. In the early
mission period—the late 1580s to the first decades of the seventeenth century—
many chiefs, chiefly officials, and their entourages made the trek to St. Augustine,
some from great distances. For instance, during one two-month period in 1597,
Governor Gonzalo Méndez de Canço entertained five different Timucua chiefs
(one of them a woman), four chiefly heirs, twenty-one chiefly officials and elites
(some were inijas who the Spaniards called mandadors), and more than one hundred other entourage members. The cost in gifts, including nearly one ton of corn
and wheat flour, was steep, but still cheaper than waging a military campaign.

The chiefs could not renege after pledging obedience. An alliance with the

Spaniards, once made, could not be broken. The cost of disobedience was military retaliation or even death.

EARLY SUCCESSES

Only a small handful of friars brought to La Florida by Father Reynoso in 1587 and 1590 had entered the La Florida mission fields and remained. Prior to these early efforts, the only Christian Indians lived in one of two towns on the north and south ends of St. Augustine: Nombre de Dios and San Sebastián. Both were ministered to by priests from St. Augustine. It is likely that both towns were inhabited by Indians relocated to provide labor for the Spanish townspeople. San Sebastián's villagers were linked to the town of Tocoy due west of St. Augustine on the St. Johns River. Both San Sebastián and Tocoy were governed by the same chief, whose Christian name was Pedro Márquez. Tocoy itself may have been positioned to provide ferry service for travelers wishing to cross the St. Johns River.

The first Franciscan missionaries who had come with Father Reynoso served Indian towns from Cumberland Island down to St. Augustine, the remnants of the Timucua alliance in the region of Mocama, a Timucuan word meaning "saltwater." The chiefs of these towns had already rendered obedience to the Spaniards. During this period—the late 1580s and early 1590s—tentative steps to reestablish contact with the Guale Indians also took place.

The eleven friars who arrived with Father Juan de Silva in 1595 provided renewed vigor to mission efforts. Father Francisco Marrón, the superior of the Florida Franciscans, assigned the friars to their missions in consultation with the governor of La Florida, Domingo Martínez de Avendaño. Some of the friars would staff two missions in Mocama where conversion of the Indian population was already under way: San Pedro de Mocama on the southern end of Cumberland Island and San Juan del Puerto on Ft. George Island just north of the mouth of the St. Johns River. The Mocama friars also visited Timucuan chiefdoms on the mainland in southeast Georgia, though more permanent missions would not be built there for several more years.

After 1595 friars would also venture back up the Georgia coast to the Guale Indians, who now seemed willing to accept them and whose chiefs renewed their pledges of obedience. Still, nothing was left to chance. Governor Martínez de Avendaño and a detachment of infantry accompanied the friars in a show of pomp and force meant to impress the native people and give notice that the priests were under the protection of the Crown. The Guale missions were Nuestra Señora de Guadalupe de Tolomato (which may have been christened with this saint's name later), Santa Catalina de Guale, Santa Clara de Tupiqui, and Santo

St. Augustine in 1595. Mission Nombre de Dios is the cluster of thatched houses just above and to the right of the wooden fort. Several of St. Augustine's buildings and its pier are to the left (south) of the fort. (Courtesy P. K. Yonge Library of Florida History, University of Florida)

Domingo de Talaje (sometimes called Santo Domingo de Asao). A mission was also established at the town of Ospo.

Missions would never again be attempted in the Orista region where Santa Elena had earlier been abandoned. The chain of coastal Franciscan missions north of St. Augustine would never extend farther than near the mouth of the Ogeechee River on the mainland and Santa Catalina de Guale on St. Catherines Island.

In 1595 friars were also sent to some Timucua villages on the St. Johns River in what had been the region of the Outina alliance, an area that had clearly suffered severe depopulation. As in Mocama, the chiefs and villages in this region—sometimes called Agua Dulce—had realigned themselves politically in response to the changes taking place around them. The chief whose Christian name was Antonico and who lived near modern Palatka, Florida, had assumed the mantle of leadership as a result.

One early mission, San Antonio de Enecape, was established at the Mt. Royal archaeological site on the north end of Lake George at the Timucua town of Enecape visited by the French from Ft. Caroline in 1564–65. Some of the villages near Antonico's village and San Antonio de Enecape also received Christian names, suggesting they were visited by friars. Later San Antonio de Enecape's chief would assume the mantle of leadership for the alliance, replacing Antonico.

These early Franciscan missions included both *doctrinas* and *visitas*. Doctrinas, missions where religious doctrine was taught to the Indian villagers, featured churches in which mass was also held. Resident friars (usually just one) lived at each doctrina, often far removed from other Spaniards. Generally, there was one doctrina per chiefdom, except in the larger chiefdoms. Other missions with churches were founded, but these were only visited by friars who did not live there. They were referred to as visitas. Because mass was also held at visitas, they, like doctrinas, received Christian names.

In the early Franciscan mission period, before severe Indian depopulation, friars often visited outlying satellite villages in the countryside around the main villages where the doctrinas were located. Such satellite villages would have been politically subservient to the chief of the chiefdom's main village. For example, in 1602, Father Francisco Pareja of the doctrina of San Juan del Puerto on Ft. George Island listed nine satellite towns to his mission: Vera Cruz, Arratobo, Niojo, Potaya, San Mateo, San Pablo, Hicacharico, Chinisca, and Carabay. The towns ranged in distance 1.5 miles (2.5 kilometers) to 17 miles (28 kilometers) from San Juan del Puerto. Those with Christian names probably were visitas.

The total population of these ten villages—San Juan del Puerto and its nine satellites—was only about 500 people. By the time of the first Mocama missions the villages were significantly smaller than they had been in pre-Columbian times, owing to epidemics. As populations declined even further, the villagers within a chiefdom were consolidated into the existing satellite villages, which became fewer and fewer. Ultimately, most of the Timucuan and Guale chiefdoms were reduced to a single village.

Building on the mission efforts begun in the late 1580s through the mid-1590s, the new governor of La Florida, Gonzalo Méndez de Canço, instituted a plan in 1597 to expand the territory of Spanish influence beyond those portions of Guale, Mocama, St. Augustine, and Agua Dulce whose chiefs had rendered obedience. The word went out, along with gifts, for chiefs to come to St. Augustine to seek an alliance and render obedience. In some instances native emissaries, in others Spaniards, were sent to distant chiefdoms such as Ais on the Atlantic coast and the main town of the Aguacaleyquen chiefdom in north Florida.

For the most part the results were impressive; chiefs or chiefly heirs from interior northern Florida, including the Acuera Indians and the Ibihica Indians in southeast Georgia came and gave allegiance. All the chiefs of the Timucuan chiefdoms nearest St. Augustine, including Chief Aguacaleyquen, had now rendered obedience, and friars would soon be sent to their villages to establish visitas. At the time there were not enough friars to staff all the potential doctrinas.

Not all the native groups welcomed the Spaniards or their representatives. The chief of Surruque intercepted the Spanish emissary sent to the Ais, killed him, and reportedly had him quartered, cooked, and eaten by his vassal chiefs.

An ambitious part of the governor's plan was to make contact and befriend the Indians of central Georgia, where de Soto's army had been more than a half century earlier. In 1597 a party consisting of one soldier, two friars, and thirty Guale Indians was sent inland from the Guale coastal town of Tolomato. On their eight-day journey across the coastal plain they encountered few Indians before arriving at the town of Tama on the Oconee River, a day's march from the main town of the chiefdom of Ocute, one of the many Mississippian societies of the piedmont.

At Ocute itself, the town's chief told them to go no farther or they would be killed. These ancestral Creek Indians still remembered the depredations of the de Soto expedition. The party returned to Tama, only to be threatened with being scalped. They decided to retreat down the Oconee River to the Altamaha River and then down it to the coast to Cumberland Island, where mission San Pedro de Mocama was located.

In 1602 another expedition would be sent back to Ocute, again departing from Tolomato. Rumors of interior wealth—echoes of the Chicora legend—continued to draw the Spaniards. That expedition, like the one of 1597, failed to discover great mineral wealth. Participants on both expeditions did comment on the dense, agricultural populations of the region, new fields for chiefly pledges of obedience, and souls to be saved. But no missions would ever be established in the Georgia piedmont, despite the region's continuing interest to the Spanish.

EARLY FAILURES AND GUALE RENEWAL

The initial success of Governor Méndez de Canço's diplomatic initiatives and the efforts of the friars themselves was dramatically offset by events in Guale in 1597. What has become known as the Guale Rebellion erupted in September of that year and resulted in the closing of all the Guale missions. Much of what we know about the rebellion was recorded by a Peruvian-born Franciscan, Father Luís de Gerónimo de Oré, who visited La Florida in 1614 and 1616 and talked firsthand with his fellow Franciscans.

According to Father Oré, the revolt was precipitated when Father Pedro de Corpa, who served at Nuestra Señora de Guadalupe de Tolomato on the Georgia mainland, perhaps in the general vicinity of modern Harris Neck, forbade a chief's heir to have more than one wife, a traditional native practice. The disgruntled Guale man fled the mission, only to return several nights later with a group of non-Christian Indians painted for war. In the morning they killed Father Corpa with a stone ax while he prayed in the mission convento. The Franciscan's head was put on display and his body hidden in the woods.

The rebels then sent word to the chief of the village at mission Santa Catalina de Guale on St. Catherines Island, telling him to kill Father Miguel de Auñon and a lay brother who lived there. When the chief refused, the rebels undertook the murders themselves, but not before allowing the chief to explain to the Franciscans he could not save them. Father Auñon's body was buried at the foot of the cross he had erected in the village. Several years later Spaniards would exhume Father Auñon and transport his remains to the Franciscan convento in St. Augustine, where they were reinterred.

Santa Clara de Tupiqui, on the mainland several miles from Nuestra Señora de Guadalupe de Tolomato, was attacked next. There, after being allowed to say mass, Father Blas Rodríquez was held captive for two days while Indians ransacked the mission. Then he, too, was killed and his body taken into the woods and buried.

A fifth Franciscan, Father Francisco Dávila, living at the town of Ospo near Santa Clara de Tupiqui and Nuestra Señora de Guadalupe de Tolomato, was also attacked. (Ospo is most likely the same town later known as Ospogue or Espoque and probably was on Sapelo Island.) Father Dávila tried to escape, but he was wounded by arrows and taken captive. His mission was ransacked, and he was taken to the town of Tulafina where he was kept as a slave for ten months. During his captivity, Father Dávila, kept naked, was subjected to severe humiliations and threats of death. He survived this ordeal, however, and later wrote an account of his horrible experiences.

While the rebellion swept through the more northerly Guale missions, a sixth Franciscan, Father Francisco de Velacola of Santo Domingo de Talaje, had been in St. Augustine gathering supplies. When he returned to his mission on the Altamaha River at the southern end of Guale, he was killed. The Guale missions were devastated, and nearly all the Franciscans serving in the province were killed.

Support for the rebellion was growing among the Indians, spurred on by the destruction of the missions. In a bold move a Guale war party, in twenty canoes, paddled south to attack the Timucuan mission of San Pedro de Mocama on Cumberland Island. The raid was planned for the feast day of Saint Francis, when it was thought the mission and the few garrisoned soldiers stationed there might be caught unaware.

Having just brought supplies, a Spanish ship was anchored by the mission. Its presence, and the military threat it represented, caused hesitation among the raiders, who had landed on the southern end of the island. The Timucuan chief at Mocama counterattacked, causing the Guale warriors to retreat. Nevertheless, Governor Méndez de Canço ordered the mission to be abandoned and its villagers moved to San Juan del Puerto farther south. The Spaniards had relinquished the Georgia coast.

Franciscans serving other missions in La Florida were also withdrawn, at least temporarily. Their number had been severely reduced by the deaths in Guale; following the rebellion there were only five friars left in La Florida.

Guale was too important to the La Florida colony, however, to remain outside Spanish control. By the time of the rebellion, the English had tried twice to establish their own colony on the North Carolina coast, and French ships had continued to trade with the coastal peoples for medicinal plants and other goods. The Spaniards believed they needed to pacify the coast and reincorporate it into the colony. And they wished to punish the rebellious Guale for killing Spanish friars and breaking their bonds of allegiance.

In October and November 1597 Governor Méndez de Canço marched one hundred Spanish soldiers and twice that many Indian warriors north through Guale, intending to deliver reprisals. The army met no resistance; apparently the rebels had fled to escape the Spaniards' wrath. Indian towns—those not already destroyed by the Indians themselves—and food supplies were burned. Captives were forced to account for the whereabouts of the dead Franciscans, and Father Dávila, the lone survivor, was rescued.

The Guale managed to flee beyond the reach of the soldiers and escape retribution. For the next several years the soldiers from St. Augustine would return to Guale on several occasions to mete out punishment, destroying houses and burning crops. These attacks prevented the reestablishment of coastal settlements and forced the Guale to eke out an existence without the rich sources of shellfish and fish that constituted such an important part of their diet.

Beginning in 1600, the Guale had had enough. First one chief, then others began anew the process of rendering obedience to the Spaniards. Later, several of these newly allied chiefs would kill some of the main instigators of the rebellion, exacting the corporal retribution the Spanish military could not because they had been unable to catch the rebels. Guale was once again safe for missionaries, though it was a very different province than previously. Major villages had been destroyed, and traditional chiefly lineages and alliances altered. By 1604 the southernmost of the Guale missions, Santo Domingo de Talaje, had been reestablished. The villagers at Santa Catalina de Guale had rebuilt their church, though possibly a friar did not arrive to staff it until the next year.

From 1605 through 1620 fifty-four additional Franciscan friars arrived in St. Augustine, and several were assigned to four missions in Guale, all of which are known to have been functioning by 1616. These four were San Diego de Satuache, at or near the mouth of the Ogeechee River 35 miles (56 kilometers) north of Santa Catalina de Guale; San Phelipe de Alave, most likely on the Newport River 14 miles (23 kilometers) inland from Santa Catalina de Guale; San Joseph de Sapala on Sapelo Island; and Santa Clara de Tupiqui, which was probably rebuilt on its old location. With Santo Domingo de Talaje and Santa Catalina de Guale there were now six Guale missions. Mission Nuestra Señora de Guadalupe de Tolomato would be reestablished later in the seventeenth century, making seven.

All seven continued operation through the mid-century, though at times an individual doctrina might be without a friar due to illness or death. Over time, as the Guale population continued to drop, the need to attend visitas and other satellite villages ceased because those villages no longer existed. Typically their remnant populations were consolidated within existing mission villages, resulting in some curious political arrangements.

The sixteenth-century uprisings in Guale provided the Spanish military government with ample justification for forcing the Guale Indians into the colonial system. Despite all the problems and Spanish deaths, including those of the Franciscans, Guale was considered crucial to the well-being of St. Augustine. With a strong tradition of transportation by canoes and with maize agriculture, the Guale Indians were important suppliers of food and labor, especially in the early decades of the seventeenth century when the mission system was expanding into interior northern Florida.

Also important to the Spaniards in this early period were the two Timucuan missions established in the 1590s in Mocama: San Pedro de Mocama on Cumberland Island, served by Father Baltasár López, and San Juan del Puerto on Ft. George Island, whose friar was Father Francisco de Pareja. Sometime between 1606 and 1609 a third Mocama mission, San Buenaventura de Guadalquini, was established on the southern end of St. Simons Island to serve the Timucua living there.

Two Mocama visitas, Santa María de la Sena and Santo Domingo de Talaje, were listed in 1602 as 3.5 miles (5.6 kilometers) from San Pedro de Mocama on an island named Napuica (also Napoyca or Napa) that most researchers have equated with Amelia Island. Others have suggested that Santa María de la Sena was on the mainland by the St. Marys River (which derives its name from the visita), but that location seems highly unlikely. In the 1660s and 1670s, however, a mission named Santa María de Yamasee, a doctrina, is well documented on Amelia Island. The relation of the 1602 visita to the 1675 mission is uncertain, though it is possible that what was once a visita grew into a mission.

At the same general time that Franciscans were returning to and expanding their missionary efforts in Guale, colonial and Catholic officials were planning to extend the missions west of the St. Johns River and into south-central Georgia, the realm of the various interior Timucuan chiefdoms. Chiefs from that large region had already rendered obedience to the Crown and requested friars. Following

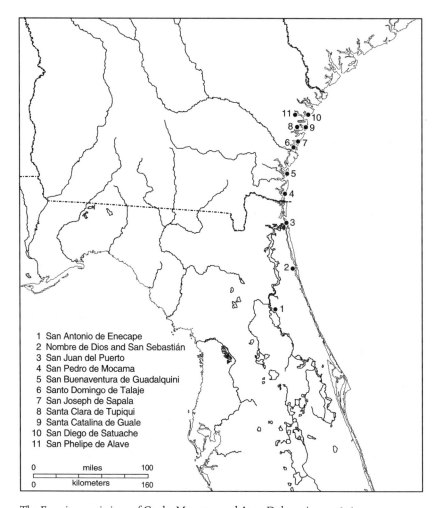

1 San Antonio de Enecape
2 Nombre de Dios and San Sebastián
3 San Juan del Puerto
4 San Pedro de Mocama
5 San Buenaventura de Guadalquini
6 Santo Domingo de Talaje
7 San Joseph de Sapala
8 Santa Clara de Tupiqui
9 Santa Catalina de Guale
10 San Diego de Satuache
11 San Phelipe de Alave

The Franciscan missions of Guale, Mocama, and Agua Dulce prior to 1606.

the rebellion in Guale, however, such an expansion at first was impossible. But the influx of the forty-four Franciscan friars in the decade and a half after 1605 would allow the Spaniards to look inland and away from the coast to enlarge their colony.

WESTWARD EXPANSION

As soon as Timucuan chiefs from interior La Florida paid their homage to Spanish authorities, Franciscan friars followed up by visiting the chiefs' villages. Villages of native officials from Potano, Timucua, and Ibihica, who had come to St. Augustine to pledge their allegiance to Governor Méndez de Canço in 1597, all received visits that same year.

Father Baltasár López made several such overland journeys into Timucua and Potano beginning in 1597, traveling more than 160 miles (258 kilometers) from his mission of San Pedro de Mocama on Cumberland Island. At the time of the Guale Rebellion, when the Guale mounted their failed attack on San Pedro de Mocama, Father López had been on such a visitation. The major town in the province of Timucua, which he visited, was probably the town of Aguacaleyquen, where de Soto had been in 1539; López called the town Timucua, though its name in the mission period was Ayacuto.

As a result of the visit to St. Augustine by an Indian delegation from Ayacuto in 1597, a hoe and two axes had been sent to the chief so that a church and convento could be built in anticipation of a friar's arrival. Although the Guale Rebellion would delay the establishment of a doctrina in Ayacuto for a decade, Father López, who spoke the Timucua language, established a visita in the town, most likely saying mass in a small chapel-like structure built by the Indians for that purpose.

In the late 1980s archaeologist Brent R. Weisman, excavating at the Fig Springs site—the location of the later mission of San Martín de Ayacuto, thought to be where Father López established the visita—excavated what may be Father López's small church. Nearly 400 years after it had been built, Weisman and his Florida Bureau of Archaeological Research field crew uncovered a small, open, pavilion-like structure. One end of it was roofed and floored and served as the sanctuary where the altar would have been. In many ways, the church resembled the first Franciscan churches in sixteenth-century Yucatán.

Father López also founded at least two additional visitas among the Potano Indians in the general vicinity of Gainesville, Florida, 35 miles (56 kilometers) south of Ayacuto. Another friar, Father Pedro Ruíz, went inland to the Ibihica Indians in southeast Georgia. But following the Guale uprising both friars were recalled.

Over the next few years, while order was restored in Guale, the Franciscans, operating from San Juan and San Pedro in Mocama and perhaps from their headquarters in St. Augustine, continued to visit the Timucua Indians in southeast Georgia and the Agua Dulce region on the St. Johns River. At some point, a mission was established south of the Agua Dulce province, south of Lake George among the Mayaca Indians. San Salvador de Mayaca seems to have been in operation only intermittently, its distance from St. Augustine being too far.

The chiefs from the interior north Florida towns still sought friars, and several made additional trips to St. Augustine to show their allegiance. They also sent laborers to work for the Spaniards as a sign of their willingness to establish an alliance. The lure of Spanish goods was great.

When twelve additional friars reached St. Augustine in 1605, the Franciscans and the military authorities were able to build on the ties already forged with the interior Timucua Indians. The founding of the first interior doctrina, in 1606 in Potano, marked the start of the westward expansion of the mission system. Efforts were made to strengthen the missions in Guale, Mocama, and Agua Dulce as well. As a result, a decade later in 1616 there would be twenty-three missions in the mission provinces of Guale, Mocama, St. Augustine, Potano, Timucua, and Agua Dulce. By the early 1620s ten additional missions existed in Yustaga and interior southern Georgia. There were still other missions that were established and soon failed, perhaps owing to epidemics among the Indians. For instance, a mission at the town of Moloa on the St. Johns River not far from modern Jacksonville, Florida, that had been associated with the Saturiwa alliance of the 1560s, lasted only a short time, as did a mission at the former visita of Santo Domingo de Talaje on Amelia Island.

The placement of all these new missions was not haphazard. As noted earlier, doctrinas where placed in the main town of each chiefdom whose chief had rendered obedience. The first doctrina west of the St. Johns River in the interior of northern Florida was San Francisco de Potano, founded in 1606. Located in modern Alachua County, several miles northwest of the University of Florida's main campus, the mission was just south of the prairie today called San Felasco Hammock on a north-south trail that crossed what would become the camino real. San Felasco is a Seminole Indian pronunciation of San Francisco, which suggests that the old site of the mission still was known when the Seminole entered north-central Florida beginning about 1750.

The governor of La Florida at the time, Pedro de Ybarra, requested the mission and was probably pleased that the Potano chief had rendered obedience and was willing to accept a mission. The Potano had long been a problem for the Spaniards. In 1567 a military detachment, sent to Potano by Pedro Menéndez de Avilés and under the command of Captain Pedro de Andrade, had been wiped out by the Indians, who perhaps remembered both the ill treatment they had received at the hands of de Soto's army and the role of European (French) soldiers in Chief Outina's raids on them in 1564 and 1565. The Spaniards had retaliated in 1584, attacking and destroying the main Potano village, causing its abandonment. Now the Potano wanted peace, and the Spaniards were anxious to cement an alliance with them by sending missionaries and establishing doctrinas.

San Francisco de Potano was therefore founded by Father Martín Prieto, who had arrived in Florida in 1605, and by Father Alonso Serrano. Father Prieto's firsthand account of his early months among the Potano chronicles the hardships and adventures of the Franciscan friars at missions far from St. Augustine. Prieto related how he also established two more missions or visitas in nearby Potano towns that he christened Santa Ana de Potano and San Miguel de Potano. All did not go well. Father Serrano was forced to return to St. Augustine because of villagers' opposition at San Francisco de Potano.

Alone, Father Prieto walked daily from his home mission at San Miguel de Potano to Santa Ana de Potano and San Francisco de Potano. He also faced some opposition from the chief of Santa Ana de Potano, who as a boy had witnessed the horrors of the de Soto expedition and hated the Spaniards. After a fierce storm leveled all of his village's buildings except the church and cross Father Prieto had erected, the chief agreed to be baptized and his people soon followed.

It is likely that Santa Ana de Potano and San Miguel de Potano were south from San Francisco de Potano within the cluster of archaeological sites just east of Moon Lake, at the west side of modern Gainesville, Florida. Mission-period Spanish and Indian artifacts have been found at several of those sites.

A year or two after Father Prieto went to Potano, a fourth Potano mission, San Buenaventura de Potano, was established closer to St. Augustine by another friar. That mission may have been at the Richardson site, believed to have been the main Potano town at the time of the 1564 and 1565 French raids and the site of a visita named Apalo, one of the early visitas Father López started among the Potano.

The four Potano missions together ministered to about 1,200 Indians, with the largest number in Santa Ana and San Francisco, whose populations each numbered about 400. Epidemics hit the Potano hard in the early seventeenth century, and the number of people living at the missions quickly fell. Within only a few years, San Miguel de Potano and San Buenaventura de Potano were abandoned. The Franciscans may have found it more expedient to consolidate their reduced populations in San Francisco de Potano and Santa Ana de Potano. Soon the Potano mission district came to be considered a part of Timucua province.

Epidemics must have hit other missions in the early seventeenth century as well. The St. Augustine mission of San Sebastián disappeared shortly after 1608, as did Tocoy west on the St. Johns River. By the mid-1620s it was replaced by San Diego de Heleca, whose villagers provided the needed ferry service across the river.

From his base among the Potano, Father Prieto traveled north several times to Ayacuto, where Father López had first been in 1597 and whose chief had been to St. Augustine to render obedience. In 1608, at the friar's urging, a new chief agreed to go to St. Augustine and pledge allegiance. As a result, Father Prieto went to Ayacuto later that year. There in the town plaza he burned twelve wooden carvings he deemed blasphemous. If Christianity was to grow, he believed aspects of the native religion that the friars called "works of the devil" had to be uprooted. In an extraordinary tour of Timucua with the chief, Father Prieto went to four other towns, burning wooden carvings in each. As John E. Worth (1998a) has noted, the friars sought to stamp out those native beliefs that they viewed as pagan and non-Christian and replace them with Christian ones. In doing so, the friars were replacing native priests with themselves.

At Ayacuto Father Prieto christened the mission San Martín de Ayacuto, and a church was erected, replacing the smaller chapel built in 1597. That church has also been found by archaeologists.

Further expansion of missions in northern Florida was hindered by warfare among the allied chiefdoms of the region and the Apalachee Indians to the west. Expansion was also blocked by a lack of friars. Both these barriers were soon removed.

In 1608 Father Prieto and an entourage of 150 Indians from Potano and Timucua, including a number of chiefs, traveled through Yustaga province, also called Cotocochuni, to the Apalachee town of Ivitachuco. The Apalachee Indians, no novices at pomp, had cleared a wide road from the town east toward the river. After a week-long journey, the friar and the Timucuan emissaries traveled along the road into Ivitachuco, where an estimated 36,000 Apalachee Indians and 70 chiefs —representatives of the 107 Apalachee towns—greeted them. It must have been an extraordinary experience, perhaps the largest assembly of Indians ever in Florida.

The seventy-year-old chief of Ivitachuco accepted the peace overtures and sent the chief of Anhaica to St. Augustine to render obedience on behalf of the entire province. Two years later the paramount chief of Apalachee, said to be eighty years old, made the trip to St. Augustine. That same year seven more Franciscan friars arrived in La Florida, while twenty came in 1612. Now that peace with the Apalachee was a reality, the expansion of missions in the several Timucuan chiefdoms north and west of San Martín de Ayacuto could begin.

The expansion around Ayacuto started with mission Santa Fé de Teleco (Holy Faith), located between San Francisco de Potano and San Martín de Ayacuto in northwest Alachua County, Florida. The Santa Fé de Teleco site was found and partially excavated by archaeologist Kenneth W. Johnson in the 1980s. It appears that the mission was next to an older village, perhaps the village of Cholupaha, where de Soto's army had been in 1539. San Juan de Guacara, in southeastern Suwannee County, and Santa Cruz de Tarihica, the Indian Pond site in western Columbia County west of Lake City—both in Florida—were established next.

At mission Santa Cruz de Tarihica, founded by Father Antonio de Cuellar, more than 4,000 Indians were baptized in only a few years. On two occasions Father Cuellar was nearly killed by native priests who recognized that the increasing power of the Franciscans and Catholicism meant the diminishing of their own power and status.

Still another mission, called Cofa, apparently the name of the Indian town where it was located (it may not have been occupied by Timucua Indians), was at the mouth of the Suwannee River on the Gulf coast. Perhaps the plan was to establish a Spanish-Christian presence there, enabling the Suwannee River to serve as a riverine highway to the north Florida missions. Via the Suwannee River and its tributary, the Santa Fe River, canoes could bring needed supplies to the missions and take corn back to the coast, where they could be loaded on boats and shipped to St. Augustine.

Provisioning the missions was always a problem. Traveling the overland routes to many of the missions was difficult and sometimes dangerous. An expedition of Christian Indians taking supplies to Cofa in 1611 was attacked by non-Christian Indians, killing seventeen. Cofa was too far removed from the other missions to be viable, and it only lasted a few years.

In 1612 the new Potano and Timucua missions, as well as those in Guale, Mocama, St. Augustine, and Agua Dulce, received a boost when a shipment of supplies for them arrived in St. Augustine. Included among the supplies were vestments, tin chrismatories, fourteen large bronze bells, and iron tonglike molds for shaping and impressing the host. The waferlike hosts were made from wheat flour, some of which was grown at the missions. In addition to wheat flour, the friars also needed a steady supply of wine, oil, and candles for religious services, though these items were often in short supply at the interior missions.

Building on the pledges of obedience made in the late sixteenth century, a friar was sent to the Acuera Indians in a town called San Blas de Avino on the Oklawaha River. By the mid-1620s the Acuera were served by Santa Lucía de Acuera. Still another mission, San Luís de Eloquale, served the Ocale Indians west of the Acuera, though the date it was founded is uncertain.

While these missions were being established in northern Florida, the Franciscans were expanding into the region of the Ibihica (San Lorenzo de Ibihica) and Icafui chiefdoms in southeastern Georgia, building on the contacts that had begun in the late sixteenth century. That expansion was a westward push out of the Mocama missions, especially San Pedro on Cumberland Island, whose chief was allied with the Ibihica and Icafui chiefs.

By 1616 Santa Isabel de Utinahica was in operation well in the Georgia interior, where the Ogeechee and Oconee Rivers meet to form the Altamaha River, north of modern Hazelhurst, Georgia, in Jeff Davis County. Santa Isabel de Utinahica was the northernmost mission serving Timucua Indians. Another southeast Georgia mission was Santiago de Ocone, founded between 1613 and 1616 among the Ocone Indians living in the Okeefenokee Swamp west of the Ibihica.

The next expansion was west of Timucua Province into Yustaga territory between the Suwannee and Aucilla Rivers through which Father Prieto had traveled in 1608 to reach Apalachee. Missionization of the Yustaga Indians brought the western Franciscan frontier to the border of Apalachee. Although the Yustaga chiefs had historical ties to the chiefs of Timucua, now Christians, the main chief

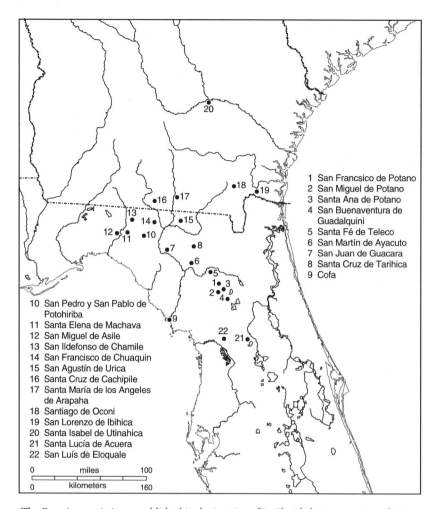

1   San Francsico de Potano
2   San Miguel de Potano
3   Santa Ana de Potano
4   San Buenaventura de
    Guadalquini
5   Santa Fé de Teleco
6   San Martín de Ayacuto
7   San Juan de Guacara
8   Santa Cruz de Tarihica
9   Cofa

10 San Pedro y San Pablo de
    Potohiriba
11 Santa Elena de Machava
12 San Miguel de Asile
13 San Ildefonso de Chamile
14 San Francisco de Chuaquin
15 San Agustín de Urica
16 Santa Cruz de Cachipile
17 Santa María de los Angeles
    de Arapaha
18 Santiago de Oconi
19 San Lorenzo de Ibihica
20 Santa Isabel de Utinahica
21 Santa Lucía de Acuera
22 San Luís de Eloquale

0   miles   100
0   kilometers   160

The Franciscan missions established in the interior of La Florida between 1606 and 1630.

of the Yustaga initially opposed the friars, delaying the process. Two friars, Fathers Alonso de Pesquera and Gregorio de Movilla, went to Yustaga in 1623. By 1628 several missions, including San Pedro y San Pablo de Potohiriba, had been founded, and by 1635 it was estimated that 13,000 Christian conversions had been made. San Pedro y San Pablo de Potohiriba was in the main Yustaga town, probably the same town where Narváez and de Soto had been a century earlier.

The site of San Pedro y San Pablo de Potohiriba in Madison County, Florida, adjacent to Lake Sampala, a corruption of San Pablo, was discovered by archaeologist B. Calvin Jones in the 1970s. The site of another mission just east of the Aucilla River has also been found. In general, though, our knowledge of the Yustaga province missions is hindered by a lack of archaeological research. What is known is that by 1630 a number of missions were in operation. In addition to San Pedro y San Pablo de Potohiriba, the Yustaga missions included Santa Elena de Machava to the west; San Miguel de Asile, located on the west side of the Aucilla River in eastern Jefferson County, Florida (possibly a Timucua-Yustaga mission in Apalachee territory); San Ildefonso de Chamile, probably north of the Hixtown Swamp in northern Madison County, Florida; and San Francisco de Chuaquin, probably on the Withlacoochee River in eastern Madison County.

The northernmost mission in the province of Timucua established about this same time, was Santa Cruz de Cachipile, probably just south of Valdosta, Georgia, and west of the Withlacoochee River in southern Lowndes County, Georgia, near I-75. Also in Timucua province was San Agustín de Urica somewhere in northern Suwannee County or southern Hamilton County, Florida. Santa María de los Angeles de Arapaha was presumably on the modern Alapaha River in southern Georgia.

By 1630 there were thirty-three Franciscan missions in La Florida, though the number of friars was slightly less. Despite a continual influx of friars into the colony, the attrition rate was high. This was owing to the rigors of colonial life and, perhaps, the same diseases that struck the Indian villagers.

The bulk of the thirty-three missions was in northern Florida and southeast Georgia, including the coast. Many fewer were in interior south-central Georgia, north of Valdosta. One reason for this may have been that it was easier to reach Yustaga, Timucua, and southeast Georgia.

Now the Spaniards could extend their control into Apalachee, the most densely populated native province with vast agricultural resources. Apalachee also fronted a considerable section of the Gulf coast, providing a means to export Spanish bounty by sea. With the colonization of Timucua and Yustaga completed, the conquest of Apalachee could begin.

THE ADVANCE INTO APALACHEE

We might expect that the founding of missions in Apalachee province occurred rapidly because of the nature of their political structure. The paramount chief could simply order his people to become Christians, and it would be done. Whether the colonization of Apalachee did occur rapidly or not is, however, uncertain; the documentary record for the first forty years of the Apalachee missions is remarkably sparse.

The advance in 1633 into Apalachee was led by Fathers Francisco Martínez and Pedro Muñoz, who followed Father Martín Prieto's 1608 visit to Ivitachuco by a quarter century. Fortunately, Father Prieto's missionary endeavors had borne some fruit. By 1612 some Apalachee chiefs had been asking that missionary priests be sent to them. In several instances churches had been built and crosses raised in readiness of such an event.

But not all the Apalachee were willing to welcome the Spaniards. On at least two occasions between 1608 and 1612, friars visiting among the Apalachee were forced to leave, and, as noted above, colonizing Apalachee was put on hold while Timucua and Yustaga received missions. In a letter sent back to Spain in 1617, the Franciscans spelled out the situation:

> The governor . . . has decided . . . not to send any religious [friars] to Apalachee because it is so far away and because it is necessary to locate a settlement or blockhouse with soldiers in that land for support and so that there would be foodstuffs for the religious, especially because it is impossible to carry those provisions overland from . . . St. Augustine or to assist them or to support them with what they need. And for this (reason) the religious, who went to see the land have returned, in addition to the fact that some of the Indians obey their chiefs poorly. (Hann 1988b, 12)

The Apalachee did not remain totally isolated from Spanish contact between 1612 and 1633. Fathers Martínez and Muñoz both spoke the Apalachee language, having learned it while living in missions on the Apalachee border. It is also known that as early as 1625 Apalachee Indians were transporting corn to St. Augustine to help relieve the food shortages that that town periodically faced. Epidemics in Guale and Timucua had left those provinces less able and willing to provide the food and labor the St. Augustine townspeople needed.

After 1612 Apalachee chiefs continued to request friars—they may have been the same chiefs who provided corn and the people to transport it to St. Augustine. The Apalachee leaders were anxious to collaborate with the Spaniards and to allow their people to become Christians for the same reasons the Timucuan and Guale chiefs accepted colonization: personal prestige, gifts, payments, and the chance to be allied with the powerful Spaniards and their new religion. Embracing Catholicism offered a chief the opportunity to participate in the La Florida colony. It also offered promise of personal access to the same power—knowledge, abilities, and material goods—that the Spaniards displayed. To be a Christian chief seemed to mean becoming a more powerful chief. It is no wonder that Apalachee chiefs, like other chiefs in La Florida, saw it in their best interest to support the missions.

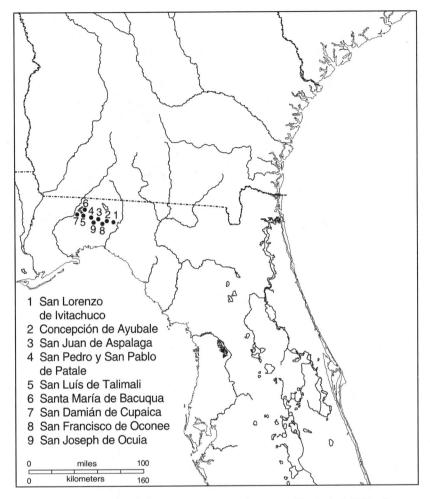

1 San Lorenzo
  de Ivitachuco
2 Concepción de Ayubale
3 San Juan de Aspalaga
4 San Pedro y San Pablo
  de Patale
5 San Luís de Talimali
6 Santa María de Bacuqua
7 San Damián de Cupaica
8 San Francisco de Oconee
9 San Joseph de Ocuia

0	miles	100
0	kilometers	160

Franciscan missions in Apalachee province 1633 to about 1650. (San Luís de Talimali was actually moved to the location shown here in 1656.)

Most likely the first mission in Apalachee, established in 1633, was San Lorenzo de Ivitachuco in the town of Ivitachuco, where Father Prieto had been. It was a major Apalachee town situated at the eastern end of Apalachee territory not too distant from San Miguel de Asile. The second mission was probably San Luís de Talimali, sometimes called San Luís de Xinayca, which suggests it was in the town of Anhaica where de Soto had been, or in the successor to that town. Documents indicate that a third mission, San Damián de Cupaica, also called San Cosme y San Damián de Cupaica, was founded in 1539, shortly after its chief went to St. Augustine to render obedience and to be baptized, receiving the Christian name Baltasar. As was the custom, the governor served as the chief's godfather.

During the late 1630s and especially in the early 1640s, at least seven other missions were founded across the Apalachee landscape, each serving a handful of satellite villages. West from San Lorenzo de Ivitachuco were Concepción de Ayubale and San Francisco de Oconee, and farther west were San Joseph de Ocuia, San Juan de Aspalaga, and San Pedro y San Pablo de Patale. Still farther west, near the Ocklocknee River, was San Damián de Cupaica. Most northern was Santa María de Bacuqua. All of these nine missions were in major Apalachee villages. Later, perhaps in the 1650s, still another mission, San Martín de Tomole, was established south from San Luís de Talimali. In 1635 the Apalachee population was estimated to be 34,000.

In 1638 Governor Méndez de Canço decided to station soldiers in the Apalachee province, a show of force intended to counter the hostility of a few of the chiefs. Several years later the soldiers were garrisoned at a recently established ranch between San Miguel de Asile and San Lorenzo de Ivitachuco. The soldiers probably helped coerce the Apalachee to provide labor for the ranch.

By the mid-1640s Apalachee had become an essential part of the La Florida colony. A deputy governor, Claudio Luís de Floréncia, took up residence in Apalachee to better represent the Crown's interests in this province so far from St. Augustine. The Floréncia family used that distance to their own advantage. At least one observer noted that the family members ran the province as if it were their own fief.

Apalachee would develop differently than the other mission provinces. In 1639 a port was in operation on the St. Marks River, providing Apalachee with a way to export and import goods far from the eyes of St. Augustine—thirteen days away by boat. Not only did the Floréncias take advantage of the situation, but the friars found the port a convenient way to export goods produced by Christian Indians to support their missions. Boats could travel between Apalachee and Havana, Cuba, and Veracruz, in Mexico, without going through St. Augustine and paying the requisite taxes. Smuggling by the Floréncias, Spanish soldiers, and even friars soon brought wealth to Apalachee that the other mission provinces did not have.

On February 19, 1647, Spaniards living in Apalachee, including eight friars, gathered at Santa María de Bacuqua for a religious celebration. A group of non-Christian Apalachee Indians and Chisca Indians (the latter also non-Christians who periodically raided Apalachee) used the occasion to attack, touching off a rebellion. The Spanish deputy general, his wife and children, and three friars were killed. Five other friars, aided by Christian Apalachee Indians, escaped and fled to Timucua.

The rebels burned seven of the eight missions, and Apalachee was no longer in Spanish hands. Almost immediately thirty-one soldiers were sent from St. Augustine to regain control. From the Timucuan missions, they took 500 warriors and marched to Apalachee. There they encountered a huge army—one account says 8,000 warriors—and a fierce, day-long battle ensued. The soldiers later recounted how they had fired 2,700 musket balls before running out of shot. Both sides suffered heavy loses. The rebels retreated, and the soldiers returned to St. Augustine with the news the rebellion had spread and included mission Apalachee Indians.

Plans were made to bring more soldiers from Cuba to retake the province. Francisco Menéndez Márquez, acting as an interim governor, journeyed to Yustaga with troops from St. Augustine to assess the situation and prevent the rebellion from spreading into that region. Much to the Spaniards' surprise, the rebels quickly lost heart. The rebels had not expected the rapid and fierce response of the Spanish soldiers and Timucuan warriors and suffered heavy losses.

With a small Spanish force and sixty Timucuan warriors, Menéndez Márquez convinced the Apalachee to hand over the leaders of the rebellion. Twelve were hung and twenty-six sentenced to labor in St. Augustine. The province again rendered obedience. The Apalachee chiefs who remained had to agree to provide laborers to work in St. Augustine, as was the practice in Timucua and Guale. The rebellion was over; a year later the missions had been rebuilt.

The Apalachee rebellion continued to reverberate through the colony amid much finger pointing. The Franciscans blamed the military government who demanded the Indians to work on the farm near Ivitachuco and serve as cargo bearers to transport goods to and from St. Augustine. Both activities caused many deaths among the Indians. A post-rebellion account noted that of 200 Indian bearers sent to St. Augustine, only ten had survived. The rest had died from hunger or the hardships of the journey. According to the friars, one more factor contributing to the rebellion was the presence of soldiers and Spanish settlers. Another factor was the lack of gifts that had once flowed to the Apalachee chiefs.

The soldiers, on the other hand, blamed the friars, citing punishments intended to turn the chiefs and other Indians away from those traditional practices that the friars viewed as anti-Christian. Certain dances and the playing of the Apalachee stick-ball game were given as examples, as well as the friars' efforts to replace native religious practitioners.

The animosity between the friars and the soldiers stationed in Apalachee mirrored similar disagreements throughout all the mission provinces. The two groups were often at loggerheads, and accusations were frequently recorded and sent to authorities in Spain. The friars continued to level charges against the soldiers and in 1651 they were successful in having the Apalachee garrison withdrawn. The farm near Asile and Ivitachuco was also closed down about the same time, although the next year friars and Christian Apalachee Indians harvested wheat from the abandoned fields and set about sowing the land themselves.

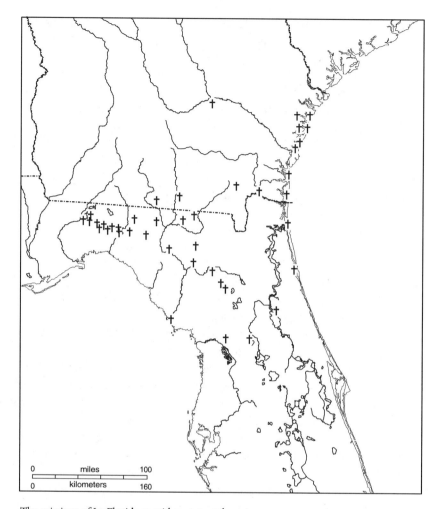

The missions of La Florida at mid-seventeenth century.

Several years later, rumors of impending British raids and the sighting of a British ship off the mouth of the St. Marks River led to the reestablishment of a garrison in Apalachee. Soldiers remained there throughout the remainder of the seventeenth century, a time when more Spaniards settled in the province.

By mid-century the Spanish considered their efforts to colonize Apalachee and the other mission provinces a success. About forty doctrinas were functioning in La Florida, serving roughly 15,000 Indians of which 12,500, nearly 85 percent, were in Apalachee. Authorities were even looking west and northwest from Apalachee to the Apalachicola and Chacato Indians, some of whom were requesting friars. Another group requesting friars was the Amacano, also located to the west.

Some scholars have referred to this period as the Golden Age of the missions. The colonization of the La Florida Indians, however, did not come without a huge cost. In Agua Dulce, Guale, Mocama, St. Augustine, and Timucua, the native population at mid-century was only a small fraction of what it had been when St. Augustine was first founded. In most cases, where once a doctrina had served several outlying villages, now only the village of the doctrina existed. No longer could Guale and Timucua provide an adequate share of labor and food for St. Augustine. As we shall see in chapter 7, during the second half of the seventeenth century, Apalachee would increase in importance while Guale, Timucua, and Yustaga would undergo great demographic changes.

6

BORN UNDER THE BELL

The goals of the Franciscan missions were to save the souls of the Indians while shaping their minds and controlling their bodies, all in support of Spanish interests. Often working in isolated locations, far from St. Augustine, and under rigorous conditions, the friars were remarkably successful. The friars and the missions brought significant numbers of southeastern Indians to the church and the Crown.

Making the initial converts was the most difficult part of the process. After one generation, children born to Catholic parents at mission villages were born into the church. Catholic beliefs, rituals, and iconography replaced native ones as Franciscan friars replaced native priests. When older generations faded away, so did many native religious beliefs that the Franciscan friars viewed as superstitions, pagan, or the work of the devil. As a consequence, much of the old and traditional was forgotten.

Writing in 1620, twenty-five years (roughly one generation) after the founding of his mission San Juan del Puerto on Ft. George Island in northeast Florida, Father Francisco Pareja noted that he had vanquished many native beliefs—he referred to them as superstitions—so effectively that the mission Indians "do not even remember them; so much so that the younger generation [who grew up under the missions] derides and laughs" at the older generation (Geiger 1937, 254).

It is important to realize that not all aspects of traditional Indian culture were replaced. The friars concentrated on changing those aspects that conflicted with Christian teachings. Much was retained, and the lives of the mission Indians became a curious blend of the old and the new.

The conversion of the Indians was a top-down strategy: first convert and co-opt the chiefs, and then use the chiefs' power to convert their people. But it was not simply political power that induced the Guale, Apalachee, and other Indians to agree to learn Catholic doctrine and labor in the fields of St. Augustine. The process of missionization was much more subtle, in one way or another permeating nearly all aspects of native life, from architecture to food, while blending with many of them.

This chapter's focus will be on the Indians who were served by the missions, people who were born, lived their lives, and died within the sound of the large, brass mission bells. Those bells, which summoned villagers to services and communicated other information, are apt symbols of the mission system. Calling villagers to work and worship, they represented the voice of religious authority.

MISSION BUILDINGS: VARIATIONS ON A THEME

The churches, with their Christian symbols portrayed in architecture, painting, and statuary, reinforced the tenets of Catholicism and the meaning of the rituals carried out within their walls. To be a Christian was to have a church or chapel in which to learn and worship—a sacred, physical place of sanctuary apart from everyday life.

The importance of the churches was well recognized by the Indians of Apalachee, Guale, and Timucua, who themselves had special buildings steeped in meaning and ritual: council houses, temples, and charnel houses. In the rebellions against the Franciscans in Guale (1597) and in Apalachee (1647), both of which occurred during the period of first-generation conversions by the Franciscan missionaries in those provinces, the mission churches and their contents, as well as the friars, were attacked. At times mission bells were also destroyed. In the rebels' eyes, the churches, their bells, and the friars represented Catholicism and the new practices that were replacing traditional beliefs. In the Timucua Rebellion in 1656, however, neither churches or friars were the objects of attack. By that time, a half-century after the first Potano missions, chiefs and villagers had accepted Catholicism, churches, and friars.

Despite their importance, we do not have a single description of what the Spanish mission churches in La Florida looked like. Documents, however, do mention churches and the other buildings and constructions found at the missions, including conventos, cocinas (kitchens), and fences. They occasionally offer information about construction practices and the tools and hardware used.

There is one late seventeenth-century plan showing the footprint of the buildings at Santa Catalina de Guale on Amelia Island, Florida, known to the Spaniards at that time as the island of Santa María. Drawn in 1691 and sent by the governor of La Florida to the Spanish Crown, the plan of the mission, moved from the Georgia coast to Amelia Island in 1684, is labeled (my translation):

> Palisade made on Santa María Island at the place of Santa Catalina in the Province of Guale; the walls are three varas [1 vara is about 3 feet] high with bastions to fire arms; the bastions have earthen ramps to half their height; around the palisade is a moat; and within it are the church, the convento of the mission, barracks for the infantry, and a small house for cooking.

As it turns out, the palisade and moat were never built, because labor and wood were in short supply. Nor is it certain that the buildings at the mission were exactly in this particular configuration. Even so, this single 300-year-old fragment provides our only documentary clues to what the size and spatial relationships of a mission may have been, and David Hurst Thomas was able to match the plan with similar buildings at his mission of Santa Catalina de Guale on St. Catherines Island, Georgia.

In the Santa Catalina de Guale drawing, the church is depicted as the largest rectangular building. On two of its sides are small plazas separating it from the other buildings in the mission compound. To the right, the two smaller rectangular buildings are the convento (the larger of the two) and the cocina. Both are oriented in the same direction as the church.

Despite having the Santa María drawing, identifying mission buildings at archaeological sites is not always an easy task. Understanding how the buildings were constructed and what they looked like is even more difficult. Despite such problems, archaeologists continue to make headway in interpreting mission buildings excavated at sites in Guale, Timucua, and Apalachee.

We have learned that not all missions were exactly like the Santa María drawing, though nearly all seem to exhibit variations of it. In every case where we have archaeological evidence from a mission site, the church is the largest rectangular building found, averaging about 60 ft. X 35 ft. (18 m X 11 m). Some mission churches were considerably larger; the San Luís de Talimali in Apalachee territory church was 110 ft. X 50 ft. (34 m X 15 m), probably the largest in La Florida.

It is likely the churches were constructed by villagers working under the watch of the Franciscan friars. Most churches combined native techniques with Spanish ones, including the use of iron tools and hardware. The first churches erected in chiefdoms whose leaders wanted to entice friars and a Spanish presence may have been built entirely by the Indians using hardware and tools they were given in St. Augustine. One example may be the small church at mission San Juan de Guacara, excavated at the Baptizing Spring site in southern Suwannee County, Florida (mentioned in chapter 1). The church was 27 ft. X 33 ft. (8 m X 10 m) with a clay

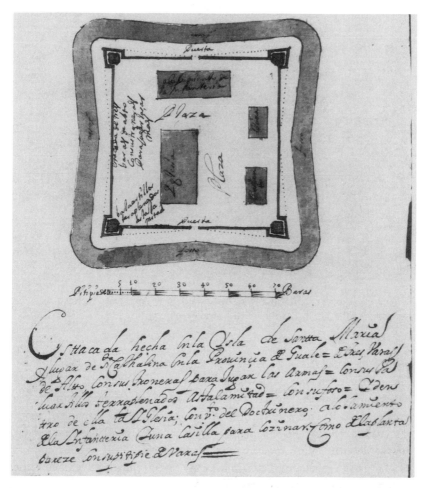

The mission of Santa Catalina de Guale on the Island of Santa María (Amelia Island). The moat and palisade depicted in this optimistic 1691 drawing were never completed. To the right of the church (*iglesia*) across a plaza are the kitchen (*cocina*) and convento. The fourth building, also separated from the church by a plaza, is a barracks for the small garrison stationed at the mission. (Courtesy P. K. Yonge Library of Florida History, University of Florida)

floor and contained a few iron spikes. It had three walls and was open on the fourth side.

A very similar early church was excavated by Brent R. Weisman at the Fig Springs site in Columbia County, Florida. As noted in chapter 5, it possibly was built when Father Baltasár López established a visita there in the late sixteenth

San Luís de Talimali's church. (Drawing by Edward Jonas; reproduced with the permission of the Florida Division of Historical Resources)

century. The same size as the San Juan de Guacara church, the Fig Springs church contained an open nave and a wooden-floored sacristy and sanctuary, both enclosed by board walls. The sacristy served as a storage room for vestments and other items used in religious services. Within the sanctuary was the altar; images of saints and other symbols and statuary were displayed there. Villagers attending mass at the small church stood around the building itself, some perhaps under the roof but most in the open. Later, in the early seventeenth century when Father Martín Prieto founded the doctrina of San Martín de Ayacuto in the same village, a much larger and more substantial church was built.

The later structure at San Martín de Ayacuto was more typical of the doctrina churches of Guale, Timucua, and Apalachee—walled, rectangular buildings with peaked roofs supported by wooden wall posts and interior support posts. Some had vertical board walls though most had walls of wattle and daub. The dried daub could be whitewashed or plastered with shell-lime plaster and then painted. In a few instances, such as with the post-1684 mission of Santa Catalina de Guale on Amelia Island, a lack of wood meant the church had no side walls; instead it was an open, pavilion-like building. Still others had walls that did not extend all the way to the roof.

Roofs were thatched with palm or palmetto fronds, while the floors in the main part of the church were packed earth or clay. Dry thatch was easily ignited, and fires may have been a constant problem. At Fig Springs, Brent R. Weisman

Constructing a wattle-and-daub wall. (Reprinted with the permission
of the University Press of Florida)

found several fire-hardened mud-dauber nests that probably had been under the
eaves of the early open church.

The largest room within each church was the nave. Villagers attending services
stood or knelt in the nave; there were no pews for sitting. Indians were used to
squatting. Kneeling was a new posture that required different muscles. One document noted that kneeling Indians at times fell forward, unable to maintain their
positions.

At the end of the church, opposite the main entrance, was the sanctuary and its
side room for storage, the sacristy. The floor of the sanctuary might be made of
wood; it was also raised. A small low barrier or fence separated the sanctuary
from the nave.

Wooden carvings, paintings, and religious items adorned the interior of the
nave and sanctuary. In some cases these were made of clay and, most likely, by

native crafts persons. Illumination came from candles and, perhaps, clerestory-like openings between the walls and roof. Some of the candlesticks were made locally of clay. As noted below, getting supplies for the missions was a continual hassle for the friars, forcing them to use makeshift items. Archaeological evidence suggests that the end walls of the churches that contained main doorways had elaborate facades, perhaps with wooden carvings and a bell tower. Just inside each doorway was the baptismal font. The objective was to create an overall ambience that was awe-inspiring. Mission San Juan del Puerto even had an organ, which some Indians learned to play.

Churches were positioned on the plazas of native villages, just as important traditional native buildings had been in the past. Atriums or courtyards fronted the main doorway, adding further elaboration to the building's outside entrance. At Santa Catalina de Guale on the Georgia coast the atrium was paved with oyster shells. These atria at the main entry of the church were the scenes for various rituals, including marriages, funerals, and baptisms. They and the adjacent plazas served as the locales for processions by *cofradiás* (religious confraternities). If the people attending religious services overflowed the nave, part of the crowd could stand in the courtyard. Fences or walls set off and enclosed areas within the mission complexes, such as a courtyard in front of the church or the convento. Some fences were wattle and daub, like most of the building walls.

In general, archaeologists have found few religious items associated with the churches. Evidently the religious precincts at the missions were swept clean. Those items that have been found most often are pieces of hardware used in the building's construction, objects such as wrought-iron nails and spikes.

At some mission sites, hundreds of small and large nails and spikes have been found, presumably transported from St. Augustine—no easy task. At San Luís de Talimali in Apalachee, the thriving Spanish-Indian mission town of the late seventeenth century, a smith was set up. Even so, the iron to be shaped into hardware had to be carried to the town. Another Apalachee mission had a small portable anvil, indicating that ironworking may have been more common than thought.

Obtaining supplies to build and operate the missions was difficult. In 1630 one friar wrote to the king asking him to order St. Augustine officials to increase the allotment of nails so more churches could be built. The king was also asked to authorize the loan of carpentry tools from St. Augustine for the construction of a mission. In the late seventeenth century a similar request was sent to the Crown asking for tools for new missions among the Jororo Indians in central Florida, south of Timucua. The tools were to be used for constructing buildings and for clearing and farming land. The list of items requested included 200 double mattocks, six large and six small saws, fifty large sickles (or scythes), and four large, four medium, and four small augers.

Communicating across the ocean with the Crown by letters was difficult at best. Military officials in St. Augustine who were quicker to support soldiers than friars only added to the friars' frustrations. Early in the seventeenth century Father Francisco Pareja complained that he and Father Pedro Ruíz had to fashion chalices out of lead. He also noted that between the two of them they had only one set of vestments, which meant only one could hold mass at a time. By skimping on meals, they were able to buy a second set. At times friars also had to come up with the money to buy wax, lamp oil, and wine, all of which were needed for services but did not always reach the missions. The friars quickly learned to use Indian labor to raise funds to support their missions.

We know much less about mission conventos and cocinas than about the churches. The information available from archaeological excavations suggests the conventos were as varied in construction techniques and sizes as the churches. At San Juan de Guacara, the Baptizing Spring site, what apparently was the convento was a dirt-floored, almost square structure about 22 feet (6.7 meters) on a side; a central hearth was used for cooking and for heat. The convento of Santa Catalina de Guale on Amelia Island was a two-roomed, wattle-and-daub building about 22 ft. × 37 ft. (7 m × 11 m). It had roofed porches on two sides, one of which may have covered a storage facility. A shell-paved floor underlay one porch and extended to a third side of the building. What seems to have been a separate cocina was nearby.

At Santa Catalina de Guale on the Georgia coast, archaeologists have identified two conventos, one probably predating the 1597 Guale Rebellion and one after. The earlier convento was quite large, about 30 ft. × 60 ft. (9 m × 11 m) and had three rooms. The later one was squarish, 27 ft. × 30 ft. (8 m × 9 m), with wattle-and-daub walls enclosing two rooms. Inside was a clay font used to hold holy water. Attached to the building was what may have been a storage bin, perhaps one raised on posts in the style favored by southeastern Indians and called a *garita* or *barbacoa* by the Spaniards.

There is still much to learn about mission buildings and their furnishings. It is safe to say, however, that the missions of La Florida bore little resemblance to the seventeenth-century adobe missions of the southwest United States or the eighteenth-century Franciscan missions of California. Life at the La Florida missions was not easy for the friars; living in damp, dirt-floored huts was hard on the Franciscans' health, extracting a high cost in lives.

CHRISTIANS IN LIFE AND DEATH

For most of the seventeenth century the Indians of Guale, Timucua, and Apalachee lived as Christians, participating in Catholic rituals. When they died,

A sixteenth-century Timucua Indian mound in which a chief was buried (engraved by Theodore de Bry in 1591).

they were afforded Catholic burial rites in sanctified ground in the floor of a mission church or in a campo santo (cemetery) close by. It is likely that the bodies of those people who lived at satellite villages were also taken to the mission compound to be interred. Friars complained that they sometimes had trouble reaching the sick and dying in those outlying villages in time to administer last rites.

With the adoption of Christianity and Catholic burial rites, the use of charnel houses and interment in lineage-maintained mounds by Guale and Timucua Indians ceased. In Apalachee, for which we know much less about pre-Columbian burial practices, the interment of elite individuals in special mounds like those at the Lake Jackson site was also halted.

In general, it may be that if a temporary chapel or church were first built when a mission was established, interments were initially made in the ground surrounding it. Then when a more permanent church was constructed, burials were placed within it. Archaeologists, however, are still undecided whether or not some missions also had a campo santo separate from the church. At any rate, it appears that the most common practice was to bury in the floor of the church nave. This came as something of a surprise both to archaeologists and Franciscan historians, because it has not been the practice for several hundred years, since the mid-eighteenth century.

Excavations outside the open church at the Fig Springs site, thought to be associated with the visita established there in 1597, uncovered a number of Christian burials around the building in a campo santo. Later, after the church was built to serve San Martín de Ayacuto, burials were made in the floor of the church nave.

Whether in a campo santo or church, Christian Indians were nearly always interred extended on their backs in shallow graves. Each individual's arms were folded on their chest, at times with hands clasped as if in prayer. In a few instances interments were made in small oval or round graves with the individual on his or her side in a flexed position, with knees and arms bent and drawn. Flexed burials were much more common in the pre-Columbian period when the ancestors of the Timucua and Guale Indians interred their dead in mounds. Perhaps such interments were made in church floors in the absence of a friar when villagers wished to bury a deceased relative in the traditional way.

Christian Indians were interred wrapped in cloth shrouds secured with brass straight pins. Because cloth was not always available, shrouds may not always have been used. A few people were buried in wooden coffins. At San Luís de Talimali bioanthropologist Clark Spenser Larsen and archaeologist Bonnie G. McEwan found interments in pine coffins in the church floor close to the altar. The people interred in that fashion were probably members of elite Apalachee families who had high social status. Once buried at the Lake Jackson site in mound tombs that reflected their high status, seventeenth-century Apalachee elites received their favored resting places in a Catholic mission church in the most important Apalachee mission and town.

A single coffin burial was found among the several hundred interments both in the Santa Catalina de Guale church on the Georgia coast and the Santa Catalina de Guale church on Amelia Island. The latter, a crudely made coffin constructed of rough timbers and large iron spikes, contained two adult males, perhaps native leaders in life. The Amelia Island coffin had been placed in the bottom of a large grave. On top of the coffin were the largely disarticulated bones of sixty-one people, mostly females, buried together in a mass grave. Exactly what this ossuary represents is uncertain. One suggestion is that the remains had been stored in a lineage charnel house and were transferred to the mass grave when Santa Catalina de Guale and its Guale Indian population were moved to the site in 1684.

Within each mission church or campo santo, individual graves and bodies all are aligned in the same direction along the long axis of the church. Excavations in the churches at San Martín de Ayacuto and Santa Catalina de Guale on Amelia Island suggest that graves were originally in ordered rows and marked or recorded in some fashion. Over time as more villagers died, the space within the nave floor became crowded. What had been rows became more chaotic and newer graves often cut into old ones, creating a jumble of bones and graves. In some instances,

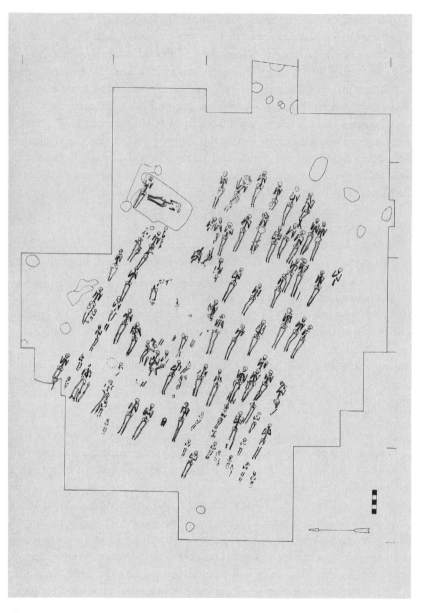

Christian Indian burials in the floor of the Santa Catalina de Guale mission church on Amelia Island.

Religious medallions from Santa Catalina de Guale. The medallion to the left, inscribed "Hail, Mary, conceived without original sin," is about 2.5 inches (6.4 centimeters) high. On the medallion on the right, the "Sorrowing Mother" of Jesus is depicted sitting on rocks at Golgotha. (Reproduced with the permission of the American Museum of Natural History)

burials literally were stacked beneath the church floor with as many as ten people interred in one 10 ft. X 10 ft. (3 m X 3 m) area of the floor. The church at Santa Catalina de Guale (in Georgia) had 400–500 people buried in the nave; San Martín de Ayacuto may have had at least several hundred. Graves containing more than one person are not uncommon. A few such graves appear to hold members of the same family, victims of some epidemic.

Christian Indians at times were buried holding or wearing items of Christian piety, such as small crosses, religious medallions, and reliquaries. Some clutched rosaries. In the early seventeenth century, Indian jewelry and ornaments, including glass beads, also occasionally found their way into graves, though the friars admonished the Timucua Indians not to put objects within shrouds, a practice presumably viewed by the church as non-Christian.

Apparently, the strictures regarding objects placed in graves did not apply to clothing. At both Santa Catalina de Guale and San Luís de Talimali, the main missions in Guale and Apalachee, respectively, tens of thousands of tiny glass beads have been found with church burials. People were interred in their finery decorated with beads in different colors.

On All Souls' Day, November 2, Christian villagers made offerings of pumpkins, beans, maize, and toasted flour to the dead. To the native people such a ritual may have echoed the traditional practice of offering gifts to the remains of their dead relatives stored in charnel houses or buried in mounds.

Certainly the archaeological study of mission burial patterns provides important information on the beliefs and rituals of the Christian Indians and the Catholic church of the time. The bioarchaeological study of the mission burials also provides a host of details about the health, diet, and causes of death of the many people who lived and died in the La Florida missions. Theirs was a story of ill-health, epidemics, and hard work.

MISSION VILLAGES

The architecture of the mission compounds, with their churches, conventos, plazas, and other features, is an interesting syncretism of new beliefs and old practices, combining Catholic ideas and iron hardware with aspects of native building techniques. In the native villages themselves, both those at the missions and, apparently, the outlying satellite areas, Spanish design influence was hardly discernible.

Within those native villages were houses for individual families and garitas, smaller food storehouses raised above ground to lessen their access to animals. Mounds were no longer constructed, but houses were still arranged around plazas as they had been in the pre-Columbian period. At the main village in each chiefdom a round council house also fronted the plaza. In the case of San Luís de Talimali in Apalachee, the council house and the mission church were located across the plaza from one another, apt symbols of old political practices and new beliefs.

Excavations at three Timucuan sites, San Juan de Guacara (Baptizing Spring), San Martín de Ayacuto, and the Richardson site in southern Alachua County, Florida, all revealed that the Indians built their round houses using traditional materials: wooden posts and palm thatch. Iron hardware was rare or totally absent, a marked contrast to the churches and conventos built to appeal more to Spanish tastes. One Spanish account describes the houses as pyramids; the wall posts were probably bent over and tied together above the center of the house, forming a pointed framework that was then thatched. The houses were relatively small, never more than 25 feet (7.6 meters) in diameter.

In contrast to the round houses were the much larger council houses, which contemporary accounts indicate were found throughout all of the mission provinces. Individual council houses were the locus of village business and where villagers met to receive and exchange information. The houses also served as lodging for visitors, including Spaniards, and it was in these houses that meetings took place between Indian leaders and Spanish officials. Council houses continued to be used throughout the seventeenth century. They were as common at mission villages as churches, reflecting the perseverance of native political structures.

Historical sources agree that council houses were circular, though estimates of size vary. One building was said to be large enough to hold 3,000 people, another only 300. Still another was said to be 81 feet (25 meters) in diameter. Entry was through a low doorway, which required people to stoop in order to pass through. A much larger opening was left in the thatched roof to allow the smoke from a central fire to escape and to let in light. Most of the accounts mention the row of benches or cabins—perhaps like box seats fronting a baseball diamond—that lined the interior wall, and some mention a second ring of seats built in line with the interior support posts, when present.

In most instances, the benches were painted in reds, yellows, and blues. The exterior walls were daubed on both sides, and murals were sometimes painted on the interiors. In their own way, the council-house interiors may have been as elaborate as those of the mission churches.

One of the many wonderful archaeological discoveries made at San Luís de Talimali was the town's council house. Excavations by archaeologists of the Florida Bureau of Archaeological Research revealed a large council house that closely resembled the historical descriptions. The circular San Luís de Talimali house was 120 feet (36.6 meters) across with two rings of interior seats. Its outer wall was marked by eight huge support posts, matched by eight others in the inner circle of seats. The paired sets of posts in the two rings supported eight radial roof rafters arranged like the ribs of an umbrella. The rafters, however, did not extend to the center of the roof, leaving an opening 46 feet (14 meters) across over the central hearth on the floor below. Around the hearth was a dance floor 65 feet (20 meters) in diameter.

Seating within the council house was according to protocol, with each individual aware of his or her status relative to the chief and everyone else.

> In this community house . . . they have its seats placed around with great
> order and arrangement, with the one belonging to the principal chief being
> the best and highest. . . . Those of the remaining leading men follow after
> this seat, without there being any confusion in it, while also having seats
> for the remaining common people, where they seat themselves without
> this order or arrangement. (Hann 1993a, 94)

LIFE AT THE MISSIONS

Though the Apalachee, Guale, and Timucua Indians retained important aspects of their ways of life during the mission period, the Indians were anxious to adopt the new Spanish ways. Because the epidemics had such devastating effects on their lives, Indians were questioning old ways that once had seemed to provide so much security. The missions offered new ways of thinking and being. Christianity and the Spaniards offered explanations for what was occurring and ways to spiritually cope with this new world in which the Indians found themselves. Friars and Spanish officials and soldiers offered opportunities and material goods that seemed to outshine traditional ones. The Indians' new life might well have appeared superior to the old ways.

Through the missions, the Indians embraced a new faith, iron tools, the Spanish language, monogamy, and peaches. Friars directed the process by condemning selected old ways and insisting on new ones. Such condemnations were especially prevalent in the early days while the initial conversions were being made. Don Juanillo, one of the chiefs involved in the 1597 Guale revolt, complained that the friars prohibited traditional "dances, banquets, feasts, celebrations, games and war," and labeled native priests as devils (Geiger 1937, 90). Friars worked hard to eradicate those aspects of Indian life they saw as morally corrupt, superstitious, or at odds with Catholic beliefs. For instance, the Timucua believed an eye twitch was an omen of bad luck, as was the sighting of an owl. Father Francisco Pareja sought to convince them that "tremors of the body and signs of birds and animals" were not to be believed (Milanich and Sturtevant 1972, 25). The friars by no means excised all that was native; native priests were expunged, but native use of herbal remedies for curing was encouraged.

As noted above, the friars worked hard to make the first generation of converts, especially among chiefs and children. Children of those first converts were born into Christian families and raised within the mission system.

The friars' education of the Indians included teaching them to read and write Spanish. As early as 1595, villagers at San Pedro de Mocama on Cumberland Island were speaking Spanish. Father Francisco Pareja devised a way to write down the Timucua language, and he translated primers and devotional books into the native language to use as teaching tools. Some of the Indians began writing letters to one another. The Spaniards recognized that literacy was important for teaching Christian discipline and doctrine. On occasion, native children were taken to St. Augustine to be raised, a means of more fully indoctrinating them into Hispanic life, culture, and language.

At the missions the Indians worked hard to learn the catechism and earn baptism and Christian-Spanish names. Often their names included both Indian clan or village names and a Christian name. Indians identified themselves both with traditional social ties and with their new religion. At times the path to achieving success was harsh. Friars whipped those individuals who skipped services or religious schooling. Only chiefs and married women were said to be exempt from such treatment.

Throughout the mission provinces the Indians learned to sing the mass—some aided friars in the celebration of mass—and to offer morning and evening prayers. Religious festivals, holy days, and feast days of obligation—including Sundays; the feasts of Nativity (Christmas), Resurrection (Easter), and Pentecost; All Saints' Day; and the days of Epiphany, the Lord's Circumcision, the Lord's Ascension, Corpus Christi, the Purification of Our Lady, the Annunciation of Our Lady, the Assumption of Our Lady, the Nativity of Our Lady, and the Apostles St. Peter and St. Paul—were marked with a mass, and the villagers were released from work duties. On fast days—all Fridays during Lent, the Saturday before Easter, and Christmas Eve—they also were given freedom from work.

The religious doctrine taught the Indians was comprehensive. As historian Amy Turner Bushnell (1994, 95) has noted, in addition to the responses to the questions of the catechism, the Indians learned the Pater Noster, Ave Maria, and Salve Regina (in Latin), and the Sign of the Cross and the Credo. They memorized the Ten Commandments, the Seven Deadly Sins, the Fourteen Works of Mercy, and other doctrine. Some of the Catholic rites were even translated into Timucua by Father Gregorio de Movilla. As a consequence, a wedding ceremony might have included words in Timucua, Spanish, and Latin.

Mission Indians who grew up in the Catholic church were Christians, just as steeped in religion as the Spanish colonists in St. Augustine. Some joined cofradías; others practiced self-flagellation on Holy Thursday before Easter. At least one friar contended that the piety of the Indians was greater than that of the colonists:

> Do they confess as Christians? I answer yes. . . . Many persons are found, men and women, who confess and who receive (Holy Communion) with tears, and who show up advantageously with many Spaniards. And I shall make bold and say and sustain my contention by what I have learned by experience that with regard to the mysteries of the faith, many of them answer better than the Spaniards. (Gerónimo de Oré 1936, 152–53)

Another friar wrote:

> They respect the Holy Cross with such great love that they never step on its shadow, if they see it on the ground. Nor is it missing from their homes. And the first thing the heathens request of us when we arrive at their villages is that we raise it and hoist it on high. (Hann 1993a, 101)

The introduction of Christianity was accompanied by a host of other novelties. Plants brought to La Florida from Spain joined corn and other crops traditionally grown by the Indians and were added to their diets. Remains of wheat, watermelons, peaches, figs, hazelnuts, oranges, and garbanzo beans all have been identified from mission archaeological sites. Historical documents also record the presence in St. Augustine of European greens, aromatic herbs, peas, sugarcane, garlic, melons, barley, pomegranates, cucumbers, European grapes, cabbages, lettuce, and sweet potatoes, all of which could well have been grown at the missions. The Spaniards worked to grow wheat in La Florida, because they greatly preferred wheat flour to flour ground from corn. Wheat was also needed for making the wafers served as the host at communion. One large, iron, tonglike wafer press has been found in southwest Florida at Mound Key, the site of Calos and the Jesuit missions of San Antonio as well as a short-lived late seventeenth-century Franciscan mission.

Mission Indians not only cultivated crops to feed themselves, but they were required to produce enough to sustain the friars and soldiers stationed in the mission provinces and help support the population of St. Augustine, a town in which corn would replace wheat as the most prevalent source of flour. Throughout the mission period corn was the chief agricultural item, as it had been in pre-Columbian times. The cultivation of wheat by Indians who had no history of growing that crop was never a big success.

During the seventeenth century, the amount of corn produced by the Indians in Apalachee, Guale, and Timucua was greater than in the pre-Columbian era. There was a conscious, successful effort to produce a surplus that could be exported from the fields of the Indians. Two factors allowed that to happen: more relative acreage was planted, and iron tools such as machetes, axes, and hoes were used to facilitate clearing and weeding of fields. There is no evidence that native agricultural methods—whether slash-and-burn or those in use in Apalachee—ever changed.

Indian chiefs and friars quickly learned that a profit could be made by exporting corn outside the colony, especially to Cuba. The surplus corn grown in mission fields was harvested, transported to St. Augustine, and collected by Spanish officials. Eventually, that practice gave way to a system of conscripted labor. In other words, rather than requiring mission villages only to supply corn, they had to supply labor to grow corn in fields surrounding St. Augustine.

Even so, large amounts—most—of mission corn was harvested, shucked, and ground into meal in the mission villages before it was sent to St. Augustine. It was more productive to carry, or transport by ship, 80 pounds (36.3 kilograms) of cornmeal than it was the same amount of unprocessed corncobs. Villagers provided the labor needed to grow, harvest, process, and transport the corn to St. Augustine overland (as from Timucua) or to coastal points from where it could be shipped (such as on the St. Marks River in Apalachee and from mission Santa Catalina de Guale on St. Catherines Island).

Evidence for the processing of increased amounts of corn is ubiquitous at every mission excavated in Apalachee, Guale, and Timucua. Hundreds, even thousands, of charred corncobs—spent fuel—have been found in small fire pits. The cobs, left after the kernels were removed, were apparently used as fuel for cooking fires and for smudge fires used to ward off insects. The number of charred cobs found at any one mission is many times the total number of cobs found in all of Florida and Georgia during the entire pre-Columbian period.

New foods may have required new methods of preparation and different serving dishes. Fired clay ceramics made by native potters in the shape of Spanish plates, pitchers, and other tableware are common at mission sites. On the other hand, such ceramics may have been made for the use of the friars who could not always get Spanish-made tablewares.

Indians were also exposed to new animals in the missions. Chickens and pigs were raised for food and export. In Apalachee some chiefs oversaw the raising of pigs and cattle that were transported to St. Augustine and Cuba in the form of tallow, pork, cowhides, and beef. Especially in Apalachee, with its larger mission-period populations, the chiefs well understood the economics of farming, livestock, and trade.

The intricacies of economic transactions were perhaps too well understood by some. John H. Hann (1988a) has uncovered documents recounting the 1695 arrest and trial of two Apalachee Indians who had been charged with counterfeiting Spanish coins out of pewter. The two were visiting St. Augustine in May when one stepped into a grocery to buy one real's worth of pastry with two counterfeit half-real coins. Emboldened when the storekeeper, Chrispin de Tapia, accepted the coins, the Apalachee man quickly returned for another pastry, passing two more fake coins. The deception was soon discovered when another customer received one of the coins in change and noted it was not silver. Several evenings later—when it was dark and difficult to see the coins—a second Apalachee offered two counterfeit half-real coins for a pastry, but the same shopkeeper, aware they were fake, apprehended him and turned him and the six coins over to the authorities.

As it turned out, the criminal was an Apalachee named Santiago, a young teen from San Luís de Talimali duped into participating in the crime. The boy had been visiting St. Augustine from a ranch outside of town where he worked. Santiago did not speak Spanish and needed an interpreter to tell his side of the story to officials. He explained receiving the money from Andrés de Escovedo, an Indian who worked as a personal servant for a soldier stationed at the fort. Jailed, Escovedo confessed that he and a third San Luís de Talimali native, Ajalap Cosme (age twenty or twenty-one), had found a pewter plate that they melted down and poured into a hand-carved half-real wooden mold. In all they had made nine coins. Cosme soon also confessed. Young Santiago was freed, and the counterfeiters were sentenced to hard labor.

This amazing story points out the extent to which some of the mission Indians were full participants in the life of the colony. A century after the founding of the Franciscan missions, Indians buying pastries at a St. Augustine store was a common occurrence.

Sometimes the friars were not certain whether an activity was compatible with Christianity or not. One example was the ball game played in Apalachee and western Timucua province in the summer while crops were in the field. (This game was quite different from the better known stick-ball game, the predecessor of lacrosse, played throughout the Southeast as well as among the Indians of the Northeast.) Players kicked a very hard deer-skin ball with their feet. One point was awarded for hitting the seven-foot-tall goalpost, two if the ball was kicked into an eagle's nest atop the post. The first team to reach eleven points won the game.

Typically the game involved just men, though women sometimes also played, and was held in the hard-packed plazas of villages. One village challenged another, set a date and place, and agreed on the number of players. One friar noted there could be fifty or even one hundred people on a side in the half-day games. Betting was intense and often injuries resulted, among players as well as spectators.

The game continued to be played throughout the mission period with friars and Spanish soldiers enjoying the spectacle. In the last quarter of the seventeenth century a debate raged for a decade about the propriety of Christian's playing the game: was it an athletic contest or was it tied to demonic practices? Documents relative to this debate, interpreted and published by Amy Turner Bushnell (1978b), paint a picture of native life quite different from that of the savvy Apalachee counterfeiters of the St. Augustine incident. When one town issued a challenge to another, they dispatched a courier whose face and torso were painted red and black, and who was adorned with bells, rattles, horns, and a badger's tail. To one friar, he looked like the devil himself.

Centuries-old rituals were used in the raising of the goalpost in the home team's plaza. Sassafras pegs anchored the wild grapevines used by six women and six men to hoist the pole up and pull its butt into the anchoring hole in which a skull or scalp had been placed. Atop the pole went an eagle's nest and shells, probably large conchs. Omens and rituals surrounded every aspect of the game, including a lot of dancing and lasciviousness the night before. A half century after the first Apalachee missions, the Christian Indians of that province still played the game in the traditional way, with all the rites and magic of the past.

At first this popular game was supported by Father Juan de Paiva. Closer examination and calls for banning the game from other Franciscans ultimately turned the friar into a staunch opponent. To bolster his case against the game, the friar recorded a lengthy Apalachee Indian story about the mythical origins of the game, noting it was dedicated to the supernatural beings associated with the sun, thunder, and rain—all elements important to a successful harvest.

The governor of St. Augustine was concerned that halting the centuries-old game might cause the Apalachee and other Indians to take it out on the Spaniards by refusing to work. The game was banned only after some of the Apalachee chiefs themselves, well-versed in the symbolism and beliefs surrounding the game, admitted it was non-Christian and should not be played.

LABOR DRAFTS

Prior to contact with the Spaniards, it was the prerogative of the chiefs of Apalachee, Guale, and Timucua to demand their vassal villagers provide labor for various projects. Tribute labor was used to build mounds and produce corn and other products for the chiefs' storehouses, or for other purposes. With the establishment of the missions Spanish officials routinely used such tribute labor for themselves in support of the colony. Working through village chiefs—usually paying them in trinkets—the Spaniards set quotas for the number of adult males each mission village would provide. This was a continuation of a traditional system, with chiefs using their power to extract labor from their people, but mounds were no longer built and the types of labors performed by the members of the labor drafts were quite different from those of the pre-mission period.

Especially demanding—and degrading—was the use of men as bearers to transport cornmeal and other foods from the mission provinces to St. Augustine. Such work was not to be done by elite individuals; manual labor was associated with lower social status. Chiefs and chiefly officials refused to carry burdens, though at times chiefs did lead groups of laborers on the trek to St. Augustine where they were feted and received gifts. Even ordinary Indians saw bearing burdens as an insult, and they frequently complained about it. It was the most onerous of the tasks demanded of the conscripted laborers. Not only was it socially demeaning, it was tremendously hard work. The bearers often suffered from cold and hunger, some dying while on the trips from the missions to St. Augustine.

Father Alonso Moral, who had served in La Florida for thirty-three years, penned this indictment of the practice in 1676:

All the natives of those provinces suffer great servitude, injuries, and vexations from the fact that the governors, lieutenants, and soldiers oblige them to carry loads on their shoulders to the Province of Apalachee and to

other areas and also to bring loads from those regions to the fort of
St. Augustine. . . . Each year from Apalachee alone more than three hundred are brought to the fort at the time of the planting of the corn, carrying their food and the merchandise of the soldiers on their shoulders for
more than eighty leagues with the result that some on arrival die and those
who survive do not return to their homes because the governor and the
other officials detain them in the fort so they may serve them. (Hann
1988b, 140–41)

The personal travails of the mission Indians forced to servitude are reflected in
their skeletal remains. More than three centuries after Father Moral offered his
testimony about the hardships suffered by conscripted laborers, bioarchaeologist
Clark Spencer Larsen and his students have studied skeletal remains from the missions and uncovered graphic evidence of the rigors of colonization. Analysis of remains from missions in Guale and Mocama show male Christian Indians are
larger in body size than their pre-Columbian counterparts, the result of performing heavy labor. Especially evident are longer and stronger leg bones, and
stronger upper torso, a result of gardening, burden bearing, and other labor.
Larsen's careful study also indicated that mission Indians suffered more broken
bones than their predecessors. Remarkably, osteoarthritis—a degenerative joint
disease—that affected less than 12 percent of pre-Columbian populations in
Guale, was present in 58 to 65 percent of the mission Indians.

At any one time, the mission provinces were required to provide 300 or more
laborers to St. Augustine. Exact figures for the various provinces by year are lack-
ing, though John E. Worth has found lists for Mocama and Guale for 1636 and several years from 1666 to 1673. Those lists, which reflect drafts for nine missions, indicate that the number of laborers for those regions dropped from fifty-four to
twenty-seven over thirty years, a 50 percent reduction probably mirroring a similar reduction in the native population. After 1647 and the Apalachee rebellion and
as the aboriginal population of Guale and Timucua declined, the number of conscripted laborers from Apalachee increased. At the time Father Moral recorded
his observations, about 80 percent of the laborers came from Apalachee.

Bearers not only carried loads to St. Augustine, they also traveled trails leading
from Apalachee and Timucua to the Gulf coast, where goods could be loaded on
boats and shipped out by water around the peninsula to St. Augustine or to Cuba.
Another way to reach St. Augustine from Apalachee or western Timucua was by
canoe down the Wacissa-Aucilla River into the Gulf of Mexico and southward to
the mouth of the Suwannee River, then up the Suwannee and Santa Fe River to
the natural bridge at modern O'Leno State Park west of mission Santa Fé de
Teleco. At the natural bridge the water route intersected with the camino real,

and there, the goods could be loaded on human backs and moved the rest of the way to St. Augustine overland. The purpose of the mission of Cofa, established at the mouth of the Suwannee River, may have been to provide a stopover for canoe travelers using this route. A variant of this route might also have seen canoes putting in at mission San Martín de Ayacuto on the Ichetucknee River, a small tributary of the Santa Fe River, rather than continuing to the natural bridge.

In the late 1940s archaeologist John M. Goggin and his students recovered hundreds of pieces of Spanish crockery and Indian pottery by the head of the spring leading to the Ichetucknee River from San Martín de Ayacuto. The huge amount of artifacts found there suggest that it was an often used canoe landing. Landing at San Martín de Ayacuto, travelers and bearers could have stayed the night at the mission and then continued their journey to St. Augustine on the camino real, which ran nearby.

Not only were goods taken to St. Augustine, supplies for the missions were brought back as well. Some travel between Guale and St. Augustine was also overland, and bearers traveled routes parallel to the coast from that province to the Spanish town. There were still other trails, some combinations of land and riverine travel, that reached into southern and southeast Georgia and northern Yustaga.

We might guess canoe travel was preferred over travel by foot, but it was not always possible. To reach some missions, it was a long overland trek. Friars complained that traveling to some missions by land routes was tedious and asked that horses be provided for them, as well as to help take the load off the Indians.

Once in St. Augustine the conscripted native laborers did not simply turn around and return to their respective villages. They were used in that town for numerous projects, sometimes spending months there before being allowed to return home. Women at the missions complained about the loss of their husbands for such long periods. In St. Augustine workers prepared fields, planted crops (especially corn), and harvested them, helping to feed the Spanish garrison. While there they may have lived in the Indian villages at Nombre de Dios and San Sebastián just north and south of the city gates, respectively.

Conscripted Indian workers also provided labor for construction projects. They helped to fell trees and cut them into timbers, then transport the lumber to town. Blocks of coquina stone used as building materials were cut from the mine on Anastasia Island and rafted to St. Augustine. The huge coquina blocks used in the construction of the Castillo de San Marcos were provided by Indians. When the massive fort was begun in the 1670s, as many as 300 Indians were involved in its construction.

Christian Indians also worked in St. Augustine as servants for Spanish families and the soldiers and officials stationed there. Some Indians may have lived in town full time, rarely traveling back to their homes.

The Indians were supposed to be paid for all of their activities—after all, they were Christian subjects of the Spanish Crown, not slaves. Payment at the rate of one real per day (the cost of one pastry) was in goods, most often trinkets. It is by no means clear that such payments were always made. However, payment or not, the Spaniards believed they were within their legal rights to summon the Indians of La Florida to work on their behalf. The practice of requiring labor in exchange for educating native people to be Christians—thus saving their souls—permeated Spanish colonial policy all through the Americas.

John E. Worth (1998a, 124–25) has found documentary evidence of still another way in which adult males served the Spanish military government: an Indian militia. Faced with the periodic threat of attack by foreign colonial powers and privateers, St. Augustine with its understaffed garrison needed to beef up its defenses. Although, for example, the Crown provided funding for 300 soldiers to be stationed at St. Augustine, the true number actually hired might have only been 150. Officers required a salary that might have been three times an enlisted man's salary. Governors and other town officials might also draw military salaries, though not actually serving as soldiers. Graft and corruption in St. Augustine was a recognized part of colonial life, but it severely weakened the colony's ability to defend itself. Using Indians to fight in defense of the colony was one way to compensate.

The militias organized in Guale and Timucua actually were drilled and armed, serving as a reserve infantry. Some of the Indians kept firearms, probably obtained through trade. Once in the late 1620s and again in the 1650s, the governor of La Florida called on the Indian militia when it was thought St. Augustine might be attacked by English forces.

Not only were Christian Indians required to bear burdens to St. Augustine, work on Spanish projects, and join the militia, they also provided labor for projects in the mission provinces. Indians maintained the camino real by clearing brush, repairing creek crossings, and building bridges. Where the camino real crossed larger rivers Indians manned canoes to ferry people across. On the Suwannee River a ferry crossing was at modern Charles Spring, while the St. Johns River crossing was near modern Picolata where the river intersected the camino real. At various times the Spaniards placed missions at both locations, intending to use the mission villagers to staff the ferry service.

Adverse winds could make crossing the St. Johns River a dangerous task. Wind could also prevent canoes having crossed from returning. Villagers of Salamototo, one of the succession of small mission towns that manned the ferry on the St. Johns River, complained that bad weather could keep them away from home for several days at a time. Ferries were also operated on the St. Johns River north of St. Augustine in Mocama, and in Mocama and Guale they provided passage between the barrier islands, such as from modern Ft. George Island and mission San Juan del Puerto, to the mission of Santa María de Yamasee on Amelia Island.

At the missions themselves, Christian Indians were servants for the friars and those soldiers stationed at mission garrisons. They tended gardens, did household chores such as cooking, and provided corn, fish, and other foods. Sometimes the soldiers paid them small amounts for these services. One account from Guale describes the Indians bringing cassina—the leaves of an ilex (holly) that could be dried and brewed into a caffeine-containing tea—to soldiers.

At mission San Luís de Talimali the wooden fort and the houses of the Spaniards living there were all built with native labor, as was a later fort at St. Marks on Apalachee's Gulf coast. Indians were even used to build a galley that explored the coast west of the St. Marks River to the bays of Pensacola and Mobile. Without the labor of Christian Indians, St. Augustine and the missions could hardly have functioned.

Corn became a sort of currency in the colonies hard pressed to feed their non-Indian population. Corn and other produce could be demanded, traded, or purchased with goods and then transported to St. Augustine or elsewhere to be sold at a profit. Royal funds provided the governors of Spanish Florida were used to buy blankets, glass beads, bells, hoes, axes, and cloth traded to the chiefs and lineage leaders in exchange for corn. Corn purchased in this fashion was for consumption in St. Augustine. Indians also traded some food directly with the townspeople of St. Augustine. The growth of Indian entrepreneurship probably introduced new social and political opportunities into the traditional fabric of native life.

As chiefdoms suffered population losses and their chiefs could no longer command respect and control lands, other native leaders were willing to take advantage and gain access to deals with the Spaniards. By the mid-1600s the decline of the Potano Indians caused that region to be placed under the control of the chief of San Martín de Ayacuto, who did not hesitate to allow Spaniards to establish ranches on Potano land in exchange for gifts.

Spaniards and Indians each sought to turn the system to their own advantage. In such entrepreneurial exchanges, however, the Indians were generally at a disadvantage. For instance, the villagers of San Juan de Aspalaga in Apalachee charged in 1677 that seven or eight years earlier their chief, who had since died, had traded 100 arrobas (2,500 pounds) of beans and corn to a Spaniard for half their worth in money plus a horse, but no payment had been received. Other villagers complained that a trade of corn for blankets was never reciprocated, and the blankets had never been delivered.

Christian Indians, as subjects of the Crown, did have rights. During the two-year term of each La Florida governor, a delegation of soldiers and officials from St. Augustine was sent to tour the missions and settle disputes like the ones mentioned above. Whether or not those legal visits substantially bettered the lot of the Indians is questionable, however.

RANCHES

Another endeavor intended to produce profits was the establishment of *haciendas* (ranches) in Apalachee and Timucua. In the late seventeenth century some ranches were established well south of the camino real and the then chain of Timucuan missions. With the labor of Indians, raising cattle, pigs, and chickens and cultivating corn and wheat were ways for Spaniards in La Florida to make money.

One of the earliest and most important ranches was in Timucua in Potano Indian territory, today Alachua County, Florida. By 1630 the ranch owned by La Florida's royal treasurer, Francisco Menéndez Márquez, a relative of Pedro Menéndez de Avilés, was raising cattle. Named La Chua ("chua" was the Timucuan word for "sinkhole"), the ranch was on the north side of Paynes Prairie not far from the Alachua Sink, a famed sinkhole through which the prairie drains and which today is named for the ranch. Menéndez Márquez's ranch was on a huge piece of land—87 square miles (225 square kilometers).

To operate the ranch, Menéndez Márquez needed the permission of Lúcas Menéndez, the Indian chief of the San Martín de Ayacuto village 50 miles (81 kilometers) to the northwest, who had apparently usurped the land from the Potano Indians, hit hard by epidemics. In exchange for allowing the ranch, Lúcas Menéndez received gifts and was feasted. Menéndez Márquez served as the chief's godfather at his baptism. The two men and their families would remain close for many decades.

Menéndez Márquez used Timucua Indians to staff the ranch, as well as at least one Indian from Mexico and two African slaves. African slaves were legal in the colony. Pedro Menéndez de Avilés had been granted permission by the Crown to keep a small number, and, according to documentation obtained by John E. Worth, between five and seven worked for royal officials in St. Augustine throughout the 1650s; two of those slaves may have been assigned to the ranch. Such deception, some might say corruption, was apparently common to Menéndez Márquez. He was arrested and served time for misusing royal funds intended to support the colony. After his death in mid-century an audit of his records revealed that he had embezzled 16,165 pesos from the royal treasury in St. Augustine. The ranch was probably started with some of his ill-gotten gains. Menéndez Márquez's son, Thómas, continued to operate the ranch after his father died.

The earliest cattle drives in what is now the United States were in northern Florida when African and Indian "cowboys" drove the cattle from La Chua to St. Augustine. There, the cattle were slaughtered, the beef sold, and the hides and tallow exported. Thómas Menéndez Márquez would carry on a lively trade with Havana, exchanging cattle products for Cuban aguadiente—a rum distilled from sugarcane.

A second ranch, between San Miguel de Asile and San Lorenzo de Ivitachuco west of the Aucilla River, was owned by Governor Benito Ruíz de Salazar Vallecilla. Beginning operation in 1645, the Asile ranch grew corn and wheat and raised pigs, all endeavors that required a much larger labor force than did raising cattle. As with La Chua, the Asile ranch operated with the permission of the local village chief.

The land on which the ranch operated was about one-third the size of La Chua, covering more than 30 square miles (78 square kilometers). Horses and oxen, with iron plows, were used to cultivate fields under the supervision of the soldiers garrisoned there and, later, an overseer. After Governor Salazar Vallecilla died, the farm was sold. By 1652 it was no longer in operation, owing to a controversy over its ownership and protests by the Indians of San Miguel de Asile and San Lorenzo de Ivitachuco, who complained that men, women, and children all had to work there.

Following the 1656 Timucua Rebellion (described in chapter 7), it became much easier for Spaniards to gain access to land in La Florida to start ranches. Land grants became common, and taxing them became a way to raise funds for St. Augustine's coffers.

One ranch—owned by Juan de Hita who was married to Antonia, a daughter of Thómas Menéndez Márquez—was near the San Francisco de Potano mission and perhaps included the dry prairie today called San Felasco Hammock. A second—named Chicharro and owned by Francisco Romo de Uriza, married to another of Thómas's daughters—was on the south side of Paynes Prairie and could be seen from La Chua across the flat prairie.

Other ranches were scattered about, many closer to St. Augustine on the east side of the St. Johns River, some as far south as Mosquito Inlet on the coast, and one in Mayaca Indian territory. John H. Hann (1996, 194) has documented twenty-five cattle ranches in northern and east Florida east of the Aucilla River in the late seventeenth and early eighteenth centuries. Most were small, but all probably used native laborers. Indeed, Santiago, the young Apalachee who had fallen in with the counterfeiters in St. Augustine in 1695, worked on a ranch owned by a soldier.

In the second half of the seventeenth century it was Apalachee, with its fine agricultural soils and large native population (relative to Guale and Timucua), where ranching was the biggest success, especially from the 1670s on when a number of Spanish settlers moved into the province. In 1675 several land grants for ranches were made, and soon there were nine ranches in Apalachee growing corn and wheat or raising cattle, hogs, and horses. A few ranches were owned by elite Apalachee Indians.

The most prominent of the Spanish families in Apalachee was the Floréncias, some of whom lived at San Luís de Talimali. Other Spanish ranches were owned by Diego Ximénez and by Marcos Delgado, whose ranch, Our Lady of the Rosary, was established in 1677. From their ranches livestock and crops were regularly shipped from the port at St. Marks. A trading boat was sent from St. Augustine to coastal Apalachee to load goods. Similar voyages to Guale also took place, since that province could be reached by sea, but the amount of ranch products (corn, for instance) exported from there was much less.

Like corn and other foods, deer hides were a commodity of exchange in seventeenth-century La Florida, though we do not have figures on the scale of the trade. Because hides were probably purchased with nongovernment funds, mention of them in official documents is rare. Yet, there are hints that Spaniards, including friars, were more than willing to obtain hides to export for a profit. For instance, in 1677 pirates entered the St. Marks River port, where they stole a small frigate as well as deer hides and "amber" (probably ambergris), all goods owned by Spanish soldiers stationed in the province. The soldiers had readied the goods for export, perhaps planning to have then smuggled out without paying the requisite duties.

The amount of goods flowing out of Apalachee was immense. In 1685 a ship left there with 100 chickens, 110 hams, 35 jars of lard, 300 deerskins, 44 bushels of corn, and 60 arrobas (approximately 25 pounds) of pine tar. In Apalachee and Guale trade may have been organized through each province's main town from where the goods could be transported by ship. Indians, friars, Spanish soldiers, and settlers in Apalachee probably all participated in this trade, acting as middlemen in dealing with other Indians, some of whom lived outside the mission provinces. Apalachee especially carried on a vigorous trade with destinations outside of Florida. As a result of their positions in local and regional trade networks, especially those involving corn sales, San Luís de Talimali and Santa Catalina de Guale acquired wealth.

This wealth is reflected in the vast array of trade goods that have been found by archaeologists at both mission sites. All the glass beads found in all the Timucuan missions excavated thus far equal only a minute percentage of those found at Santa Catalina de Guale. The wealth of San Luís de Talimali was even greater. Based on the array of artifacts found in the town's Spanish quarter, archaeologist Bonnie G. McEwan (1991) concluded the town's Spanish inhabitants lived as well, if not better than, some of their compatriots in St. Augustine. Ultimately, the wealth of both missions was extracted from the labors of Indians.

7

EPIDEMICS, REBELLION, AND CHANGE

Tens of thousands of Indians died. In La Florida epidemics were such a commonplace occurrence that they drew little mention in official documents. The trial of two Apalachee Indian counterfeiters in St. Augustine in 1695 generated more words in documents than did all the disease-related deaths of the entire mission period. The epidemics created demographic devastation. Although the Spaniards and the Franciscans could save souls, they could not save lives. All their efforts to repopulate the missions, especially those in Timucua between Apalachee and St. Augustine, would go for naught.

Epidemics, which periodically swept through mission villages and, sometimes, St. Augustine itself, were not solely responsible for devastating the native population of the mission provinces. Villagers weakened by forced labor, malnourishment, and battling epidemics were left susceptible to secondary infections such as pneumonia and other viruses. Epidemics and secondary diseases were a lethal combination.

Another contributor to mission depopulation was the system of repartimiento. Conscripted Indian laborers suffered horridly from the work assigned them, often dying away from home or on the trails to and from the mission province. John E. Worth (1998b, 21–22) has suggested that a lower birthrate, caused both by the rigors of colonialism and by a labor system, which took males away from home was still another cause of reduced mission populations.

To deal with the problem of Indian depopulation—a problem that threatened the labor force that the colony had come to rely on—the Spaniards employed a number of initiatives. All, unfortunately, were short-term and ineffectual. Sending soldiers to catch Indians who had fled the missions and bring them back was one example. Another was the occasional use of non-mission Indians—usually taken by force—as laborers in St. Augustine. Such efforts brought in only handfuls of Indians, not enough to make up for the ongoing depopulation.

DISEASE AND DEPOPULATION

Prior to the founding of St. Augustine in 1565, the documentary record for the vast region that would become the mission provinces is spotty at best. Only infrequently was the region visited by Europeans, and those who did left no information on the impact of diseases introduced. For example, the Pánfilo de Narváez and Hernando de Soto expeditions provide important descriptions of Indian societies, but neither stayed in one place for more than a few days or weeks, except for de Soto's camp at Tampa Bay and his winter camp in the Apalachee town of Anhaica. These early Spanish expeditions were not able to observe the effects of their own presences. Even while wintering at Anhaica, the people of de Soto's huge entourage saw little outside their own encampment.

Many archaeologists and historians believe that in the eighty years between Juan Ponce de León's first voyage to La Florida in 1513 and the first major thrust of the Franciscan missions into Guale and Timucua after 1595, epidemics ripped through the native populations. Most of that impact might well have occurred in the generation and a half following 1564 and the settlement of Ft. Caroline. The depopulation zone surrounding the site of that French settlement and St. Augustine to the south, as well as the lack of early missions along the upper third of the St. Johns River (mentioned in chapter 2), offer evidence of the impact of sixteenth-century, pre-mission epidemics.

There are also other hints of pre-mission impact. We know, for example, that mound building, common in pre-Columbian times in the Southeast, had stopped in northern Florida and coastal Georgia by the time of the first Franciscan doctrinas. The cessation of mound building likely reflects social and behavioral disruption and uncertainty associated with disease-caused depopulation. Had the Jesuit missionaries of the late 1560s ventured into the interior of northern Florida, they probably would have witnessed the demographic devastation that was being wrought.

Many aspects of life other than mound building would have been impacted, especially when epidemics appeared again and again in succeeding generations. Archaeologist Marvin T. Smith (1987) has cited several cultural changes that occurred among southeastern Indian societies in the aftermath of disease-caused population reductions. In addition to a cessation of mound construction, there was a reduction in the number of Indian towns, reduction in town size, relocation of towns (as people left old areas for new ones), and an increase in graves with multiple burials. Also, artifacts associated with elite individuals became fewer in number, a reflection of the decline in the power of leaders as complex chiefdoms broke down into simpler ones. Settlement hierarchies, such as those found in pre-Columbian Apalachee, also began to break down as political structures became less centralized.

There is little concrete archaeological evidence—clues on the bones of the victims themselves—of epidemics in Spanish Florida. People who die of smallpox, the plague, or measles, for example, die quickly, before the diseases can etch evidence on human skeletons, leaving little to be interpreted by scientists. Even from the mission period, when we are certain epidemics killed thousands of people, at least some of whom must be interred under the floors of mission churches, analyses of skeletal remains have failed to yield definitive evidence of disease-caused mortality. The deaths of infected mission Indians were simply too swift.

Bioarchaeologists, however, are able to consult the mortal remains of mission villagers and better understand other impacts of colonization on individual lives. For example, Lisa M. Hoshower's analysis of the remains of people buried at mission San Martín de Ayacuto in Timucua shows that they lived in relatively poor health. Though an individual might have survived measles and smallpox, he or she still may have had to cope with other infections that left evidence of physiological stresses on bones.

Historians are also working to improve our understanding of the impact of diseases, like bubonic plague, measles, smallpox, chicken pox, dysentery, diphtheria, influenza, malaria, scarlet fever, typhoid, typhus, and yellow fever. Documents indicate an epidemic struck the missions in Mocama and Guale in 1595, almost as soon as the Franciscan efforts in those provinces began. And not long after the interior missions in Timucua province came into existence—between 1613 and 1617—a number of "great plagues and contagious diseases" killed half the mission Indians in Potano and Timucua (Hann 1988b, 175). During the several years in which epidemics ravaged the interior missions (Apalachee had yet to be colonized), one friar, Father Antonio de Cuellar, who served at newly founded Santa Cruz de Tarihica, baptized more than 800 dying Indians at that mission alone.

Apparently the epidemics were not wavelike pandemics that quickly swept through the entire southeastern United States or even through all the mission provinces. Instead, they seem to have been more localized, a trend observed in the colonial period northeastern United States as well. These epidemics were simply too lethal to spread over vast distances. With their high mortality rates, most of the diseases did not have time to spread outside the region they infected. Carriers grew sick and quickly died, unable to travel great distances.

There is evidence, however, that the use of the camino real for travel across northern Florida made the spread of diseases easier. Travelers, infected in St. Augustine while serving on labor gangs, could transport germs back to their home villages in only a few days. This is most likely what happened to the Indians of Potano, the closest of the interior mission provinces to St. Augustine. By 1617, only a few years after they had started sending laborers to St. Augustine, the Potano missions were hit particularly hard by epidemics. Depopulation was so severe that for a time there was not a sufficient number of adult males to fill the labor quotas demanded by Spanish officials. As Father Francisco Pareja observed, these early epidemics resulted in "a very great harvest of souls."

Between 1649 and 1651 epidemics struck down not only Indians but friars and two La Florida governors. During this same period, a horrible epidemic struck Seville, Spain, where many ships destined for the Americas originated, suggesting that it may have been the ultimate source of the epidemics that reached St. Augustine and the missions.

In the winter of 1654–55 a severe epidemic thought to be smallpox hit. It lasted much of 1655, ravaging St. Augustine and all of the mission provinces. Two years later the governor of Spanish Florida, Diego de Rebolledo, wrote that the epidemic had killed half the population of Timucua and Guale. Apalachee, up to this time shielded somewhat from the epidemics by its more remote geographical location and the fact that it had not sent many laborers to St. Augustine until after the 1647 rebellion, also suffered. In 1659 a new governor alleged that 10,000 Indians had died recently from measles, which suggests that the terrible epidemics continued (though that governor, Alonso de Aranguiz y Cotes, might have been referring to the earlier epidemics).

By mid-century 30,000 Apalachee Indians had been reduced to about 10,000 in about twenty years. That is only 20 percent of the 50,000 Apalachee in 1513, when Juan Ponce de León first had anchored off La Florida's Atlantic shore. The Timucua Indians, whose total population near the end of the sixteenth century was between 20,000 and 25,000, numbered between 2,000 and 2,500 following the mid-seventeenth-century epidemics. Guale, similarly devastated and with a smaller number of people to begin with, probably ended up with even fewer Indians, somewhere between 1,000 and 2,000. The once flourishing chiefdoms consisting of multiple villages among the Guale and Timucua Indians were each reduced to a single mission village. Individual chiefdoms could no longer provide St. Augustine with anything near the number of laborers they once did. As a consequence, Spanish officials increasingly would look to Apalachee to provide the support the colony needed.

THE TIMUCUA REBELLION AND
MID-CENTURY CHANGES

The mid-seventeenth century was a rough time for the Timucua chiefs of the mission villages in interior northern Florida. Their chiefly ancestors each had presided over several villages and hundreds, usually thousands, of people. By the 1650s things had changed. The epidemics had reduced the number of their people, and they no longer controlled multiple villages. As Apalachee grew in importance, the Timucuan chiefs saw their own power and status diminish. Some chiefdoms, like Potano, had almost disappeared. Even the recognition and presents they had once been able to claim from the Spaniards were not the same. Their future as chiefs under the thumb of the colonial powers in St. Augustine promised more of the same.

In early 1656 rumors reached St. Augustine of an impending English raid. St. Augustine, however, was not prepared to ward off any attack. The ability of its wooden fortifications—the stone Castillo de San Marcos was not yet built—to withstand a cannon attack from ships was dubious. Repairs were being made, but would take time. Worse, the number of soldiers stationed in the town was well below what it should have been, mostly because of corruption and a failure by the authorities to assign soldiers to the garrison.

Corruption and laxness had also left the town's food stores low. A protracted siege would have been disastrous. Faced with these serious shortcomings, Governor Diego de Rebolledo took drastic action to ensure the safety of his colony and prevent La Florida from falling into English hands. First he called up the Indian militia from the mission provinces. He also ordered the chiefs of Apalachee, Guale, and Timucua to assemble 500 men, some members of the Indian militia, and march with them to St. Augustine to help defend it. Furthermore, the governor commanded the warriors and their chiefs to carry their own supplies, including the corn and food they would need for the overland trek to and from St. Augustine and for a stay of at least one month in town.

One Timucuan chief, Lúcas Menéndez, the same individual who had been involved with Francisco Menéndez Márquez and his descendants, owners of the La Chua cattle ranch, flatly refused: chiefs and other high-ranking males did not carry burdens. The chief was probably also well aware of the hardships suffered by bearers who made the trip to and from St. Augustine; carrying six weeks or more of food in addition to weapons would have been a difficult task at best. To make it even worse, the Indians and chiefs would not be paid for their labors.

Lúcas Menéndez disliked the governor, who had treated him and other chiefs badly on previous visits to St. Augustine. The chiefs had not been feasted or given gifts by the governor when in town, as had been done in the past, a public slight

Lúcas Menéndez and the other chiefs must have felt deeply, especially in view of the deteriorating state of the Timucua province. As chief of San Martín de Aya-cuto, traditionally one of the major Timucuan villages, Lúcas Menéndez was able to convince other Timucuan chiefs to join in openly defying the governor's orders —a rebellion.

Lúcas Menéndez worked to strengthen his rebellion, and he issued orders to kill the Spaniards in Timucua province. The Franciscan friars were excluded from this order; after all, they were now an integral part of native society, having long since replaced traditional native priests. The rebellion was not against Catholi-cism, which had become now the Timucuas' own religion; it was against the military government and its mistreatment of the chiefs and their people.

Timucuan warriors prepared for war and went out from the mission villages. At the farm near Asile, a Spanish soldier stationed there as part of the military government's presence in Apalachee province was killed. A second soldier at San Pedro y San Pablo de Potohiriba, east of the Aucilla River in Yustaga (western Timucua), was also slain. Next to be killed were a Spanish servant and a Mexican Indian, likely a laborer at one of the ranches. The pair had chosen to camp on the west side of the Suwannee River, while traveling eastward to the La Chua ranch, perhaps from the ranch at Asile. These victims of the rebellion were scalped, though later some of their killers buried the scalps, obvious evidence of their crimes. Led by Chief Lúcas Menéndez, a war party next raided La Chua itself, killing a third Spanish soldier and two African slaves. At the time of the raid, the ranch's owner was in residence, but because he was the chief's patron he was spared.

After the death of these seven people, the killing stopped, but the rebellion con-tinued. It may have been that all the potential victims in the province had been killed. Many villagers in Timucua abandoned their missions, refusing to provide labor for the Spaniards. Spring crops were not planted; St. Augustine would have less to eat. Because not a single friar had been harmed, military officials later ac-cused some friars of abetting the rebellion—they could not believe that the Indi-ans had chosen not to kill the religious leaders.

Well-versed in Spanish ways, the rebellious Timucua knew it was only a mat-ter of time before there was retribution. To prepare for the inevitable, some of the rebels congregated at Santa Elena de Machava, east of the Aucilla River close to Apalachee. No doubt they hoped to convince the Apalachee to join them against the Spanish military. But the Apalachee, as well as some Timucuan chiefdoms such as Arapaha, chose not to take part. Somewhere near Santa Elena de Machava in modern Madison County, Florida, the rebel Timucuas built a wooden, palisaded fort for protection and waited for the Spanish soldiers. In building their fort, the In-dians might well have used techniques they had learned working in St. Augustine.

That was not all they had learned as members of the Spanish colony. Documents found by John E. Worth indicate that the rebel chiefs communicated with one another by writing letters in the Timucua language. At one point rebels intercepted a dispatch being circulated among the Spaniards and were able to read its contents, written in Spanish.

In September 1656 Governor Rebolledo planned a military expedition to quell the rebellion and restore order. He had delayed doing so because it was not certain how extensive the rebellion was and whether or not the Apalachee Indians were involved. He also had to make certain that the Guale remained loyal. If all the provinces had rebelled, the military power of the St. Augustine garrison may not have been enough to prevent defeat. In addition, Rebolledo had to determine whether the rumored English attack that had helped to touch off the rebellion was still a possibility.

The governor's initial military response was to order a detachment of sixty Spanish infantry and some 200 Apalachee Indians to march into Timucua province. The latter were possibly laborers caught in town during the rebellion. Guale Indians, some with firearms, had assembled in St. Augustine in response to the governor's earlier order, but they were disarmed and sent home as insurance against their rebelling too. Marching west from St. Augustine, the joint Spanish-Apalachee army headed for eastern Apalachee, avoiding the camino real and other main trails so they would not encounter any hostile Timucua Indians. They did not know the state of the province nor the strength of the rebel forces.

Reaching Apalachee, they were reinforced with Spanish soldiers who had been stationed there. From Indians they learned of the fort near Santa Elena de Machava in which the rebels had fortified themselves. Wisely, the sergeant in charge opted to negotiate rather than storm the fortification. After protracted talks the Indians surrendered and walked out of their fort. Most were allowed to go free, but leaders and several of the Indians who had participated in the murders were arrested. One confessed on the spot and was executed. The other arrested Indians were taken first to Ivitachuco, then marched to St. Augustine and jailed to await trial.

Toward the end of November, Governor Rebolledo and a second, smaller military force entered Timucua, intending to punish more rebels. Probably traveling along the camino real, he arrested nearly two dozen Indians, including a number of chiefs, and took them to Apalachee, where he held a trial. About half of the Indians were sentenced to hard labor in St. Augustine. The other half were sentenced to death. Those under a death sentence were hung at various locations in Timucua, graphic and grisly reminders of what befell those who opposed the Crown's representatives.

Order was thus restored, but Timucua was devastated. Many of its chiefs were dead or serving time in St. Augustine. Missions had been burned. Recognizing

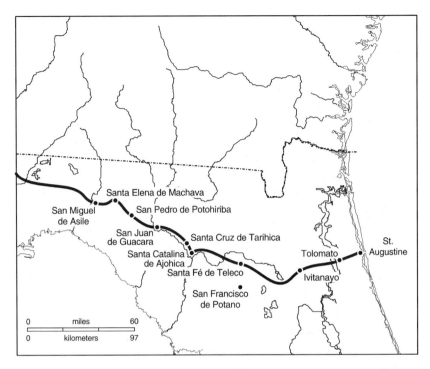

The reorganized missions of Timucua province following the 1656 Timucua Rebellion.

that the province was only a shadow of what it had been a half century earlier, Rebolledo decided to reorganize the missions and the remaining Timucua Indian
population: Timucua's missions would become way stations along the camino
real between Apalachee and St. Augustine. Mission villagers would continue to
work for the Spaniards, maintaining the road and river crossings and aiding in the
transport of people and goods along the road.

To implement this plan, some missions were abandoned, others were shifted
along the road, and a few new ones were founded. Ultimately eleven Timucuan
missions were spaced roughly one day's travel apart along the camino real, the
linear arrangement later described by Bishop Calderón on his 1674–75 visit (see
chapter 1). This chainlike configuration of missions along the camino real recalls
the north-south chain of California missions established a century later along another camino real.

The Timucuan mission chain ran from Santa Fé de Teleco to San Miguel de
Asile near the Aucilla River. Efforts to keep another mission (Ivitanayo) east of
Santa Fé de Teleco were problematic, as was maintaining a mission (Tolomato) at
the St. Johns River where villagers were needed to run the ferry.

DEALING WITH DEPOPULATION—THE LATER SEVENTEENTH CENTURY

Throughout the remainder of the seventeenth century disease and fugitivism plagued the Timucuan missions, and the Spaniards were almost constantly faced with shifting people from more populous locales to keep the mission way stations on the camino real open. This practice of moving and consolidating Christian Indians in Timucua province actually had begun in the early part of the seventeenth century. Following the 1613–17 epidemics that had severely impacted Potano, Franciscan friars had written a letter to the king asking permission to consolidate small villages into larger ones, increasing the efficiency of the conversion process. At other times in the first half of the 1600s, as satellite and mission village populations were reduced, the Spaniards had found it desirable to move other villagers. One reason was to assure there were enough villagers to operate the St. Johns River ferry.

Following the Timucua Rebellion, more extensive moving of Christian villagers was necessary to implement Governor Rebolledo's plan. As the populations of the Timucuan missions continued to drop in the last half of the 1600s, it became necessary to shift still more people to make certain the way stations on the camino real could fulfill the role envisioned by the governor. The more northern and western reaches of Timucua territory that had numerically larger populations in the early 1600s were the sources of the villagers moved southward to the camino real missions following the rebellion.

Archaeological evidence from both pre- and post-rebellion sites suggests that the movement of Timucua Indians from Georgia to the north Florida missions may have been much more extensive than revealed in archival records. At sites such as Baptizing Spring (San Martín de Ayacuto) the amounts of nonlocal Indian pottery found by archaeologists may indicate that nonlocal Indians in significant numbers were living there. Because most of the nonlocal pottery resembles that found in south-central and central Georgia, some archaeologists believe the pottery reflects the presence of Georgia Timucua Indians. Nonlocal pottery is also prominent at missions in Mocama. The source of that pottery appears to be the southeast Georgia Indians and may reflect movements of Timucua from the Georgia mainland to the coastal missions.

It is possible—some researchers would say likely—that over time the Timucua Indians across north Florida adopted these new pottery types as their own. One thing that is certain is that compared to the sixteenth century, there is almost a complete change in the types of Indian ceramics found at seventeenth-century missions in Mocama and Timucua provinces.

A 1681 census, fifteen years after the rebellion, lists just less than 1,000 Timucua living in the camino real missions. Remarkably small numbers of people lived at each of the missions, perhaps less than 100 at most. It is likely that these 1,000 Indians and those living at the Mocama missions, certainly less than 1,000 in number, were all the remaining Timucua Indians. Colonization had been cruel to a people who once had numbered as many as 200,000.

While Timucua's population continued to drop during the second half of the seventeenth century, that of Apalachee stabilized at about 8,000 to 10,000 people. As a result, the Spaniards worked hard to assure Apalachee's role as the main producer for the colony and the source for the bulk of its human labor needs. Mission San Luís de Talimali was moved to a new location and soon became the largest settlement outside of St. Augustine.

Apalachee's missions did suffer from diseases and fugitivism, but with a significantly denser population to begin with, it better withstood the mid-century epidemics. Even so, by 1675 the Spaniards found it necessary to move non-Apalachee Indians into the province to help maintain the population. New missions were established to serve these newcomers. San Carlos de los Chacatos and San Nicolas de Tolentino were occupied by Chacato Indians from west of Apalachee; Nuestra Señora de la Candelaria was occupied by Indians from Tama, originally on the Georgia fall line; and San Pedro de los Chines's and San Antonio de los Chines's villagers were Chine Indians, whose origin is uncertain, probably from the region north or west of Apalachee. Even some Tocobaga Indians from Tampa Bay resettled on the southern fringe of Apalachee, as did Amacano Indians thought to be from the lower Withlacoochee River region in west-central Florida north of Tampa Bay.

Another initiative to place additional Indians under the banner of the colony was to expand the missions west and north of Apalachee into the Apalachicola, Flint, and Chattahoochee Rivers' drainage. Contacts were made with Indians in the region, some of whom had once been antagonistic toward the Spaniards and the Christian Indians of Apalachee (and some who still were). The Chine Indians were one such group who had been visited by friars before moving into Apalachee.

Missionaries were sent to other groups west of Apalachee, such as the Sabacola Indians, some of whom, by 1675, were living at mission La Encarnación a la Santa Cruz at the intersection of the Flint and Chattahoochee Rivers. La Encarnación a la Santa Cruz, however, functioned only intermittently. Attempts to colonize west and northwest of Apalachee did not fare well, though they were continued beyond the third quarter of the seventeenth century. It was more effective to move Indians into Apalachee, where they could work for the colony.

One problem with western mission efforts was simply the sheer distance from St. Augustine. After the Timucua Rebellion the Spaniards found their La Florida capital on the Atlantic coast and the bulk of their Indian colonists on the opposite side of northern Florida. Further expansion beyond Apalachee would only exacerbate the geographical situation.

There was another problem. Indians, some ancestors to the later Creek Indians, were moving into the panhandle and southwest Georgia to take advantage of trade with the Spaniards and their Indian allies. Some groups raided others, at times threatening the missions. In order to retain control and keep options open for expanding the colony west or north out of Apalachee, the Spaniards strengthened the existing wooden fort at San Luís de Talimali in Apalachee and established a second fort on the St. Marks River near the coast. A third fort was built on the Apalachicola River and a fourth, Santa María de Galve, was constructed at Pensacola in 1698. The Pensacola area had the potential to become an important entry for Spanish colonization into the interior of the Southeast (a fact that had been noted by Tristán de Luna well over a century earlier). The establishment of English colonies on the Atlantic seaboard and, later, the French in the northern Gulf of Mexico region threatened all such plans.

In the early decades of the eighteenth century, Spain again attempted inroads into the Gulf region by establishing a chain of presidios and missions from northeastern Mexico north of the Rio Grande River across what today is Texas. The easternmost settlement, Los Adaes, was near modern Natchitoches, Louisiana, about 360 miles (580 kilometers) from Pensacola. By the time Los Adaes came into existence, French settlements from Mobile to the Mississippi River had already driven a wedge between La Florida and the northeasternmost outpost of New Spain.

After looking north and west of Apalachee for Indians to colonize, the Spaniards tried other options to assure the success of the La Florida colony. One was to bring in native people from outside La Florida. Officials even considered moving families from the Canary Islands to La Florida. Later, they thought about bringing in Indians from Mexico. Individual Mexican Indians already had found their way to La Florida as laborers. Resettlement of large numbers of Mexicans with their traditions of agriculture and expert weaving would have added immeasurably to La Florida's profits, but neither of these initiatives were carried out.

Another option was to look southward down the peninsula, a region largely ignored by the Spaniards. In 1697 a contingent of Franciscans was sent to Calos, the main town of the Calusa Indians, which had been visited by Juan Ponce de León in 1513 and Pedro Menéndez de Avilés in the mid-1560s, as well as being the site of one of the early Jesuit missions (San Antonio). The Calusa proved no friendlier to Spaniards in the late seventeenth century than they had been to Ponce de León 180 years earlier. The friars were ridiculed, insulted, and literally run out of town. Calusa hecklers mooned the friars and sent them fleeing south down the coast toward Cuba in a small boat. Along the way Indians took their clothes and food.

Nearly dead from exposure, the friars were finally rescued by a Spanish ship in the Florida Keys.

The Spaniards thought that perhaps missions could be placed among other groups in peninsular Florida south of Timucua province. Although the Indians of that area were not agriculturists, they might be taught how to farm and then moved to north Florida, presumably to repopulate Timucua. Because the demographic catastrophe that had hit Timucua and Guale had also been felt by the Ais, Mayaca, and other native people in the northern part of central Florida, the Spaniards were forced to look farther south, to south-central Florida and the Jororo Indians. In the late seventeenth century three missions were therefore established in existing Jororo villages roughly 20 miles (32 kilometers) from one another.

In 1696 the Indians at the mission in the Jororo town of Atissimi killed Father Luís Sanchez, the doctrina's friar, and two young Indian altar boys. A contingent of soldiers and Guale Indians sent from St. Augustine was unable to find the rebels to punish them. The Jororo missions quickly failed, and further attempts to expand the colony southward halted, although some Jororo were enticed to move northward to the St. Johns River colonies.

The Spanish presence in south-central Florida in the late 1690s may be reflected in the glass and metal beads, iron tools (scissors, knives, and such), and reworked metal objects found in several archaeological sites thought to date from that time in Osceola and Highland counties. It is interesting that these items have come from mounds. Like the Calusa, the Jororo, who were living beyond the realm of the missions in the seventeenth century, apparently continued to use mounds and, most likely, maintained a more traditional way of life than did the Indians of the mission provinces.

INDIAN AND PIRATE RAIDS:
ABANDONMENT OF GUALE

At the time that Timucua was being reorganized and populations were being moved to missions in both that province and in Apalachee, the Spaniards sought to revitalize Guale, whose population had also been devastated. The mid-century epidemics had left those missions as severely depopulated as the Timucua ones.

There were also pressures growing out of the international competition between England and Spain to control the Atlantic coast. The 1604 establishment of the Jamestown colony, in Virginia (the land known as Jacán to Pedro Menéndez de Avilés in the sixteenth century) posed a serious threat to La Florida. That threat grew in 1670, when Charles Towne was settled by English colonists in the very lands Spanish Jesuit missionaries had once traveled.

The threat was not mere saber rattling. In 1661 *Chichimecos*—a term often used by the Spaniards for native raiders who attacked Spanish interests all across the colonial frontier from Mexico to Georgia—canoed down the Altamaha River and destroyed Santo Domingo de Talaje near the mouth of the river on its north bank. Villagers who survived the attack fled to San Joseph de Sapala on Sapelo Island.

The raiders, said to number as many as 2,000 (though one account gives the number as 500), came down the river in 200 canoes. Scholars believe these particular Chichimecos were Rechahecrian Indians from Virginia who had been armed by English traders and pointed southward. Some think originally they were Erie Indians forced out of their own lands bordering the Great Lakes as a result of Iroquoian infighting and pushed south to Virginia. At any rate, by 1559 they had swept into interior Georgia and had been capturing Indian slaves to sell or trade to the Virginians. Reports from Apalachee had them prowling the northern borders of that province.

Shocked by the raid on the Guale mission, the governor of La Florida, Alonso de Aranguiz y Cotes, sent soldiers to San Buenaventura de Guadalquini on St. Simons Island to guard against further attacks and rid the coast of the Chichimecos. Soldiers were also sent to protect San Joseph de Sapala where Guale Indians and friars had fled for protection after more raids were rumored.

Before the soldiers could reach San Joseph de Sapala, a Chichimeco war party approached the mission by water. Seventy of the attackers aboard a makeshift boat fashioned from boards taken from the church and convento of Santo Domingo de Talaje were blown out to sea and drowned in full view of the Spaniards and Christian Guale huddled at San Joseph de Sapala. The remaining Chichimecos were driven off, and by the time the Spanish soldiers arrived, they had fled back up the Altamaha River. Eventually, four Chichimecos were captured and interrogated. They revealed that they had indeed come from Jacán—the Virginia region—and had been slave hunting in interior Georgia.

With the threat of the Chichimecos lifted, Santo Domingo de Talaje was reestablished. This time it was not on the mainland, where it was difficult to protect, but on the opposite end of St. Simons Island from San Buenaventura de Guadalquini, the Timucua Indian mission on the south end.

Having found slaving lucrative, the Chichimecos soon returned and, by late 1662, were living along the Savannah River. From that location they continued to raid the non-Christian Indians north and west of Guale, including one village only a few miles north of San Diego de Satuache. Alarmed, the Spaniards reinforced Guale by moving a garrison of soldiers to the mission on St. Catherines Island. They also moved San Diego de Satuache from its precarious location on the mainland to that island, merging it with Santa Catalina de Guale.

Indians continued to flee the interior of South Carolina and Georgia to the

A Yamasee Indian ceramic pot from Amelia Island. Fourteen
inches (35.6 centimeters) high, the pot's surface is stamped
with a motif characteristic of Yamasee pottery. (Courtesy
Florida Museum of Natural History)

coast north of Guale, primarily to the old Orista region and the area around the
former location of Santa Elena. These newcomers to the coast were called Yamasees. Exactly who the Yamasee Indians were has long puzzled several generations of modern researchers. Most believed the Yamasee were the aboriginal inhabitants of the Georgia coastal plain west of Guale. But John E. Worth has
presented evidence indicating that the Yamasee were a new group, a confederation of the remnants of Georgia and South Carolina Indians forced to band together to deal with the problems of depopulation and the Chichimeco raids. By
the mid-1660s some of the Yamasee had moved south to the Guale missions, hoping the Spaniards could offer protection. At that time Guale's population was only
several hundred people who were divided among the five missions still functioning (six, if Santo Domingo de Talaje is counted).

The appearance of the Yamasee on the coast and their apparent willingness to move to the missions provided the Spaniards with new souls to save and more labor, a palliative to the depopulation of Guale. Fleeing the Chichimecos and enticed by the Spaniards, several hundred more Yamasee moved into Guale and Mocama. Two abandoned missions—San Pedro de Mocama on Cumberland Island and Santa María on Amelia Island, both in Mocama—were reopened to serve the Yamasee, and new Yamasee towns were put on St. Simons Island (San Simón and Ocotonico) and Amelia Island (Ocotoque and Tama).

More turmoil followed the 1670 establishment of Charles Towne. Recognizing that serious conflicts with the Carolinians were inevitable, the Spaniards shifted San Phelipe de Alave south to the northern end of Cumberland Island, and moved Santa Clara de Tupiqui from the mainland to mission San Joseph de Sapala. As a result, Santa Catalina de Guale and its military garrison were at the northernmost end of the Guale and Mocama missions, all of which were now located on barrier islands.

With the new Yamasee towns, the resettlement of old missions by Yamasee Indians, and the moving of other missions, Guale and Mocama were quite different than they had been in 1661, before the Chichimecos had raided Santo Domingo de Talaje. The Guale missions had been shifted southward and their southern extent now overlapped with Mocama. (As a result, it became common for the Spaniards to refer to both provinces as Guale.) By 1675 there were more Yamasee Indians living in Guale and Mocama than there were Guale and Timucua Indians: 350 Yamasee (not yet Christians) versus 326 Christian Guale and Timucua Indians. Not surprisingly, the number of Yamasee Indians conscripted to work in St. Augustine and tend its fields was greater than the number of indigenous Indians from Guale and Mocama. Once the home of Guale and Timucua Indians, the coastal mission provinces were now home to the Yamasee, an Indian group that may not have even existed in the 1650s.

From their new base at Charles Towne, the Carolinians set about making allies with nearby Indian groups, intending to use them to pressure the Spanish missions and, ultimately, to wrest La Florida from the Spanish Crown. One group they befriended was the Chichimecos (whom they called *Westos*) who were continuing slave raids over a large region of the Southeast.

Abetted by their new Carolinian trading partners, the Westos allied themselves with the Uchise Indians, a group that later became part of the Lower Creek Indians, and the Chiluque Indians, probably from somewhere in the Carolinas. In 1680 this Indian coalition struck the Yamasee town of San Simón on St. Simons Island. Though the raid resulted in only a few deaths and was quickly thwarted by Spanish soldiers from Santa Catalina de Guale aided by Indian warriors, the nineteen years of relative calm in Guale following the 1661 Chichimeco raid were shattered.

The Westos and their allies retreated, then moved north, and prepared to attack Santa Catalina de Guale. The raid on St. Simons Island may have only been a feint, intended to draw away the garrison on St. Catherines Island. At dawn 200 to 300 warriors in war paint attacked Santa Catalina de Guale, killing five lookouts before an alarm was raised. The soldiers, who, fortunately, had returned, and armed Guale Indians barricaded themselves in the mission convento and held off the raiders from dawn until four o'clock in the afternoon. Before they finally withdrew to another part of the island, the attackers torched the town.

Spanish soldiers sent from St. Augustine to reinforce the garrison arrived several days later to find the Santa Catalina de Guale villagers homeless, fearful, and demanding to be moved to a safer place. As a consequence, the Guale inhabitants of Santa Catalina de Guale, including the former residents of San Diego de Satuache, who had merged with Santa Catalina de Guale's population in the early 1660s, were taken south to mission San Joseph de Sapala on Sapelo Island. Despite some talk that it should be reoccupied, Santa Catalina de Guale was abandoned. Spain's northern frontier had been moved southward another notch. The total population of Guale and Mocama was down to only 420 people, most of whom were Yamasee Indians.

The year 1680 also saw a falling-out between the Westos and their Carolinian allies. Aided by Savannah Indians, the Carolinians nearly wiped out the Westos, sending the survivors fleeing west out of the Savannah River valley. However, new adversaries threatened the fragile mission populations on the Atlantic coast between St. Augustine and Sapelo Island. In 1683 a pirate fleet that included both French and English ships landed at Matanzas inlet, killed the garrison in the watchtower there, and threatened to attack St. Augustine itself. Spanish soldiers marched south from St. Augustine to ward off the pirates. They captured one ship and its entire crew, executing all of them in a reprise of the Matanzas massacre ordered by Pedro Menéndez de Avilés nearly 120 years earlier.

The remaining pirates sailed past St. Augustine to attack the mission towns to the north. San Juan del Puerto (on Ft. George Island) and San Phelipe de Alave (on Cumberland Island), and probably towns on Amelia Island, were raided. Many of the Yamasee inhabitants of the region fled. John E. Worth (1995, 36–37) has convincingly argued that these fugitive Yamasee went north to modern Hilton Head Island, off the South Carolina coast, most likely in anticipation of shifting their allegiance from the Spanish Crown.

Practically overnight, the population of Guale (and Mocama) had been halved, and the towns still occupied were spread out too far for effective protection. The leaders of the remaining Indians met with Spanish officials to work out a withdrawal plan. The populations of Santa Catalina de Guale, San Diego de Satuache, Santa Clara de Tupiqui, and San Joseph de Sapala, all of which were on Sapelo Island, would be moved to Santa María de Yamasee on Amelia Island, recently abandoned by its Yamasee inhabitants. By fall 1684 the villagers of Santa Catalina

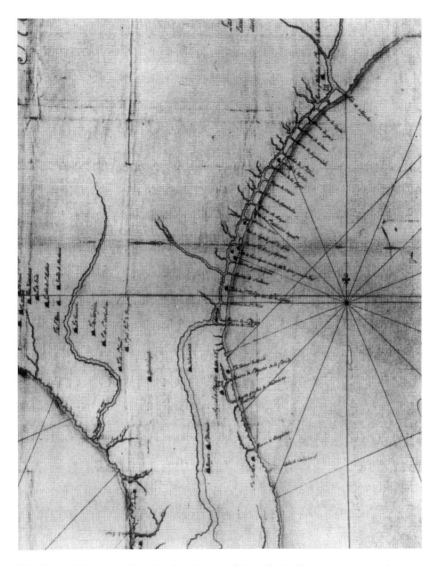

The Alonso Solana map showing the missions of Spanish Florida in 1683, prior to the abandonment of Guale province. (Courtesy P. K. Yonge Library of Florida History, University of Florida)

de Guale and San Diego de Satuache had arrived at their new home, and soon a new church, also called Santa Catalina de Guale, was built next to the old Santa María de Yamasee church. Both the Santa María de Yamasee church and the Santa Catalina de Guale church were adjacent to Harrison Creek and have been found by archaeologists (see chapter 1). The other Christian Indians from Sapelo Island were to move there later.

The plan also called for Santo Domingo de Talaje (on northern St. Simons Island) and San Phelipe de Alave (on the north end of Cumberland Island) to move to San Pedro de Mocama on the southern end of Cumberland Island, also abandoned. San Buenaventura de Guadalquini on St. Simons would be merged with San Juan del Puerto on Ft. George Island. All of what had been Guale and northern Mocama north of southern Cumberland Island was to be relinquished.

The plan, however, did not go smoothly. In October 1684 another fleet of pirate ships arrived off the coast of Guale and Mocama. The pirates hoped to take food and any other supplies they could seize. San Juan del Puerto was hit first. Then the pirates landed on Sapelo Island intending to sack the mission there, whose remaining inhabitants were caught in the midst of moving south to the new Santa Catalina de Guale mission. Those Indians, as well as the villagers from San Pedro de Mocama on Cumberland Island, fled to the mainland to escape the raiders. The mission settlement on Sapelo Island was destroyed. Next, the pirates attacked and burned San Buenaventura de Guadalquini on St. Simons Island, wiping the Guale population out completely.

La Florida's northern border had been pushed back still another notch. The entire Georgia coast was now abandoned, reduced to a no-man's-land between La Florida and the Carolinas.

Some of the refugees from the 1684 pirate raid agreed to move south to towns in the vicinity of the resettled Santa Catalina de Guale mission on Amelia Island and towns near San Juan del Puerto. Cumberland Island and its mission of San Pedro de Mocama, however, were not reoccupied. Other refugees fled northward to the South Carolina coast, forsaking the Spaniards for the English.

By 1685, the northernmost Spanish-controlled town was on the northern end of Amelia Island, where some of the refugees from Santa Clara de Tupiqui had resettled. Manned by a handful of soldiers, a watchtower was established nearby in what today is Fernandina Beach. That fragile outpost would guard the northernmost tip of Spain's American empire for a mere seventeen years before it, too, would fall.

8

A PEOPLE DESTROYED; A LAND FORGOTTEN

By the end of the seventeenth century La Florida was a changed colony from what it had been seventy-five years earlier. In 1700 St. Augustine's resident population was about 1,500 people, nearly three times as large as it had been in 1625. Many of the Spaniards maintained modest houses in town and actually lived on small haciendas outside the city gates. Guale was gone, and Mocama contained mostly refugees, including several hundred Yamasee Indians. Timucua was reduced to a few hundred Indians living along the camino real, the largely isolated, threadlike trail that led to the only bright spot in the colony, Apalachee.

Apalachee province and the Indians who lived there were thoroughly integrated into the colonial system. In the province entrepreneurialism flourished among both elite Indians and Spaniards, while Christian Indians, mostly Apalachee, provided the labor. By La Florida's standards, some Spaniards, mainly members of the Floréncia family, were growing quite wealthy, though there were accusations that the Floréncia's success came at a high cost to the Indians.

With the demise of Guale and the severe depopulation of Timucua, it may well have been that Pensacola would have grown in importance and the mission frontier might have moved west from Apalachee to that town, effectively shifting the entire colony west. But that would not occur. As the seventeenth century came to a close, colonial La Florida was becoming a prominent pawn in the conflicts among European monarchies, especially Spain, England, and France.

To understand the events of the eighteenth century that would affect La Florida and its missions, the state of colonization in North America and the interplay of European politics should be reviewed. One direct threat to La Florida, touched on earlier, was the settlement of Charles Towne in 1670. Its largely

Protestant population hated the Catholic Spaniards and the Indians living at their missions as fervently as Pedro Menéndez de Avilés had hated Jean Ribault's Huguenots. Slave hunting and pirating set in motion by the Carolinians at Charles Towne had turned Guale into a land of contention between these old European enemies.

In 1685 a new colonial power appeared in the La Florida equation when French explorer Robert Cavelier La Salle traveled down the Mississippi River to the northern Gulf coast. France, which had attempted settlements in La Florida in the 1560s, was now exerting colonial influence in northeastern North America. Its military power, which at this time exceeded that of either Spain or England, represented a potential threat to both colonies. Only recently had France and England reached a standoff in the King William's War fought in northeastern North America, a nine-year conflict that had failed to oust France from that region. The outcome had emboldened France and sent shivers through the English colonies from the eastern seaboard down to the Carolinas.

By the end of the seventeenth century, France was also moving to secure the Mississippi River, the waterway leading from the Gulf coast to its interests in the Great Lakes and eastern Canada. Spain sought to oust the French, sending no less than eleven expeditions along the northern Gulf coast between 1685 and 1690 in search of La Salle. The establishment of Pensacola in 1698 was in part an attempt to stymie the French from moving east from Mobile Bay in Alabama. As the first decades of the eighteenth century dawned, France, England, and Spain all held lands in southeastern North America, forming an uneasy triangle.

After the death of Spain's Charles II in 1700, Louis XIV of France claimed the vacant Spanish throne for his grandson, Philip, forming a powerful Franco-Hispanic alliance that threatened the Carolinas and other English interests. Plans, perhaps frivolous ones, were drawn up for a French attack on Charles Towne, a campaign to be anchored in Louisiana and carried out through St. Augustine and La Florida.

Other European powers were loathe to allow an alliance of France and Spain, setting the War of Spanish Succession in motion on the east side of the Atlantic Ocean. When news of that conflict, also known as Queen Anne's War, reached Charles Towne in 1702, the governor of the Carolina colony, Colonel James Moore, urged a preemptive attack on St. Augustine to prevent French soldiers from ever occupying that town's fort. His first attack was not a success, but he led other armies into north Florida on bloody ventures to destroy the missions, devastate the labor on which St. Augustine depended, and end the threat of an allied Franco-Hispanic attack on South Carolina. Though Moore's aggressive military forays were effective, the fort in St. Augustine did what it was intended—it protected the town and colony against a total takeover by the Spanish Crown's enemies.

DESTRUCTION AND ABANDONMENT OF MOCAMA

One late afternoon in 1985, I stood on the bank of Harrison Creek on Amelia Island, enjoying the sunset across the salt marsh and the mainland of what was once La Florida. Unknown to me at the time, I was standing on the site of the church of the Santa María de Yamasee mission, which had been abandoned by its Indian congregation 300 years earlier after the 1683 pirate raids on Guale and Mocama. A short distance behind me were the recently located ruins of the church that had served the refugees of the Santa Catalina de Guale mission, who moved there in 1684. Over the next few years we would excavate both these churches and learn a great deal about the missions and events of the late seventeenth century. For the moment, though, I was content looking and listening. I wanted to hear the cries of Indian children and the breaking of crockery, the sounds generations of the owners of the property, the Harrison family, sometimes heard as ghostly relics of Colonel Moore's destruction of Santa Catalina de Guale in 1702.

As the setting sun turned the salt marsh into a palette of greens, it did not take long for the calling of gulls and the scurrying of crabs to conjure up the past. History is a powerful element of the present, and Amelia Island is a wonderful place for an archaeologist to experience history—not just to imagine sounds and take in a spectacular vista, but to find and interpret the material remains of the missions of Spanish Florida. Near where I stood were pieces of the distinctive stamped pottery made by the Yamasee Indians. Close by were potsherds left behind by the Timucua Indians, who had been living in Mocama for hundreds of years by the time the first Europeans arrived. Eroding out of the storm-cut bank above which I was standing, were oyster shells that had once been packed around the bottoms of wooden posts anchored in deep holes, used to support the Santa María de Yamasee church.

The scientific delight I initially experienced at the Harrison Creek site was soon tempered by other realities. Beside those eroding oyster shells, we would find the skeletal remains of Indians buried beneath the floor of the church and now exposed by nature. Our excavations of the Santa Catalina de Guale buildings would uncover the charred scars of the violent confrontations between the English-backed Carolinians and the Spaniards that destroyed the remnants of that mission and scattered its occupants.

A few short years after 1700, Santa Catalina de Guale and all the other missions of Mocama, Apalachee, and Timucua fell victim to the international rivalries of France, Spain, and England. The death of the La Florida missions did not come quickly, but in fits and starts: at times a single, devastating attack, and at others diseases slowly took their toll.

The end of the Mocama missions, in particular, came in one giant convulsion—Colonel Moore's invasion. In late August 1702 Moore had been given per-mission and funding to carry out the preemptive attack on St. Augustine he had wanted. Accounts are contradictory, but it appears that 500 Carolina colonists, some African slaves, and 300 Indians, mainly Yamasee but also Apalachicolas and Chiluques, sailed from the port near Charles Towne bound for St. Augustine. Colonists who agreed to join Moore's army were promised slaves and plundering rights. This was not to be a mere raiding party. Moore intended to administer St. Augustine a killing blow. That goal, however, would not be reached. The unpaid Carolinian militia, composed of townsmen and even recent visitors to Charles Towne pressed into military service, was not an army of well-trained soldiers. Many of the fourteen boats that transported the militia—the Indians traveled overland—were civilian craft, not armed warships.

Under the cover of darkness on November 3, the Carolinian army reached Amelia Island. The small Spanish garrison stationed at the fortified tower was caught totally by surprise, and the two soldiers on guard duty were killed in a fu-tile attempt to defend it. The tower's garrison and the relocated Guale mission Santa Clara de Tupiqui nearby were overwhelmed and destroyed. The residents fled in fear into the night.

There is evidence that the Spaniards should have been expecting an attack. Two weeks earlier, a Christian Chacato woman from Apalachee had been in an Apalachicola Indian village northwest of that province. While there she learned that the Apalachicola were preparing to join their Carolinian allies in an attack on St. Augustine. Returning home, she related the news to the Spanish soldiers at the San Luís de Talimali garrison, who quickly sent word to the governor in St. Au-gustine, Joseph de Zúñiga y Zerda. Upon hearing an attack was likely, Zúñiga y Zerda began to shore up his defenses. He sent word to San Luís de Talimali, Pen-sacola, French Mobile, and Havana asking for reinforcements. Then he set about trying to put the St. Augustine garrison—poorly armed, supplied, and trained—on a war footing. One fear was that if the Carolinians did attack, Christian Indians thought to be friendly to the Spaniards might well switch sides and join the attack, as had happened in Guale.

While the Spaniards were making plans, Colonel Moore had acted. He had at-tacked Tupique and then marched part of his Carolinian army down Amelia Is-land, sending the remainder by sea to stage a land-and-sea attack on the Spanish garrison at Santa Catalina de Guale on the south end of the island. Along the way, the militia destroyed the Indian settlement San Phelipe de Alave, on the inland side of the island, sending the Indians who lived there fleeing.

Word of the attack on Tupiqui reached Santa Catalina de Guale within hours. Well before dawn on the morning of November 4, the garrison commander at the mission, Captain Francisco Fuentes de Galarza, and two Franciscan friars, Fathers

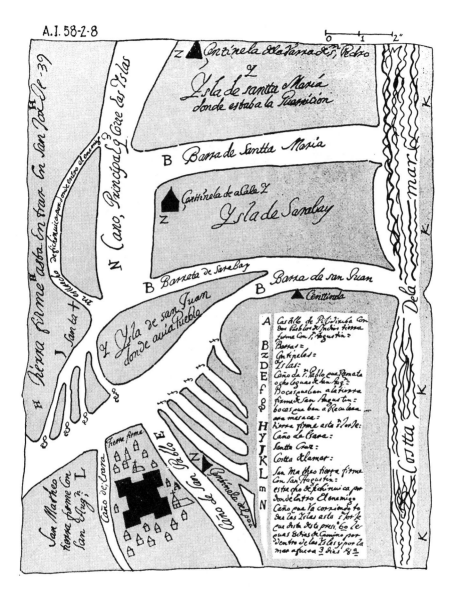

This facsimile of an early eighteenth-century Spanish map shows places raided by Colonel James Moore's army in its 1702 attack on Mocama and St. Augustine. At the top is Amelia Island ("Santa María Island where the garrison was"); just south is Talbot Island ("Sarabay Island"); below that the tear-shaped Ft. George Island ("San Juan Island where there was a village," i.e., the mission of San Juan del Puerto). On the south bank of the St. Johns River ("San Juan") is the fort called Piribiriba, with two new refugee Indian villages beside it, each with a church. (Reprinted with the permission of the University Press of Florida)

The 1.5-inch (3.8 centimeter) impression on the end of this metal
seal depicts Santa Catalina, Martyr of Alexandria, who was tortured
to death on a wheel, when she would not disavow her Christian
beliefs. The seal was found near the convento of the Santa Catalina
de Guale mission on Amelia Island, where it might have been lost
during the November 1702 raid that destroyed the mission.

Manuel de Urisa and Domingo Santos, rang the mission bell to warn of the militia's approach. Panicked by tales of atrocities carried out against Tupique, many
of the Indians of Santa Catalina de Guale ran into the woods and salt marsh to
hide, rather than accede to the pleas of the Spanish soldiers and friars to stay and
defend the town. Other Indians fled south to villages closer to St. Augustine.

Captain Fuentes de Galarza ordered an evacuation, and he, the garrison's soldiers, and friars collected the church's statues, vestments, and ornaments and es-

The Santa Catalina seal (see page 180) is identical to the one
on the desk of San Agustín in this mid-seventeenth-century
painting by Antonio Rodríquez. The seal is the object with
the doorknoblike handle on one end; the oval impression
would have been on the opposite end.

caped south down the island, probably traveling by canoe to San Juan del Puerto
on Ft. George Island. The Carolinians arrived almost immediately after and set
Santa Catalina de Guale ablaze. Captain Fuentes de Galarza and his party made it
to San Juan del Puerto, where they decided to make a stand against the invaders.
An urgent report was sent to St. Augustine.

Receiving the message the next day, Governor Zúñiga y Zerda immediately
sent twenty soldiers to reinforce San Juan del Puerto and defend the St. Johns
River crossing to its south. If the Carolinian militia reached the mainland on the
south side of the St. Johns River there was nothing to block their marching on St.

Augustine. The governor, essentially declaring martial law, set in motion the strategy he had devised over the past week: the town was put on alert and all men—Spaniards, Africans, Indians, and anyone else—were armed. Food supplies were taken to the fort of San Marcos in the likelihood the town was besieged. Messages were sent to Havana pleading for reinforcements and weapons.

In the meantime, the Carolinian land and sea forces rolled over San Juan del Puerto and the adjacent villages and crossed the St. Johns River. Resistance from the Spaniards was token at best; their small company of soldiers was routed in short order. The two friars from Santa Catalina de Guale and Captain Fuentes de Galarza and his family were captured. The Carolinians poised themselves to move against St. Augustine.

The fall of San Juan del Puerto had alerted Governor Zúñiga y Zerda that it was time to order everyone to take refuge in the fort, abandoning the town to the attackers. All of the townspeople, including African slaves and freedmen, Indian servants, and the Indians from Nombre de Dios mission, poured into the fort with their belongings. In all, they numbered between 1,500 and 1,600 people. From captured members of the militia, the Spaniards obtained frightening information on the size of the approaching army. The good news was that the Carolinians were not armed with exploding shells, bombs that could be shot into the fort and explode among the people clustered inside. The bad news was that Moore was said to have sent a ship to Jamaica for such armaments.

Soon the sails of the Carolinian ships appeared in the Atlantic east of the fort, and the infantry arrived by land. Moore set up headquarters in the church at the Franciscan convento at the south end of town, a direct slap at Catholicism. Over the next month and a half, the Carolinians held the population of St. Augustine in a medieval-like siege, surrounding the fort on the land side while occupying the entire town. Only light losses occurred on both sides as the attackers periodically shelled the fort, and the Spaniards sallied out to retaliate. The most devastating loss of Spanish life happened when an old cannon exploded, killing three and injuring five.

Sustained in part by cattle they had driven into the fort moat, the Spaniards waited out the siege. In late December Spanish ships with soldiers arrived from Cuba, blockading Moore's small fleet. Faced with the possibility of his makeshift army taking serious loses, Moore opted to lift the siege and withdraw. Moore and his army were forced to walk back to Charles Towne, no small feat. On December 30 St. Augustine was back in Spanish hands, though the town was in ashes. More than one hundred buildings, and possibly twice that number, had been destroyed, including Nombre de Dios and the Franciscan convento.

At least some of the Indians who had fled the destroyed Mocama missions congregated at two small villages near a wooden fort called Piribiriba on the south bank of the St. Johns River, north of St. Augustine. By the end of 1704, though, Indian raids on those refugee settlements forced them even farther south.

MORE RAIDS AND THE DESTRUCTION OF TIMUCUA AND APALACHEE

The raids that plagued Guale in the early 1660s and the 1680s were not the only seventeenth-century attacks on La Florida missions. Chiscas and other non-Christian Indians who had previously been allied with the Spaniards quickly learned of the English trade goods that could be theirs in exchange for slaves taken from the mission provinces. The poorly defended farmsteads of Apalachee were especially easy targets. In part, the post-1670 attempts to establish missions west and northwest of Apalachee had been attempts to counter this growing Indian threat.

In the fall of 1677, following the harvest, a war party of nearly 200 Apalachee went west across the Apalachicola River to punish the Chisca Indians for past attacks. In the 1680s other war parties were sent to apprehend the Carolinian traders known to have been consorting with the Indians that raided Apalachee. Those actions and the building of the forts at San Luís de Talimali and on the St. Marks River caused some of the raiders to move well east to the Ocmulgee River in central Georgia—at the time called Uchisi Creek (from which the name Creek Indians would be derived). These Creeks, still allied with the English, would continue to raid the Apalachee missions from their new location. A few of the Apalachee Indians, unhappy with the inability of the Spaniards to protect them, switched sides and joined the Creeks.

To the east of Apalachee in Timucua, the La Chua ranch and the Timucua missions also posed tempting targets for Indian raiders. The first attack on La Chua was by French buccaneers who had established a camp on Anclote Key on the Gulf coast north of Tampa Bay. In 1682 the French pirates came up the Suwannee and Santa Fe Rivers to raid the ranch. Two years later they again attacked the ranch, this time traveling on the Withlacoochee River a short distance before moving overland through modern Marion County. Spain was unable to protect the missions and ranches in Timucua and Apalachee, a fact that did not escape the Indian allies of the Carolinians.

In 1685 Yamasee Indian slavers, armed and abetted by the Carolinians, attacked Santa Catalina de Ajohica, a mission located in southern Suwannee County, Florida. Twenty-one Timucua Indians were captured and taken to South Carolina, where they were traded for shotguns and cutlasses. Eighteen other villagers were killed, and Santa Catalina de Ajohica's church, convento, and most of the houses were burned to the ground.

The blatant attack on Santa Catalina de Ajohica, one in the growing number of attacks on the missions of Apalachee, Timucua, and Guale, drew Spanish retaliation. A contingent of soldiers was sent from St. Augustine to attack Stuarts Towne, an outpost of Charles Towne, but instead decided to hit nearby Port Royal. Carolina plantations were burned, and buildings in the port were torched. The raid did nothing to halt the attacks on the missions. In 1691 San Juan de Guacara on the Suwannee River was next. Then, in early 1702, it was Santa Fé de Teleco in Timucua. In a three-hour battle much of the mission was destroyed by Apalachicola Indians, though the small Spanish garrison stationed at the mission drove off the attackers. Feeling bold, the Spanish soldiers gave chase to the Apalachicolas, only to walk into an ambush in which ten Timucua Indians and the Spanish lieutenant were killed, no small loss in view of the small number of Indians and Spaniards remaining in the province.

In part, the raids by the Apalachicola and other Creek Indians on the missions were reprisals for an earlier, murderous attack by Francisco de Floréncia (of the Floréncia family) and forty Chacato warriors against a trading party of Indians from the town of Taisquique (Tuskegee). The traders, headed toward Apalachee with buffalo hides and deer-hide shirts, had been camped when Floréncia and the Chacatos killed sixteen of the two dozen men, stole their goods, and took the loot to the mission town of Ayubale.

To retaliate for the Santa Fé de Teleco raid and the attacks on Apalachee Indians, the Spaniards assembled an army to attack the Apalachicola Indians on the lower Chattahoochee River. Led by Captain Francisco Romo de Uriza, a handful of Spanish soldiers and 800 Apalachee, Chacato, and Timucuan warriors were marching toward their goal, when they were ambushed on the lower Flint River in southwest Georgia. The Spanish-led force was smashed. Only 300 warriors escaped, many of them without their weapons. It was a devastating blow.

As a result of the raids, deaths suffered in battles, and consolidation of mission populations, the Timucua missions were reduced, by 1703, to only Santa Fé de Teleco and San Francisco de Potano, which soon merged, and some of the more western missions between the Aucilla and Suwannee Rivers in Yustaga. A garrison was stationed at San Francisco de Potano, where a stockade had been built. Nearby were the ranches of Chicharro, Santa Cruz, and La Chua, the last also fortified.

The raids on the missions became a torrent. In January 1704 Colonel James Moore commanded an army of 50 Carolinians and 1,000 Creek Indians—Apalachicolas and others—in an attack on Apalachee. La Concepción de Ayubale, where the murdered Creek traders' goods had been taken, was the first target, probably no coincidence. The villagers fought until their ammunition was gone and the church in which they had sought cover set ablaze. Some of the town's residents

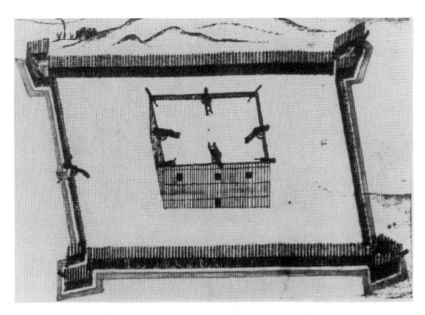

An early eighteenth-century drawing of the fort at San Luís de Talimali. Within the moat and palisade was a strong house armed with four cannons and four smaller *pedreros,* artillery pieces that swiveled and shot stone balls or bags of rocks. The gate and corner bastions were similarly armed with cannons and pedreros. Unfortunately, this formidable arsenal could not protect the Apalachee missions. (Courtesy P. K. Yonge Library of Florida History, University of Florida)

were burned at the stake; others chose to switch allegiances and join the attackers.

Moore's joint Creek-Carolinian army then marched on other Apalachee missions, though they stayed clear of San Luís de Talimali and its wooden fort. Ivitachuco was spared when the village chief turned over the church silver and provided food for the attackers. Disillusioned with the Spaniards, two missions surrendered without a fight and the villagers agreed to accompany Moore back to South Carolina. Other missions were destroyed. When Moore withdrew, he had with him 1,300 Apalachee who had agreed to surrender and nearly another 1,000 taken as slaves. San Luís de Talimali and San Lorenzo de Ivitachuco survived, along with San Pedro y San Pablo de Patale, San Cosme y San Damian de Cupaica, San Juan de Aspalaga, and one of the Chacato missions. Some of the refugees and a few of the friars fled into the woods.

In late June another large attack by Creek warriors captured the mission villages at Patale, Aspalaga, and Cupaica. In the 1704 raids Spaniards and Christian Indians were horribly tortured; some individuals were skinned alive. Father Juan de Parga, killed near Ayubale, was beheaded and his head displayed by Creek war-

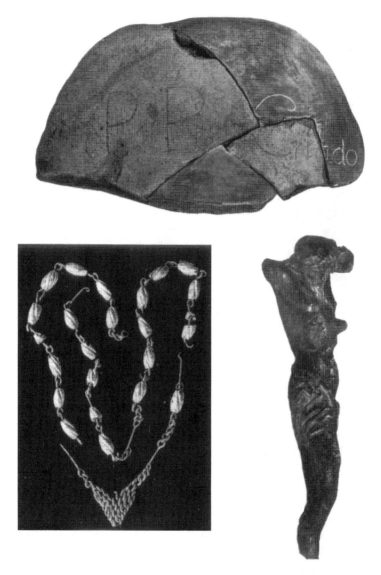

Artifacts from Apalachee missions, all attesting to the destruction of the province.
Top: pieces of a Spanish olive jar (7 inches [17.8 centimeters] wide) inscribed *Pe Pre
Criado* ("Padre Predicador"—Preaching Father—Criado). In 1704 Father Domingo
Criado and the Christian Indians he served fled San Francisco de Oconee—the
Scott Miller site—where these pottery fragments were found. The next year their
refugee village 35 to 42 miles (56 to 68 kilometers) from St. Augustine was raided by
Indians and the friar taken captive. Forced into servitude, he died. Bottom left:
portions of a rosary found in the moat of the San Luís de Talimali fort. Bottom
right: a partially melted corpus from a crucifix (4.5 inches [11.4 centimeters] high),
also from the Scott Miller site. (Reprinted with the permission of the University
Press of Florida)

riors in that town's council house. Other friars and hundreds of Indians were also killed, many more were taken as slaves, and still more simply surrendered. At one point at least fifty Apalachee joined the attackers en masse.

Following the June devastation, the Indians of San Luís de Talimali decided that if the province were attacked again, they would switch sides because the Spaniards were unable to protect them. When a third raid was rumored, Spanish authorities ordered the nearly destroyed Apalachee province abandoned rather than face more desertions.

A large number of Indians, nearly 800, including the populations of San Luís de Talimali and Cupaica, as well as Chacato and Yamasee Indians, choose to migrate west to Pensacola. With them went most of the Spaniards who had been living in Apalachee. Pensacola, poorly supplied and not in a region well-suited for agriculture, did not appeal to most of the Apalachee Indians, who chose to move farther west to French Mobile in Alabama. Later, one group of Apalachee migrated even farther west to Louisiana, where a few of their descendants still live today. Others returned to Pensacola. By 1718 Apalachee Indians were living in a village named Nuestra Señora de la Soledad y San Luís about 15 miles (24 kilometers) east of Pensacola.

In 1704, at the same time many Apalachee moved west, the villagers of Ivitachuco, under their chief Don Patricio de Hinachuba, decided to resettle to the east at a place they named Abosaya, one day's travel east of San Francisco de Potano not far from La Chua. There, the Apalachee built a palisaded fortification, hoping it would protect them from future raids. They planned to live off the crops and livestock of the abandoned ranches in the region until their own fields could be planted.

The destruction of Apalachee and the abandonment of the fort at San Luís de Talimali, burned by the Spaniards when they withdrew, had left Timucua wide open to additional attacks. In August 1704 San Pedro y San Pablo de Potohiriba, San Matheo de Tolapatafi, and Santa Elena de Machaba, perhaps the only remaining Yustaga missions, were destroyed and their chiefs burned at the stake. Many villagers were killed and others taken as slaves. Survivors fled east to St. Augustine. The Creek attackers next hit La Chua, where they captured and dismembered an African slave.

By the end of 1704, the last of the Apalachee and Timucua Indians still in northern Florida were living as refugees in the woods near Apalachee, or clustered at San Francisco de Potano and Abosaya, both of which were fortified and whose total population was estimated at 600. Nearby was the La Chua ranch, also with a fortified strong house. Farther east, Timucua Indians were living at Salamototo, another stockaded settlement, on the east bank of the St. Johns River at the camino real crossing.

The wooden forts, strong houses, and handfuls of Spanish soldiers were not enough to withstand the onslaught of slavers and raiders from the north. In late 1705 the remaining settlements in what had been Timucua province, as well as the ranch of La Chua, were attacked. Abosaya was besieged for twenty days before the raiders withdrew. Skirmishes took place all across northern Florida, even east of the St. Johns River as the Creek Indians grew bolder. Refugee Indians and friars living in the woods were captured or killed.

The chief of Abosaya moved his Apalachee villagers to a new location south of St. Augustine. In one year, however, Indian warriors, including Apalachee who had previously joined the Carolinians, killed Don Patricio de Hinachuba and most of his people. The Timucua at San Francisco de Potano moved to Salamototo in 1706, but by the end of that year raids had forced them farther east to the outskirts of St. Augustine. La Chua was abandoned. Apalachee and Timucua, like Guale and Mocama, were no more. By the end of 1706 interior northern Florida, from the St. Johns River to Pensacola, was abandoned by the Spaniards. The Indians who had lived there for centuries were gone. They had either been killed or they had fled La Florida to South Carolina or French Mobile. Others had been taken to South Carolina as slaves or had resettled east of the St. Johns River near St. Augustine.

REFUGEE MISSIONS AND MISSION REFUGEES

Today, tourists to the Castillo de San Marcos in Florida, a national monument open to the public, may have a difficult time envisioning the defensive strength the fort represented in the early eighteenth century, especially in this age of SCUD missiles and smart bombs. Against the weaponry available at the time, the fort was almost impenetrable. It was a state-of-the-art defensive structure, though the art was still late medieval. Moore had not been able to breach its thick coquina walls in 1702, nor would other attackers in the 1730s.

Refugees from the missions soon would be joined near the fort by other Indians who wanted to escape the raids of the Yamasee, Creek, and other Indians, attacks that continued after the demise of Apalachee and Timucua. The populations of the refugee villages around St. Augustine and Pensacola waned and waxed as epidemics and raids took more lives, and as Indians from regions beyond what had been the mission provinces sought sanctuary with the Spaniards and the Franciscan friars.

Because the fall of the Mocama missions had left St. Augustine exposed to raids from the north, Spanish authorities arranged the refugee Christian Indians into a line of five towns outside St. Augustine's northern gates, north of mission Nombre de Dios. Timucua Indians lived in (relocated) San Francisco de Potano, Salamototo (also relocated), and Nombre de Dios; Guale and Yamasee Indians were in Santa María and Tolomato (both relocated); and the few remaining Apalachee Indians who had moved east—a total of forty-eight—inhabited the recently relocated Abosaya. Several years later, in 1711, those towns had been joined by others that housed Ais Indians and other Indians from the coast south of St. Augustine, themselves refugees from native slavers who were ravaging peninsular Florida. Even with the new arrivals, the total number of men, women, and children in the nine refugee towns was only 416.

While the Spaniards tried to use the refugee towns as a barrier to protect St. Augustine's northern approach, slavers were looting the rest of Florida. The abandonment of Apalachee and Timucua now allowed Creek and Yamasee Indians, as well as other groups, to roam the length of the peninsula unimpeded. Even Pensacola was attacked. Groups like the Calusa, who had retained their own way of life, living in relative isolation in the lower peninsula, were no match for the raiders armed with rifles. In a few years after the collapse of the missions, the surviving Calusa and other indigenous people were pushed south toward the tip of the peninsula.

Suffering heavy losses and driven from their traditional territories, these refugees sent word to Cuban authorities that they wished to be moved to that island, where they could become Christians and escape certain destruction. In early 1711, 270 Florida Indians, including Calusa, Jobe (originally from the southeast Florida coast), and Mayaimies (originally from the Lake Okeechobee basin), were taken by ship to Havana. In a letter written later that year to the Spanish Crown, the bishop of Cuba, Bishop Gerónimo Valdés, summarized the situation in Florida and requested permission to bring more refugees to the island:

> In the past month . . . a ship entered this port, which had come from the keys. . . . The heathen Indians of the chiefs, Carlos, Coleto, and others live in those keys. And some of the above-mentioned Indians who came in the aforesaid ship told me about very serious persecutions and hostilities, which they are experiencing and which they have experienced on other keys, which the Indians whom they call Yamasees have destroyed. That the Yamasees have killed some of the aforementioned Keys Indians; have made others flee; and that they have captured the greater part of the latter, whom, it is said, they carry off and sell, placing them into slavery at the port of [Charles Towne]. . . . And as a remedy for these injuries they gave an account to me of their very strong desire that I should assist in transporting them to this city with their families, wives, and children to receive the holy sacrament of baptism and to follow Christianity. (Hann 1991, 335–36)

The bishop noted that if the ship had had room, 2,000 more people could have been rescued, while the total population in Florida who wished to become Christians in Cuba was 6,000. It took nearly four years for the king to pen his response, giving permission to use whatever resources were available to accomplish the task. His letter may have never reached Cuba. In December 1720, nine years after he first wrote the Crown, Bishop Valdés again sent for permission. By then it was too late for most of the Indians, victims of Indian slavers, the ponderous Spanish bureaucracy, or the uncertainties of transatlantic mail delivery. The question of moving Florida Indians to Cuba would resurface in the early 1730s.

While the Indians waiting to be rescued in peninsular Florida became fewer and fewer in number, the population of the St. Augustine refugee towns was actually increasing, the result of the 1715 Yamasee War fought in South Carolina. Following an unsuccessful uprising, the rebellious Indians, mainly Yamasees but also Apalachee, Apalachicola, and Creeks, were forced to leave that colony, and many entered Spanish Florida. Yamasees, who once had been living under the Spaniards and fled to South Carolina in the late seventeenth and early eighteenth centuries, thus returned.

Desperately in need of Indian allies, the Spaniards welcomed them, and several Yamasee towns sprang up around St. Augustine among the other refugee villages. As a result, the number of villagers in 1717 was between 900 and 1,000. In addition to Nombre de Dios (Timucua and Apalachee Indians), the Christian Indians among them were served by Santa Catalina de Guale (Guale Indians), San Buenaventura de Palica (Timucua Indians), Nuestra Señora de la Candelaria de Tamaja (or Tama) (Yamasee Indians), San Joseph de Jororo (Yamasee Indians), and Nuestra Señora del Rosario de Abosaya (Apalachee Indians). Old mission names were still retained, though the actual missions were in villages far from their namesakes of a century earlier.

Refugee villages, most of which were associated with missions, became a curious mixture of both Christian and non-Christian Indians with various languages and ethnic identities. The troubled times that had befallen La Florida had began to break down tribal divisions. Marriages between adults of different ethnicities also began to occur, a result of a lack of suitable marriage partners from within tribes. No longer were people only Yamasee or Timucua Indians, they were also Spanish Indians. Even so, most still spoke their native languages, and some towns adhered to traditional patterns of chiefly inheritance.

Not all of the refugees from the Yamasee War went to St. Augustine. Groups of Indians fled to Apalachee or elsewhere in northern Florida, places where some of them had once lived but were now devoid of people. The result on the landscape was a quiltlike pattern of Indian groups living in small, isolated settlements where they hoped to avoid attacks or from where they could mount their own attacks on neighbors.

Newcomers continued to arrive into the state, even while some of the indigenous Indians, tired of being prey for predatory Indians, were giving up life in the countryside and resettling in St. Augustine's refugee towns. Alafia and Pohoy Indians, who had lived on Tampa Bay, joined the Indians at the missions in St. Augustine, while some of the Pohoy opted to become raiders. Such was the case in 1718 when Pohoy Indians raided a village of Tocobaga Indians, their former Tampa Bay neighbors who were then living near the mouth of the Wacissa River. The Tocobaga, who had lived as non-Christians on the fringes of Apalachee in the late seventeenth century, had escaped the 1704 raids. After the 1718 Pohoy attack, the Tocobaga resettled again, this time near the mouth of the Aucilla River, southeast of San Marcos de Apalachee, a fort Spanish soldiers had just built in an attempt to retake control of Apalachee province. Other Indians, including refugee Apalachees who had been living near Pensacola, were also drawn to San Marcos de Apalachee for protection. There, by 1723, Fathers Domingo Garza and Joseph de Hita, traveling from St. Augustine, had baptized 116 people, mostly adults. The fort continued to be occupied until 1764, when the Spaniards withdrew from La Florida.

At the time baptisms were taking place around San Marcos de Apalachee, at least a dozen Franciscans, including Fathers Garza and de Hita, ministered to the Indians in the villages around St. Augustine, who numbered just over 1,000 in 1726. From that time on, the population of the refugee missions, though fluctuating a bit, began a steady decline, as did the number of missions and refugee villages. Disease and raids continued to claim lives. Though only the distance of two musket shots from St. Augustine's stone fort, even Nombre de Dios was sacked by Creek Indians in 1727. By then it sheltered the shrine of Nuestra Señora de la Leche, as it does today. A census of the refugee towns taken the next year listed only 436 people, all but eleven Christians; by 1738 the mission population was down to 350.

Indians in south Florida were faring as poorly as those around St. Augustine. The king's order, originally issued in 1716 and reissued in 1720, to move the surviving south Florida Indians had never been implemented. Church officials pressed the issue, and in 1730 the king repeated his order. In the early 1730s a ship was finally sent to south Florida from Cuba. Aboard were six Indians from Havana, the only survivors of the 272 Indians brought to Cuba in 1711.

The small expedition was successful in convincing Don Diego, chief of the Keys Indians, and thirteen of his high-ranking men to return to Havana. There Don Diego, who did not speak Spanish, agreed to the resettlement of his people in Cuba, where they were to be baptized and become Christians. Two ships were subsequently chartered and sailed back to Florida with Don Diego and his entourage. The ships anchored while the Indians returned to their village. Over several days the Spaniards waited, while Don Diego and the others traveled back and forth between the ships and their village, negotiating at the latter, partaking of rum and the Spaniards' provisions at the former. On the fourth day the Indians failed to return from their village—the deal was off.

Another attempt was later made to bring the south Florida Indians to Christianity, this time led by Jesuits seeking to establish a new mission at old Tequesta at the mouth of the Miami River—the same place Jesuits had raised the cross during the governorship of Pedro Menéndez de Avilés 176 years earlier. The plan to build a mission among the south Florida Indians represented a change in thinking by Cuban authorities, who admitted that bringing Indians to Cuba had been a mistake because of their susceptibility to diseases. Another reason for keeping the Indians in southern Florida was to form a buffer between the mainland and the Florida Keys to protect Spanish fishing interests from raids. Also, in the past, the south Florida Indians had rescued shipwrecked Spaniards, and they had stood up against English sailors who had intruded into Spanish territory in the Keys. Lastly, the mission was requested by the Indians themselves. Researchers who have studied the documents have noted, though, that the letter requesting the mission was written in remarkably good Spanish by someone who was conversant with the bureaucracies of the Catholic church and the government of Cuba, probably not an Indian.

The governor of Cuba wrote to the king in July 1743 to inform him of the plan to send the Jesuits to La Florida. Fathers Joseph María Monaco and Joseph Xavier Alaña had departed Havana in late June bound for the mouth of the Miami River, which they finally located after three weeks. There, they found about one hundred Indians living in five large houses in the village of Santa María de Loreto, as the Jesuits named their mission. The Jesuits reported that many of the adult men spoke Spanish, a result of their working for Cuban fishermen. The refugees living at Santa María de Loreto included Keys Indians (the remnants of the Tequesta), Calusa, Boca Ratones (from the southeast coast), Mayaimies, Santaluces, and Mayacas.

The Indians of Santa María de Loreto were well-versed in the material benefits of association with Spaniards. According to the Jesuits, the Indians wanted good cloth, not burlap, for clothing, and they asked to be supplied with rum. Furthermore, if they were to become Christians and allow a church to be built in their village, the Indians wished to be paid a daily salary and for their chief to receive gifts. The Indians had once been armed by the Spaniards, so they could stand up to the raiders from the north, but they had traded many of their arms for rum. Rum was also obtained from Cuban fishermen. While at the town the friars witnessed firsthand the problems alcohol was causing. As much to protect themselves from the local Indians as from possible raids, the two Jesuits suggested that a small fort be built and manned with a dozen Spanish soldiers.

The Santa María de Loreto Indians were quite different from the Guale Indians that the Jesuits had first proselytized in the sixteenth century. Even so, many of the fiercely devout Jesuits' observations sound a great deal like those of their earlier counterparts as well as the early Franciscans. In the Jesuits' view, the Indians were engaging in practices that were idolatrous and associated with the devil. They also worshiped wooden idols, at least one of which the Jesuits smashed and burned. The Jesuits derided the native priest, portraying him as a drunk. Conversion to Catholicism would "root out" the Indians' superstitions and conquer their souls, just as colonialism and Catholicism had done elsewhere in the Americas.

But the Jesuits were less than successful. Spanish authorities decided that the cost of a mission and fort in south Florida was too steep. The Jesuits returned to Havana, and Santa María de Loreto passed into history.

The Indians of Santa María de Loreto were not the only native people to work in the fishing industry. In the eighteenth century numerous Cuban and some St. Augustine–based boats plied the coastal waters for fish. The fish were dried and processed on shore at small fishing ranchos by Indians and a few Spaniards. Ranchos were found on southern Florida's coasts from Tampa Bay, around the tip of Florida, through the Keys, and up the Atlantic coast to Jupiter Inlet. Indians were paid for their labor and probably used the salaries to buy supplies and goods. This was quite a different livelihood than their ancestors'. At times Indians from the ranchos were taken by boat to Cuba, where it was likely they were just as at home interacting with Spaniards on the docks of Havana as with their native friends and families in their home communities.

While Jesuits attempted to bring Christianity to the Indians of Santa María de Loreto at the small settlement in the middle of what would become Miami, Franciscan friars continued to serve the dwindling number of Indians living in the refugee villages around St. Augustine. Like their counterparts to the south, some of St. Augustine's native population also suffered social problems stemming from drunkenness. Aguadiente, rum from Cuba, was too easily obtained by Indians whose lives had been turned inside out by colonialism and warfare.

By 1752 only five Christian villages, plus Nombre de Dios, remained. Tolomato, Pocotalaca, Punta, La Costa, and Palica together only housed between 150 and 200 people. The Spanish Indians living in these towns had names that either combined a Spanish Christian name with a native name, or they simply had Spanish names, like Miguel Hicapuca, María Casipuya, Juan Alonso Cavalo, and María de la Cruz Uriza.

It seems that all these Indians spoke some Spanish. However, the friar who served Palica and its small Timucuan population may have held some confessions in the Timucua native language. The New York Public Library's copy of Father Francisco Pareja's 1613 *Confessionario en Lengua Castellana y Timuquana* (*Confessional in Spanish and Timucuan*) contains a certificate stuck in its pages that reads (in Spanish): "On the _____ day of the month of _____ in 1755 _____ confessed. He knows the doctrine." To be filled in by the friar when a person confessed and exhibited knowledge of Catholic tenets, the certificate suggests the

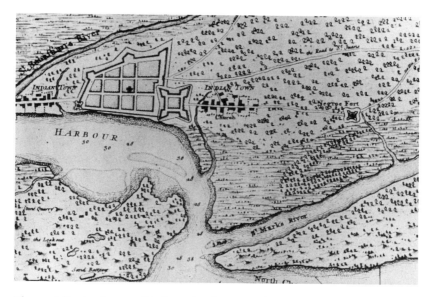

Thomas Jeffrey's 1762 map of St. Augustine shows Nombre de Dios ("Indian Town") to the north side (right) just beyond the walls of the Castillo de San Marcos, its same location for nearly two centuries. The "Indian Town" on the south side of St. Augustine is most likely Tolomato, the other remaining mission village. North of Nombre de Dios is a small "Negroe Fort," a community of African fugitives who had escaped from Carolina plantations. (Courtesy P. K. Yonge Library of Florida History, University of Florida)

friar may have found it necessary to use Father Pareja's 142-year-old dual-language book to communicate.

The refugees and their mission towns continued to disappear. In 1759 only two missions, Tolomato and Nombre de Dios, were left serving ninety-five Indians. They represented all that remained of the La Florida Indians: Yamasee, Chiluque, and Casipuya Indians (probably Cusabo), all latecomers to the Spanish missions from the Carolinas; Timucua and Guale Indians, the latter called Ibaja in the Timucua language; and Costa and Chickasaw Indians, refugees who came to St. Augustine in the mid-eighteenth century.

The disappearance of the last two La Florida missions did not come from epidemics or raids, but from international treaties, which resulted from wars fought in Europe that spilled over into the Americas. Ultimately involving most of the major European powers of the time, the Austro-Prussian War began in 1756 as a conflict between Austria and Prussia. France, which recently had been an antagonist in the French and Indian War in North America against the British, allied with Austria, and Britain joined on the side of Prussia. This brought on a new French-

British conflict: the Seven Years' War. In early 1762, near the end of the war, Spain threatened to enter on the side of France, which led to a British retaliatory declaration of war. Spain immediately invaded Portugal, a British ally. Abroad, Britain took Manila in the Philippine Islands and Havana, both Spanish holdings. The war soon wound down, and treaties were signed. According to one agreement, the Treaty of Paris, in exchange for regaining control of Havana and Manila, Spain would give up its La Florida colony to Britain.

The exodus of the Spaniards from the colony to Cuba began in 1763. From Pensacola, forty Apalachee families who had been living in two nearby villages, Punta Rasa and Escambe, were taken to a village in Veracruz, Mexico. Eighty-nine Indians, the remaining residents of Tolomato and Nombre de Dios, left with the Spaniards from St. Augustine and were resettled in the Cuban town of Guanabacoa. There, their names were carefully written in the city-hall registry, a testament to the end of the Spanish La Florida missions.

Following the end of the Revolutionary War in 1783, Florida once again became a Spanish colony. The indigenous Indians were gone and the missions were already turning into ruins. Creek Indians, the ancestors of the Seminoles who live there today, were colonizing interior northern Florida, often settling where Spanish missions and ranches had once been. These Creeks, some descendants of earlier raiders, were aware of the association of the landscape and the abandoned missions.

Even so, the missions themselves became lost. Their history was largely ignored by the settlers from the southern United States who moved into Florida after it was officially handed over to that new country in 1821. Names in English replaced the Spanish, Timucua, and Apalachee ones, further obscuring the missions. In large part, it is thanks to the Seminole Indians and their continued use of old names that a few of the mission-period place-names survive into the present.

SELECT BIBLIOGRAPHY

Alegre, Francisco Javier. 1956. *Historia de la Provincia de la Compañia de Jesus de Nueva España, Vol. I.* Bibliotheca Instituti Historici S. J., Vol. IX. Rome: Institutum Historicum S. J.

Arnade, Charles. 1965. *The Siege of St. Augustine in 1702.* Gainesville: University of Florida Press.

Bolton, Herbert E. 1921. *The Spanish Borderlands: A Chronicle of Old Florida and the Southwest.* New Haven: Yale University Press.

———, ed. 1925. *Arredondo's Historical Proof of Spain's Title to Georgia: A Contribution to the History of the Spanish Borderlands.* Berkeley: University of California Press.

Bolton, Herbert E., and Mary Ross. 1925. *The Debatable Land: A Sketch of Anglo-Spanish Contest for the Georgia Country.* Berkeley: University of California Press.

Boyd, Mark F. 1938. "Map of the Road from Pensacola to St. Augustine, 1778." *Florida Historical Quarterly* 17:1–23.

———. 1939. "Mission Sites in Florida." *Florida Historical Quarterly* 17:255–80.

———. 1948. "Enumeration of Florida Spanish Missions in 1675." *Florida Historical Quarterly* 24:181–88.

———. 1953. "Further Considerations of the Apalachee Missions." *The Americas* 9:459–79.

Boyd, Mark F., Hale G. Smith, and John W. Griffin. 1952. *Here They Once Stood: The Tragic End of the Apalachee Missions.* Gainesville: University of Florida Press.

Bushnell, Amy Turner. 1978a. "The Menéndez-Marquez Cattle Barony at La Chua and the Determinants of Economic Expansion in 17th-Century Florida." *Florida Historical Quarterly* 56:407–31.

———. 1978b. " 'That Demonic Game': The Campaign to Stop Indian Pelota Playing in Spanish Florida, 1675–1684." *The Americas* 35:1–19.

———. 1979. "Patricio de Hinachuba: Defender of the Word of God, the Crown of the King, and the Little Children of Ivitachuco." *American Indian Culture and Research Journal* 3(3):1–21.

———. 1981. *The King's Coffer: Proprietors of the Royal Treasury, 1565–1702.* Gainesville: University Presses of Florida.

———. 1989. "Ruling 'the Republic of Indians' in Seventeenth-Century Florida." In *Powhatan's Mantle: Indians in the Colonial Southeast,* edited by P. H. Wood, G. A. Waselkov, and M. T. Hatley, 134–50. Lincoln: University of Nebraska Press.

———. 1994. *Situado and Sabana: Spain's Support System for the Presidio and Mission Provinces of Florida.* American Museum of Natural History, Anthropological Papers 74. Athens: University of Georgia Press.

Caldwell, Sheila K. 1953. "Excavations at a Spanish Mission Site in Georgia." *Southeastern Archaeological Conference Newsletter* 3(3):31–32.

———. 1954. "A Spanish Mission Site near Darien." *Early Georgia* 1(3):13–17.

Chamberlain, Robert S. 1948. *The Conquest and Colonization of Yucatan, 1517–1550.* Publication 582. Washington, D.C.: Carnegie Institution of Washington.

Chapman, Samuel. 1996. "Archaeological Testing of the Indian Pond Site, Columbia County, Florida." Master's thesis, University of Florida.

Coe, Capt. Charles H. 1941. *Debunking the So-Called Spanish Mission near New Smyrna Beach, Volusia County, Florida.* Privately printed.

Coulter, Ellis Merton, ed. 1937. *Georgia's Disputed Ruins.* Chapel Hill: University of North Carolina Press.

Covington, James W., and A. F. Falcones, eds. 1963. *Pirates, Indians, and Spaniards: Father Escobedo's "La Florida."* St. Petersburg, Fla.: Great Outdoors Publishing, Co.

Deagan, Kathleen A. 1972. "Fig Springs: The Mid-Seventeenth Century in North-Central Florida." *Historical Archaeology* 6:23–46.

———. 1978. "Cultures in Transition: Fusion and Assimilation among the Eastern Timucua." In *Tacachale: Essays on the Indians of Florida and Southeastern Georgia during the Historic Period,* edited by Jerald T. Milanich and Samuel Proctor, 88–119. Gainesville: University Presses of Florida.

———. 1983. *Spanish St. Augustine: The Archaeology of a Colonial Creole Community.* New York: Academic Press.

———. 1987. *Ceramics, Glassware, and Beads.* Vol. 1 of *Artifacts of the Spanish Colonies of Florida and the Caribbean, 1500–1800.* Washington, D.C.: Smithsonian Institution Press.

Floyd, Marmaduke. 1937. "Certain Tabby Ruins on the Georgia Coast." In *Georgia's Disputed Ruins,* edited by Ellis Merton Coulter, 1–189. Chapel Hill: University of North Carolina Press.

Ford, James A. 1937. "An Archaeological Report on the Elizafield Ruins." In *Georgia's Disputed Ruins,* edited by Ellis Merton Coulter, 193–225. Chapel Hill: University of North Carolina Press.

Gannon, Michael V. 1965. *The Cross in the Sand: The Early Catholic Church in Florida, 1513–1870.* Gainesville: University of Florida Press.

Geiger, Maynard J. 1937. *The Franciscan Conquest of Florida, 1573–1618.* Washington, D.C.: Catholic University of America Press.

———. 1940. *Biographical Dictionary of the Franciscans in Spanish Florida and Cuba (1528–1841).* Franciscan Studies 21. Paterson, N. Y.: St. Anthony's Guild Press.

Gerónimo de Oré, Luís. 1936. *The Martyrs of Florida (1513–1616)*. Translated by Maynard J. Geiger. Franciscan Studies 18. New York: Joseph F. Wagner.

Goggin, John M. 1953. "An Introductory Outline of Timucua Archaeology." *Southeastern Archaeological Conference Newsletter* 3(3):4–17.

Gold, Robert L. 1965. "The Settlement of the Pensacola Indians in New Spain in 1763–1770." *American Historical Review* 45:567–76.

Gradie, Charlotte M. 1988. "Spanish Jesuits in Virginia, the Mission That Failed." *The Virginia Magazine of History and Biography* 96:131–56.

Griffin, John W. 1952. "The Addison Blockhouse." *Florida Historical Quarterly* 30:276–93.

———. 1955. "A Preliminary Report on the Site of the Mission of San Juan del Puerto, Fort George Island, Florida." Typescript. St. Augustine: St. Augustine Historical Society.

Hann, John H. 1986a. "Church Furnishings, Sacred Vessels, and Vestments Held by the Missions of Florida: Translation of Two Inventories." *Florida Archaeology* 2:147–64.

———. 1986b. "Demographic Patterns and Changes in Mid-Seventeenth Century Timucua and Apalachee." *Florida Historical Quarterly* 64:371–92.

———. 1986c. "Translation of Alonso de Leturiondo's Memorial to the King of Spain." *Florida Archaeology* 2:165–225.

———. 1986d. "Translation of Governor Rebolledo's 1657 Visitation of Three Florida Provinces and Related Documents." *Florida Archaeology* 2:81–145.

———. 1987. "Twilight of the Mocamo and Guale Aborigines as Portrayed in the 1695 Spanish Visitation." *Florida Historical Quarterly* 66:1–24.

———. 1988a. "Apalachee Counterfeiters in St. Augustine." *Florida Historical Quarterly* 67:52–68.

———. 1988b. *Apalachee: The Land between the Rivers*. Gainesville: University Press of Florida.

———. 1989. "St. Augustine's Fallout from the Yamasee War." *Florida Historical Quarterly* 68:180–200.

———. 1990a. "De Soto, Dobyns, and Demography in Western Timucua." *Florida Anthropologist* 43:3–12.

———. 1990b. "Summary Guide to Spanish Florida Missions and Visitas with Churches in the Sixteenth and Seventeenth Centuries." *The Americas* 46:417–513.

———. 1991. *Missions to the Calusa*. Gainesville: University of Florida Press.

———. 1992a. "Heathen Acuera, Murder, and a Potano Cimarrona: The St. Johns River and the Alachua Prairie in the 1670s." *Florida Historical Quarterly* 70:451–74.

———. 1992b. "Political Leadership among the Natives of Spanish Florida." *Florida Historical Quarterly* 71:188–208.

———. 1993a. "1630 Memorial of Fray Francisco Alonso de Jesus on Spanish Florida's Missions and Natives." *The Americas* 50:85–105.

———. 1993b. "Visitations and Revolts in Florida, 1656–1695." *Florida Archaeology* 7:1–296.

———. 1995. "The Indian Village on Apalachee Bay's Rio Chachave on the Solana Map of 1683." *Florida Anthropologist* 48:61–66.

———. 1996. *History of the Timucua Indians and Missions*. Gainesville: University Press of Florida.

Hann, John H., and Bonnie McEwan. 1998. *The Apalachee Indians and Mission San Luis.* Gainesville: University Press of Florida.

Hoffman, Paul E. 1983. "Legend, Religious Idealism, and Colonies: The Point of Santa Elena in History, 1552–1566." *South Carolina Magazine of History* 84:59–71.

———. 1984. "The Chicora Legend and Franco-Spanish Rivalry." *Florida Historical Quarterly* 62:419–38.

———. 1990. *A New Andalucia and a Way to the Orient: The American Southeast during the Sixteenth Century.* Baton Rouge: Louisiana State University Press.

———. 1994a. "Lucas Vázquez de Ayllón's Discovery and Colony." In *The Forgotten Centuries: Indians and Europeans in the American South, 1521–1704,* edited by Charles Hudson and Carmen Chaves Tesser, 36–49. Athens: University of Georgia Press.

———. 1994b. "Narváez and Cabeza de Vaca in Florida." In *The Forgotten Centuries: Indians and Europeans in the American South, 1521–1704,* edited by Charles Hudson and Carmen Chaves Tesser, 50–73. Athens: University of Georgia Press.

Hoshower, Lisa M. 1992. "Bioanthropological Analysis of a Seventeenth-Century Native American–Spanish Mission Population: Biocultural Impacts on the Northern Utina." Ph.D. diss., University of Florida.

Hudson, Charles. 1976. *The Southeastern Indians.* Knoxville: University of Tennessee Press.

———. 1990. *The Juan Pardo Expeditions: Spanish Explorers and the Indians of the Carolinas and Tennessee, 1566–1568.* Washington, D.C.: Smithsonian Institution Press.

———. 1994. "The Hernando de Soto Expedition, 1539–1543." In *The Forgotten Centuries: Indians and Europeans in the American South, 1521–1704,* edited by Charles Hudson and Carmen Chaves Tesser, 74–103. Athens: University of Georgia Press.

Johnson, Kenneth W. 1990. "The Discovery of a Seventeenth-Century Spanish Mission in Ichetucknee State Park, 1986." *Florida Journal of Anthropology* 15:39–46.

———. 1991. "The Utina and the Potano Peoples of Northern Florida: Changing Settlement Systems in the Spanish Colonial Period." Ph.D. diss., University of Florida.

Jones, B. Calvin. 1970. "Missions Reveal State's Spanish-Indian Heritage." *Archives and History News* 1(2):1, 3.

———. 1971. "State Archaeologists Unearth Spanish Mission Ruins." *Archives and History News* 2(4):2.

———. 1972a. "Colonel James Moore and the Destruction of the Apalachee Missions in 1704." *Florida Bureau of Historic Sites and Properties Bulletin* 2:25–33.

———. 1972b. "Spanish Mission Sites Located and Test Excavated." *Archives and History News* 3(6):1–2.

———. 1982. "Southern Cult Manifestations at the Lake Jackson Site, Leon County, Florida: Salvage Excavation of Mound 3." *Midcontinental Journal of Archaeology* 7:3–44.

Jones, B. Calvin, John Hann, and John F. Scarry. 1991. "San Pedro y San Pablo de Patale: A Seventeenth-Century Spanish Mission in Leon County, Florida." *Florida Archaeology* 5:1–201.

Jones, Charles C. 1883. *Aboriginal and Colonial Epochs.* Vol. 1 of *The History of Georgia.* Boston: Houghton, Mifflin, and Co.

Jones, Grant D. 1978. "The Ethnohistory of the Guale Coast through 1684." In *The Anthro-*

pology of St. Catherines Island. 1. Natural and Cultural History, 178–210. Anthropological Papers 55, pt. 2. New York: American Museum of Natural History.

Kapitzke, Robert. 1993. "The 'Calamities of Florida': Father Solana, Governor Palacio y Valenzuela, and the Desertions of 1758." *Florida Historical Quarterly* 72:1–18.

Kerrigan, Anthony, trans. 1951. *Barcía's Chronological History of the Continent of Florida: From the Year 1512, in Which Juan Ponce de Leon Discovered Florida, until the Year 1722.* Gainesville: University of Florida Press.

Lanning, John Tate. 1935. *The Spanish Missions of Georgia.* Chapel Hill: University of North Carolina Press.

Larsen, Clark Spencer. 1990. "Biological Interpretation and the Context for Contact." In *The Archaeology of Mission Santa Catalina de Guale: 2. Biocultural Interpretations of a Population in Transition,* edited by Clark Spencer Larsen, 11–25. Anthropological Papers 68. New York: American Museum of Natural History.

———. 1994. "In the Wake of Columbus: Native Population Biology in the Postcontact Americas." *Yearbook of Physical Anthropology* 37:109–54.

Larsen, Clark Spencer, and George R. Milner, eds. 1994. *In the Wake of Contact: Biological Responses to Conquest.* New York: Wiley-Liss.

Larsen, Clark Spencer, Hong P. Huynh, and Bonnie G. McEwan. 1996. "Death by Gunshot: Biocultural Implications of Trauma at Mission San Luis." *International Journal of Osteoarchaeology* 6:42–50.

Larson, Lewis H., Jr. 1953. "Coastal Mission Survey." Mimeographed. Atlanta: Georgia Historical Commission.

———. 1978. "Historic Guale Indians of the Georgia Coast and the Impact of the Spanish Mission Effort." In *Tacachale: Essays on the Indians of Florida and Southeastern Georgia during the Historic Period,* edited by Jerald T. Milanich and Samuel Proctor, 120–40. Gainesville: University Press of Florida.

———. 1980. "The Spanish on Sapelo." In *Sapelo Papers: Researches in the History and Prehistory of Sapelo Island, Georgia,* edited by Daniel P. Juengst, 35–45. Studies in the Social Sciences 19. Carrollton, Ga.: West Georgia College.

Lewis, Clifford M., and Albert J. Loomie. 1953. *The Spanish Jesuit Missions in Virginia: 1570–1572.* Chapel Hill: University of North Carolina Press.

Loucks, Lana Jill. 1978. "Political and Economic Interactions between the Spaniards and Indians: Archeological and Ethnohistorical Perspectives of the Mission System in Florida." Ph.D. diss., University of Florida.

Lowery, Woodberry. 1905. *The Spanish Settlements within the Present Limits of the United States, Florida, 1562–1574.* New York: G. P. Putnam's Sons.

Lyon, Eugene. 1976. *The Enterprise of Florida, Pedro Menéndez de Avilés and the Spanish Conquest of 1565–1568.* Gainesville: University Presses of Florida.

———. 1988. "Pedro Menéndez's Strategic Plan for the Florida Peninsula." *Florida Historical Quarterly* 67:1–14.

Marrinan, Rochelle A. 1985. "The Archaeology of the Spanish Missions of Florida: 1566–1704." In *Indians, Colonists, and Slaves: Essays in Memory of Charles H. Fairbanks,* edited by Kenneth W. Johnson, Jonathan M. Leader, and Robert C. Wilson, 241–52.

Florida Journal of Anthropology Special Publication 4. Gainesville: Florida Anthropology Student Association of the University of Florida.

McEwan, Bonnie G. 1991. "San Luis de Talimali: The Archaeology of Spanish-Indian Relations at a Florida Mission." *Historical Archaeology* 25:36–60.

———, ed. 1993. *Spanish Missions of La Florida*. Gainesville: University Press of Florida.

McEwan, Bonnie G., and Charles B. Poe. 1994. "Excavations at Fort San Luis." *Florida Anthropologist* 47:90–106.

McMurray, Judith A. 1973. "The Definition of the Ceramic Complex at San Juan del Puerto." Master's thesis, University of Florida.

Milanich, Jerald T. 1971. "Surface Information from the Presumed Site of the San Pedro de Mocamo Mission." *Conference on Historic Site Archaeology Papers* 5:114–21.

———. 1972. "Excavations at the Richardson Site, Alachua County, Florida: An Early 17th-Century Potano Indian Village (with Notes on Potano Culture Change)." *Florida Bureau of Historic Sites and Properties Bulletin* 2:35–61.

———. 1978. "The Western Timucua: Patterns of Acculturation and Change." In *Tacachale: Essays on the Indians of Florida and Southeastern Georgia during the Historic Period*, edited by Jerald T. Milanich and Samuel Proctor, 59–88. Gainesville: University of Florida Press.

———. 1994. *Archaeology of Precolumbian Florida*. Gainesville: University Press of Florida.

———. 1995. *Florida Indians and the Invasion from Europe*. Gainesville: University Press of Florida.

———. 1996. *The Timucua*. Oxford, U. K.: Blackwell Publishers.

Milanich, Jerald T., and Charles Hudson. 1993. *Hernando de Soto and the Florida Indians*. Gainesville: University Press of Florida.

Milanich, Jerald T., and William C. Sturtevant. 1972. *Francisco Pareja's 1613 Confessionario: A Documentary Source for Timucuan Ethnography*. Tallahassee: Florida Department of State.

Pareja, Francisco. 1613. *Confessionario in Lengua Castellana, y Timuquana*. . . . Mexico City: Viuda de Diego López Davalos.

Pearson, Fred Lamar. 1968. "Spanish-Indian Relations in Florida: A Study of Two Visitas, 1657–1678." Ph.D. diss., University of Alabama.

Phinney, A. H. 1925. "Florida's Spanish Missions." *Florida Historical Quarterly* 4:15–21.

Quinn, David B., ed. 1979. *Major Spanish Searches in Eastern North America. Franco-Spanish Clash in Florida. The Beginnings of Spanish Florida*. Vol. 2 of *New American World: A Documentary History of North America to 1612*. New York: Arno Press.

Ross, Mary. 1926. "The Restoration of the Spanish Missions in Georgia." *Georgia Historical Quarterly* 10:171–99.

Ruhl, Donna S. 1993. "Old Customs and Traditions in New Terrain: Sixteenth- and Seventeenth-Century Archaeobotanical Data from La Florida." In *Foraging and Farming in the Eastern Woodlands*, edited by C. Margaret Scarry, 255–83. Gainesville: University Press of Florida.

Saunders, Rebecca. 1996. "Mission-Period Settlement Structure: A Test of the Model at San Martín de Timucua." *Historical Archaeology* 30:24–36.

Seaberg, Lillian M. 1955. "The Zetrouer Site: Indian and Spanish in Central Florida." Master's thesis, University of Florida.

Shapiro, Gary, and Bonnie G. McEwan. 1992. "Archaeology at San Luis, Part One: The Apalachee Council House." *Florida Archaeology* 6:1–173.

Smith, Hale G. 1948a. "Results of an Archaeological Investigation of a Spanish Mission Site in Jefferson County, Florida." *Florida Anthropologist* 1:1–10.

———. 1948b. "Two Historical Archaeological Periods in Florida." *American Antiquity* 13:313–19.

———. 1956. *The European and the Indian.* Florida Anthropological Society Publication 4. Gainesville: Florida Anthropological Society.

Smith, Marvin T. 1987. *Archaeology of Aboriginal Culture Change in the Interior Southeast: Depopulation during the Early Historic Period.* Gainesville: University of Florida Press.

Solís de Merás, Gonzalo. 1964. *Pedro Menéndez de Avilés, Adelantado, Governor and Captain-General of Florida.* Translated by J. T. Connor. Gainesville: University of Florida Press.

Sturtevant, William C. 1962. "Spanish-Indian Relations in Southeastern North America." *Ethnohistory* 9:41–94.

———. 1964. "A Jesuit Missionary in South Carolina, 1569–70." In *The Indian and White Man,* edited by Wilcomb E. Washburn, 167–75. New York: New York University Press.

———. 1993. "The First American Discoverers of Europe." *Native American Studies* 7(2):23–29.

———. 1996. "The Misconnection of Guale and Yamasee with Muskogean." *International Journal of American Linguistics* 60:139–48.

Swanton, John R. 1922. *Early History of the Creek Indians and Their Neighbors.* Bulletin 73. Washington, D.C.: Smithsonian Institution, Bureau of American Ethnology.

Symes, M. I., and M. E. Stephens. 1965. "A-272: The Fox Pond Site." *Florida Anthropologist* 18:65–72.

Thomas, David Hurst. 1987. *The Archaeology of Mission Santa Catalina de Guale: 1. Search and Discovery.* Anthropological Papers 63, pt. 2. New York: American Museum of Natural History.

———, ed. 1990. *Archaeological and Historical Perspectives on the Spanish Borderlands East.* Vol. 2 of *Columbian Consequences.* Washington D.C.: Smithsonian Institution Press.

True, David O. 1944. "The Freducci Map of 1514–1515, What It Discloses of Early Florida History." *Tequesta* 4:50–55.

———, ed. 1945. *Memoir of D. d'Escalante Fontaneda Respecting Florida, Written in Spain, about the Year 1575.* Coral Gables, Fla.: Glade House.

Weber, David J. 1992. *The Spanish Frontier in North America.* New Haven: Yale University Press.

Weisman, Brent R. 1992. *Excavations of the Franciscan Frontier: Archaeology of the Fig Springs Mission.* Gainesville: University Press of Florida.

Wenhold, Lucy L., ed. and trans. 1936. "A Seventeenth-Century Letter of Gabriel Díaz Vara Calderón, Bishop of Cuba." *Smithsonian Miscellaneous Collections* 95(16):1–14.

Williams, Emma Rochelle. 1927. "The Bell of a Florida Spanish Mission." *Florida Historical Quarterly* 5:159.

Worth, John E. 1992a. "Revised Aboriginal Ceramic Typology for the Timucua Mission Province." In *Excavations of the Franciscan Frontier: Archaeology of the Fig Springs Mission,* by Brent R. Weisman, 188–205. Gainesville: University Press of Florida.

———. 1992b. "The Timucuan Missions of Spanish Florida and the Rebellion of 1656." Ph.D. diss., University of Florida.

———. 1994. "Late Spanish Military Expeditions in the Interior Southeast, 1597–1628." In *The Forgotten Centuries: Indians and Europeans in the American South, 1521–1704,* edited by Charles Hudson and Carmen Chaves Tesser, 104–22. Athens: University of Georgia Press.

———. 1995. *The Struggle for the Georgia Coast: An Eighteenth-Century Spanish Retrospective on Guale and Mocama.* Anthropological Papers 75. New York: American Museum of Natural History.

———. 1998a. *Assimilation.* Vol. 1 of *The Timucuan Chiefdoms of Spanish Florida.* Gainesville: University Press of Florida.

———. 1998b. *Resistence, and Destruction.* Vol. 2 of *The Timucuan Chiefdoms of Spanish Florida.* Gainesville: University Press of Florida.

Zubillaga, Felix. 1941. *La Florida: La Misión Jesuitica (1566–1572) y la Colonización Española.* Rome: Institutum Historicum S. J.

———, ed. 1946. *Monumenta Antiquae Floride.* Monumenta Historica Societatis Iesu 69, Monumenta Missionum Societatis Iesu 3. Rome: Monumenta Historica Soc. Iesu.

INDEX